Praise for Vitali Vitaliev

'Vitaliev drinks his way through Easte...
draught redolent of the company, and ...
more by the author's gift of observ...
Riesling, Vitaliev's travelogue cultiv...
turns what is essentially an excuse for a ...
portrait of post-Communist Europe. A prolonged moment of clarity'
OBSERVER

'He has a sharp and sardonic eye; and his observations are informed by his
humanity and compassion. He has written a funny and sad book which
seems to be about drinking, but is really about people, suffering, tyranny
and foolishness. He is an engaging fellow and his book puts you at his
companionable elbow'
DAILY TELEGRAPH

'An ironic and witty commentator on life. He writes with a humanist's
appetite, and an outsider's discrimination, for social oddity. There is great
charm in his emotional roller-coasting'
SPECTATOR

'With the charm of Michael Palin and the wit of Clive Anderson,
this man is adorable'
TIME OUT

'Vitaliev transcends his genre, producing a new travel-writing of the soul,
a journey with lessons about what really matters in life. That makes
it literature'
LITERARY REVIEW

'I admire his writing which gets better and better. We're both interested in
the history of the 20th century, but he's lived it, and I've been a spectator'
Clive James

'Imagine Michael Palin, Clive Anderson and Bill Bryson all rolled into one
and you'll have some idea of what to expect'
EGO

Amazon.co.uk
A reader in Sussex, England
Intoxicating stuff
Extraordinarily funny account of travels in Eastern Europe, seen through
the bottom of a vodka glass. Vitali, a former Soviet Journalist of the Year
who was expelled from the USSR, is a wonderful raconteur and has the
true humourist's genius for illuminating darkness with laughter

Also by Vitali Vitaliev

King of the Bar
Special Correspondent
Dateline Freedom
Vitali's Australia
The Third Trinity
Little is the Light
Dreams on Hitler's Couch

BORDERS UP!

Eastern Europe Through the Bottom of a Glass

Vitali Vitaliev

Scribner

First published in Great Britain by Scribner, 1999
This edition first published by Scribner, 2000
An imprint of Simon & Schuster UK Ltd
A Viacom Company

1 3 5 7 9 10 8 6 4 2

Simon & Schuster UK Ltd
Africa House
64-78 Kingsway
London WC2B 6AH

Simon & Schuster Australia
Sydney

A CIP catalogue record for this book is available from the British Library

ISBN 0-684-85180-6

Printed and bound in Finland by WSOY

To Jacinta Negri

CONTENTS

A 'Thank You' Toast from the Author   ix
One for the Road   1

I: BEER LANDS
The Czech Republic, with a touch of East Germany
1   My Pint of View   17
2   Playing it by Beer   23
3   Baby and Bully   27
4   Pub-crawling in Prague   35
5   Professor of Brewing   44
6   Stalin's Ear   48
7   Life Beerage in Plzen   54
8   U Bronku   65
9   The Inglorious End of Bohumil Sol, the Father
      of Semtex   72
10 The Last Few Drops of Beer   81

II: SPIRITS LANDS
Poland and Slovakia, with a dash of East Germany
11 Aqua Vitae – East and West   87
12 Pre-drinking Exaltation in Krakow   95

13 Vodka 'Auschwitz'   103
14 A Deer in Blue Underwear   111
15 'Libido' Hotel   119
16 How Angels Puke   127
17 Polish Scrabble   136
18 My Grandad's Travelling-bag   147
19 Slovakian 'Rampage'   162
20 A Lesson in Self-applied Narcology   173
21 I Saw Them Drink and Fight   185
22 The Last Eighteen Drops of Spirits   193

III: WINE LANDS
Hungary, Bulgaria and Romania, with a hint of East Germany

23 Wine Lands Begin in South Ruislip   199
24 Igor's Nitty-gritty   209
25 'Bruderschaft' Sneezing in Budapest   216
26 Of Noble Rot and Ignoble Snot   228
27 A Couple from Hell   242
28 Balaton Reflections   247
29 Dinner with Sceptics   264
30 The Stony Alyosha   273
31 Squiffy Notes in My Tasting List   278
32 Rediscovering Old Buddies and Old
        Taste-buds   285
33 The Quaintest City in the Balkans   292
34 Shiatsu of the Soul   296
35 Ceausescu's Plonk   306
36 Bumpy Wine Roads of Romania   317
37 The Last Few Drops of Wine   336

The Final Toast with Mineral Water   341
Postscript   347

A 'THANK YOU' TOAST FROM THE AUTHOR

'Can I be your taster?' my London friends asked me before the start of my East European journeys. They all thought it was going to be great fun – travelling, meeting interesting people, tasting wines and spirits. They were obviously unaware of all the hardships and masochistic deprivations of a drinking travel writer's life.

After the first several months of my peripatetic and bibulous research, my head started spinning, and not so much from the booze (as a stomach-ulcer-sufferer of many years' standing, I often had to fluctuate between total abstention and very moderate drinking when I had to chase every glass of wine with two Pepcidin pills – I was even playing with the idea of subtitling this book 'Travels with my Pepcidin'), but from all those planes, trains, faces, borders, names, wineries, distilleries, monuments, cars, hotels, twisted roads, near head-on collisions, politicians, sibilant languages, appalling toilets, etc. I had to start taking Stugeron, British-made travel sickness pills (which I had prudently bought in Boots before the trip), whose side-effects, according to the instructions on the box, included 'dizziness' and 'feeling queasy'.

The index finger on my right hand was parabolically bent due to the constant pressure of a ball-pen. And the blasted cold which I caught somewhere in Pardubice, or maybe in Sarospatak, did not let go of me for several months (which was not very conducive to wine-tasting) and bluntly refused to be cured either with crude Hungarian Panadol or with peculiar Romanian nasal drops, Bixtonim.

Instead of spending a week in bed sipping raspberry tea (or heavily peppered vodka – an old Russian folk remedy for colds), I had to grab my suitcase and dash to the railway station to board an overnight trans-European express called *Mozart* or *Einstein*, only to be woken up every half-hour by the stern, vigilant guards of some newly invented (or scrapped, but still functioning) borders who were desperate to have a look at my dog-eared Australian passport.

I had to taste dozens (if not hundreds) of wines, beers and spirits, including a new Polish vodka, Gold Wasser, with flakes of real gold, imported from Switzerland, floating in the bottle like fragments of the glorious Polish past; a dark Hungarian liqueur, Swack Unicum, made (allegedly) of forty different healing herbs and giving you a splitting headache in the morning, and Nicolae Ceausescu's favourite wine, Galbena Odobesti – as tasteless, unremarkable and naff as Ceausescu himself. By the end of my journeys, multiple wine-spots on the pages of my multiple notebooks felt like dried stains of my own blood.

'Drinking *is* my work,' the late *Spectator* columnist Jeffrey Bernard used to say. I know exactly what he meant. Drinking can be a bloody hard job, too, especially if a worker (ditto a drinker) is constantly on the move. This is why my mission would not have been completed without generous, and often over-generous, help from other people, not necessarily my drinking companions, and organisations, not necessarily wineries and distilleries.

Before starting my literary journey, I want to propose a heartfelt (and liver-felt) 'thank you' toast to some of them.

I toast my elder son Mitya, who – inadvertently – prompted the idea of this book.

I raise my hard-working wine glass to my dear friends Alexander Kasjanov of Bratislava, Theodor Troev of Sofia, Tony Paterson of Berlin, Joanna Rushby of London and Igor Pomerantsev of Prague, whose help, hospitality and knowledge were absolutely invaluable.

I say 'cheers' to Neil Taylor of Regent Holidays, Kate Catleugh of the Hungarian Tourist Office, Krystyna Rees of the Polish National Tourist Office, Agatha Suess of the German National Tourist Office and Doug Goodman of Doug Goodman PR for their active (and totally teetotal) participation in the project.

My pure and genuine, Polish-vodka-like, thanks to Domaine Boyar (Bulgaria), Vinexport (Romania), German Wine Information Service and Halewood International (UK), the companies, which bravely volunteered to take me through the drinking part of my travels; as well as to the Czech Centre, Hungarian Tourism Service, Warsaw Tourist Information Centre, Berlin Tourismus Marketing GmbH and Leipzig Tourist Service which assisted with the travelling part of my drinking.

A special multi-lingual 'thank you' ('koszonom', 'dekuji', 'dziekuje', 'multumesc', etc.) toast to Lonely Planet, whose superb *Eastern Europe Phrasebook – Language Survival Kit* indeed helped me to survive the Hungarian part of my trip, whereas the excellent *Eastern Europe on a Shoestring* guidebook was helpful throughout.

A big 'thank you' sip from my weather-beaten travel flask to my publisher and editor, Martin Fletcher, for his faith, flexibility and understanding of my ever-changing circumstances, and to my champagne-like (lovely, lively and bubbly) literary agent, Anthea Morton-Saner of Curtis Brown.

A boiling-hot salute with a steaming cup of espresso to the staff of Caffé Uno in Muswell Hill, who helped me unwind and de-toxicate in-between the trips to Eastern Europe, a largely espresso-less part of the world.

My main – strictly non-alcoholic and caffeine-free – thanks are reserved for my wife Jacinta and my newborn son Andrei, who kept my spirit (I mean my soul, of course) alive while I was doing the hardest bit of this book, writing it.

Vitali Vitaliev
London, May 1998

... But they also have erred through wine, and through strong drink are out of the way; the priest and the prophet have erred through strong drink, they are swallowed up of wine, they are out of the way through strong drink; they err in vision, they stumble in judgement ...

Isaiah

It was the Thirty Years War and we went to ground
under the debris
fearing
that we might be found by Wallenstein mercenaries

When the Great Hunt was on
we kept hiding in the cellars
fearing
that we might be found by the blonde supermen
from Goethe's land

Today
we leave our rooms and walk the corridors
fearing
that nobody
will find us

Jerzy Jarniewicz,
modern Polish poet

ONE FOR THE ROAD

The six nations that registered the greatest per capita consumption of alcohol in liquor since 1991 are Germany, Hungary, Poland, Czechoslovakia (prior to its break-up), Romania and Bulgaria.

Compton's Interactive Encyclopedia

How can I forget those Moscow drinking sessions with my friends: a bottle of vodka in the centre of the table, and the telephone covered with a cushion to give us an illusion of privacy . . . We believed naïvely that a cushion could somehow neutralise the KGB's ubiquitous bugging devices.

Drinking under communism was far from a hedonistic occupation. It provided us with an outlet – a coveted, even if short-lasting, escape from the gloomy reality and the all-permeating political dogma. A bottle of vodka was therefore a sort of a liquid hard currency, much more reliable (and certainly much more stable) than money. Anything, from a trip abroad to difficult-to-obtain roof tiles, could be bought and sold for alcohol, and had its inflation-free vodka equivalent.

A Moscow colleague of mine was suffering from a bleeding stomach ulcer, but kept drinking vodka, washing it down with Almagel, a nauseous lime-like medicine. 'What are you doing? You are killing yourself!' I told him off once as he was coughing up blood after another glass of vodka. 'I don't care if I die tomorrow,' he grimaced, swallowing a spoonful of Almagel. 'I don't care whether I survive for another twenty years of queuing. I don't like this life. Do you?'

What could I say? By that time, like most of my friends, I had acquired a duodenal ulcer myself. In a tragicomical arrangement, a bottle of Almagel was routinely put in the middle of the table during our friendly get-togethers. Next to a bottle of vodka, of course. But the tragedy of our heavy drinking by far outweighed its comedy: several of my university mates and fellow-hacks died of alcoholism in their twenties and thirties. Such was the vicious circle of our Soviet existence, which only death or vodka could break.

Westerners implicitly assumed that with the collapse of communism in Eastern Europe, people in that part of the world would drink less – a democratic society would provide many more means of escape than alcohol, such as books, free press, foreign travel and the cornucopia of consumer goods. The reality, however, has been different. As statistics show (see the epigraph), drinking in the post-communist Eastern Europe has increased dramatically since the fall of the Berlin Wall.

And isn't it more than just a coincidence that *all* the new democracies of Europe (except Albania, which *Compton's Encyclopedia*'s researchers must have simply overlooked on the map, and conflict-torn former Yugoslavia, which they were probably too scared to survey) are now at the top of the list of the world's fastest-growing drinking nations?* What is it? A paradox? A curious historic aberration? Or a logical result of years of social turmoil, lies and double standards that have

* You might wonder why Russia doesn't figure in this authoritative encyclopedic entry. The only explanation I can think of is that Russia had reached the absolute human limit of per capita drinking under the communists called 'Bolsheviks'. This is why now – under the communists called 'democrats' – no significant growth in alcohol consumption has been recorded.

created a vacuum in people's souls – a Torricellian spiritual emptiness, which spirits alone can fill?

I spent eleven months trying to answer these questions travelling around Eastern and Central Europe.* It was a journey not so much through the countries, whose old political borders had largely become blurred, ill-defined and often irrelevant, but rather through drinks – through vodka and beer, palinka and slivovitz, zubrovka and riesling, Tokaji and cabernet sauvignon – whose spheres of influence and areas of consumption were as stable and impregnable as ever before. Each of the countries had its own 'endemic' drinks, with which every single aspect of its bewildering reality was somehow connected. In fact, by the end of my journey, I had come to believe that the only real present-day borders of Eastern Europe were those of drinks, not of states – hence the title of this book.

'Not for the first time, it struck me that the only way to make sense of the cultural map was to ignore the political boundaries and go back to the oldest divide of all,' wrote Nicholas Crane in his magnificent travel book *Clear Waters Rising: A Mountain Walk Across Europe*. And although his 'divide' was 'between plains people and mountain people and coast people – and of course the nomads', my proposed drinking divide is no less old and no less well manifested: different geographical areas have been characterised by different drinks since time immemorial.

Let's face it: for many Westerners, Eastern Europe has

---

* As a fairly vague and ill-defined concept, the term 'Eastern Europe' is used in this book in its Western meaning to denote the countries of the former Soviet bloc, including East Germany. I am well aware of how reluctant East Europeans themselves are to be called 'East Europeans'. They very much prefer to call their part of the world 'Central Europe' or 'Mitteleuropa'. I apologise to all East European (sorry, Central European) readers of this book, and want to assure them that no offence was intended.

largely lost its attraction. At least under the communists
it was different and hence exciting (so they thought).
The dominating perception of Eastern Europe in the
West has not changed much since 1910, when *Near
Home or Europe Described*, the pride of my collection
of old travel books, was published in London by
Longmans, Green & Co (to provide you with a retro-
spective, I've used extracts from this extraordinary
volume, aimed at dumb and hooray-patriotic turn-of-
the-century English teenagers, as epigraphs to some of
the chapters).

A similar attitude prevails among a number of
modern travel writers, who make up for their lack of
knowledge and insight with pseudo-omniscient arro-
gance and unusual means of transport: they travel
around Eastern Europe by bicycle, they criss-cross it in
old Trabants, they fly over it in colourful balloons, or
walk across it on their hands, whereas the only thing
they really need is a pair of sharp and compassionate
eyes.

A stereotypical paragraph from a stereotypical
Western travel book on Eastern Europe would read
approximately like this:

On a dull rainy morning, my Hungarian (Polish, Czech)
unemployed friend Gyula (Stanislaw, Bohumil) kindly –
for just a hundred US dollars, the equivalent of his salary
for ten years – offered me a lift to Warsaw (Bucharest,
Bratislava) in his dilapidated Skoda (Dacia, Polish Fiat).
We are chugging towards the drab capital city along a
bumpy, pot-holed dirt-track, lined with destitute prostitutes, prostituting destitutes and corrupt, bribe-seeking
policemen in their grey uniforms. We drive past gloomy
apartment blocks with peeling stucco on their façades and
filthy washing hanging from the balconies. Hungry,
skeleton-like children, dressed in rags, play in the debris
and follow with their sad eyes the gleaming BMWs of the
new rich and the mafiosi – with sub-machine-guns and

rocket launchers sticking out of their bullet-proof windows.

And so on.

And although you might think this a pretty adequate description of some parts of present-day Romania or Bulgaria, nothing can be further from reality, for Eastern Europe these days is an extremely interesting and (yes!) exciting place which is worth visiting more than ever before. This uncomplaining and long-suffering part of Europe is now balancing precariously – like a drunk on a tightrope – between the past and the future, between so-called socialism and the so-called free market, between the so-called East and the so-called West.

In an amazing twist of history, many post-communist countries are now again ruled by the communists, who have been voted back into power by the very people who overthrew them. The post-communist hangover is being cured by a 'hair of the dog', a proven recipe. The problem with such a cure is that it usually triggers another drinking bout.

And although the communists, who used to call themselves 'communists', now call themselves democrats and champions of the free market, their mentality remains unaltered. If you stick a wine label on to a bottle of vodka, it won't affect the contents. The only way to bring about a real change is to pour the vodka out and to pour the wine in.

A traveller in present-day Eastern Europe has a unique opportunity to watch the edifice of history being built in front of his eyes (he may even be allowed to hold a trowel). And it won't stay like this for much longer: give it five or ten years, and Eastern Europe will be sucked – finally and irretrievably – into the whirlwind of Western consumerist society, like a fallen autumn leaf into a drainage pipe.

To some extent, Eastern Europe is already almost a part of the Western world, yet without political correctness, meaning that men are still men, and women are still women, and no one is particularly concerned about the burning Western issue of sexual harassment. Yes, Eastern Europe is sexy, even lewd: men are not ashamed to gape openly at pretty women, and women, rather than filing sexual harassment suits, are often willing to gape in return. Also, for a beleaguered Western smoker like myself, Eastern Europe, where everyone still happily puffs away, is like a breath of fresh, nicotine-saturated air.

Political correctness (or rather, the lack of it) and sexual harassment are the problems of a well-developed and self-satisfied (not to say 'idle') society, whereas in Eastern Europe more topical issues take priority: how to survive on a miserly salary, how to provide for the future of the children, how to save women from kitchen slavery and hard physical labour, how to protect oneself from the volatile bacteria of Western (mostly American) mass culture, and so on. 'People want to know, first, why their pockets are empty and, second, why others' are full,' as I was told by a Romanian journalist in Bucharest. Well, welcome to the free world!

A small Slovakian (or Hungarian) hamlet, where I stopped to buy cigarettes. Ramshackle little houses (sorry, but many houses in East European villages *are* ramshackle). A stunning (and no less ramshackle) baroque church. An old peasant woman carrying an armful of hay on the back seat of her antediluvian bicycle. Everything around me is painted in greyish pastel half-tints. There are only two screaming bright touches in this sombre post-communist landscape – two huge billboards advertising Marlboro cigarettes and Coca-Cola above the entrance to the hamlet's only shop, which, in accordance with an old Soviet habit, is closed for a mysterious 'Sanitary hour'. Or for an inventory. Or for goods delivery. Or . . .

Why is it that the triumphant march of Western civilisation into the former communist bloc is led by cigarettes, soft drinks and junk food, not by its cultural and intellectual pillars? Isn't it strange that the West is using these unhealthy and foul-smelling products as its ambassadors and front-runners, as if subjecting the new member-countries of the free world to a cruel survival test: if they live through this pernicious invasion, welcome to NATO and the EU.

Speaking of Westernisation, I have to admit that so far it has led to nothing more eye-catching than countless Marlboro and Coca-Cola signs on the time-beaten façades of Budapest, Bucharest, Sofia or Veliko Turnovo, a fragile medieval town in Bulgaria, the impoverished country with probably the world's highest per capita rate of Marlboro and Coca-Cola ads.

In post-communist Eastern Europe, Marlboro and Coca-Cola are like two primary-school upstarts constantly raising their impatient hands so as not to be overlooked by an elderly and myopic teacher of history. Plus, of course, the ubiquitous McDonald's fast-food restaurants, these smelly and oily ice-breakers of capitalism.

How nice it would be, for a change, to spot on the walls of a Hungarian (or Slovakian) village shop a mug-shot of kindly grandfather Freud with his sharp Lenin-style goatee, or the refined face of George Orwell, or a life-size image of Luciano Pavarotti. And commercials of the type 'Read Orwell!' or 'Listen to Stravinsky!' or even 'Don't Read Joyce: You Won't Understand a Thing!' instead of all those saying 'Drink!' and 'Smoke!' and 'Buy!' and 'Stuff Yourselves Stupid!'

To be fair, a certain amount of freedom is already there. One can travel anywhere from Liechtenstein to Australia without permission from local bureaucrats – if he (or she) has money and provided Liechtenstein and Australia do not mind him (or her) coming over. The undisguisedly bourgeois *Playboy* magazine is displayed on every news-stand, next to super-sensitive, self-adhesive and remote-controlled Japanese condoms. The Great Friend of Children (especially boys), Michael Jackson, regularly goes on East European tours carrying in his luggage his own 30-metre-high inflatable statue, and even thinks of buying himself a castle somewhere in Poland, which, as I heard, he tends to confuse with France.

True, the sticky 'socialist' word 'queue' has almost vanished from the people's lexicon. But, for the majority of East Europeans, the shops bursting with faked French deodorants and genuine American fags are hardly affordable. Just like Wacko Jacko's concerts. Or like the restaurants, now decadently offering pizzas, kebabs and other capitalist yummies, and yet routinely (and unprofitably!) *closing* for lunch, which in most East European countries is the main meal of the day and is called dinner, and sometimes for dinner, which in that part of the world is known as supper.

Yes, old habits die hard. And old drinking habits die even harder. Especially in Eastern Europe. If we look at the latest East European political and social ups and downs – swarms of purposeless political parties, chaotic changes of equally inept governments, hasty liquidation of old borders and even hastier creation of new ones, futile attempts at reinventing 'socialism with a human face' which have so far resulted in a wild capitalism with the red face of a boozer, the awakening of racism and ugly nationalism, degraded morals, an upsurge of crime – we can be forgiven for thinking that these countries are simply *drunk*.

Drunk with their sudden freedom which, as it turns out, not only gives you new rights but also implies lots of responsibilities. Drunk with alcoholic beverages which are now more accessible and more versatile than ever before. Poland alone now produces over a thousand different brands of vodka and consumes 34 million cases of it in one year – almost a case, or 20 bottles, per every single Pole (the population of the country is 34 million, including new-born babies and senile, but (presumably) still heavily imbibing, octogenarians). This is not counting 4 million cases of wine; 470 million cases of beer; 250,000 cases of brandy, thousands of cases of whisky, gin, rum, cognacs, liqueurs; and – on top of this stormy Alcoholic Ocean – a fairly insignificant 2,500 cases of tequila!

'Psychologically, the Poles didn't feel too bad under the communist yoke. Repression enabled them to protest and to express their rebellious nature. Now, when they are free and have to carry the burden of responsibility themselves, they don't know how to behave, and every imaginable extreme becomes possible,' said Stanislaw Lem, a famous Polish science fiction writer. These words can be applied in equal measure to any other country of Eastern Europe; all of them have shown a significant increase in alcohol consumption since the collapse of communism. It looks as though, instead of becoming (as we all had hoped) new European democracies almost overnight, the post-communist countries have turned into anti-totalitarian (or is it 'un-teetotalitarian'?) *dipsocracies*, countries ruled by a strong drink rather than a 'strong hand'.

'The [modern East European] state is like a drunk in a crowded bus; it stands only because there's a crowd. When the people get off, it will fall because it has no strength to stand on its own,' as one Polish official put it.

At times, however, it looked as if the 'crowd' on the bus was drunk, too. I saw hundreds of confused East Berliners drinking themselves into a stupor inside huge tarpaulin tents serving as makeshift bars in Alexanderplatz. I saw Slovaks pumping themselves up with tepid beer in the dark beer halls of Bratislava. I read the proceedings of the First International Dracula

Congress in Transylvania, which now tries to market itself as Dracula land: after all, Dracula, too, was a compulsive drinker (although he preferred red booze to white).

It is not only the people who are affected by this epidemic of massive inebriation. In Romania, I heard a story of a peasant from the village of Cuza Voda who had dumped twenty ducks in a river, thinking they were dead, only to find them later waddling happily around his yard – they had simply been in a drunken stupor after drinking from wine casks he was cleaning.

I don't want you to think, however, that East European drinking culture has undergone no change since the dismantling of the Berlin Wall. The main development is the growing consumption of wine and beer – drinks not half as effective as spirits in achieving the desired oblivion – whereas the consumption of stronger drinks, albeit still very high, keeps going down, slowly but surely.

Let me point it out again: in Eastern Europe, like nowhere else, *everything* is connected with drinks – in one way or another. By looking at the evolution of drinks and drinking habits one can understand the character of the momentous changes which have occurred there since 1989, and one of the best ways to do so is through the translucent, even if slightly distorting, bottom of a wine, beer or vodka glass.

Travelling in Eastern Europe, I have made a number of personal discoveries, the most important being wine culture, of which I had been totally ignorant. What can you expect of someone whose drinking education started at the tender age of 16 in the Soviet Ukraine under the expert guidance of an 18-year-old youth called Evgeny Bulavin – a sportsman, a provincial intellectual, a draft-dodger (he simulated dromomania, an irrepressible passion for purposeless travel) and a consummate alcoholic, thrown out of the Pedagogical

Institute (where he studied swimming) for intemperate drinking after his second year? We used to work together as dishwashers at a sports camp near the village of Gaidary on the bank of the Severski Donets river.

Bulavin's favourite toast was 'To this glass not being the last one, to more frequent drinking – long live alcohol – hooray!' On seeing a dead-drunk man lying in the gutter, Evgeny would note jealously, 'Happy guy! Look, he is already enjoying himself, and we haven't drunk anything yet!' Once he got so smashed that he lost the minute-hand from his wristwatch, whereas the hour-hand remained intact under the glass and kept showing hours properly. He could never explain that enigmatic incident.

It was under Evgeny's tutorial influence that for the first and last time in my life I drank perfume. It was called Russian Forest. We diluted it with water, and the opaque liquid in the glass was immediately covered with soapy foam. The taste was disgusting, and for the rest of the evening we stank like two walking barber's shops.

A muscular lad and an excellent swimmer, Evgeny often dog-paddled across the river with a bagful of empty vodka bottles tied to his head. Then he would hitch-hike (once, he flagged down an ambulance) to the nearest vodka-shop town, where he would deposit a couple of dozen empty bottles in exchange for a full one. During one such expedition, he dropped a newly acquired bottle, which broke to smithereens. He stood there for two hours crying and wondering whether they would replace the bottle if he picked up all the fragments and showed them as evidence to the shop assistant.

Evgeny and I developed a measuring unit for drunkenness: one bout. The mathematical formula for it was as follows:

$$\frac{gram \times \% \text{ of alcohol}}{person \text{ per second}} = 1 \text{ bout}$$

No wonder my taste buds, ruined by Russian Forest and other 'high-bouted' drinks, were not particularly sensitive to wine.

After a short stint as a dishwasher, Evgeny Bulavin found himself a full-time position as a porter at a milk factory (he tried a vodka factory first, but it had no vacancies). The main perk of that job was that he could drink as much milk as he wanted. Evgeny consumed up to twenty litres a day, assuring me that ten litres of milk on an empty stomach had an effect similar to a shot of vodka.

I don't know what happened to him in the end. One day – just like the fifteenth-century French poet (and drunkard) François Villon – he simply disappeared, and nothing further is known of him.

During my East European wanderings, I often thought of Evgeny Bulavin, the home-grown vodka philosopher, the plonk intellectual and the great pundit of Soviet-style drinking, both in theory and in practice. At times, it felt as if he was travelling with me around Eastern Europe, and together we were discovering the pleasures of the grape.

Having started my travels as a reluctant ulcer-challenged teetotaller, I had to give up my teetotalitarian ways after several wine tastings. The reason was that in Hungary and Bulgaria they provided me with a spittoon ('What a waste!' Evgeny would say), but in Romania – because of the dire economic situation, I presume – they often didn't. Since it was inappropriate for a visiting London scribe to spit on the floor, I had to start swallowing – and came to enjoy it in the end . . .

Spit – sorry, split – into three parts, 'Beer Lands', 'Spirits Lands' and 'Wine Lands', this book is nevertheless not so much about the drinks as about the people – the long-suffering people of Eastern Europe – and the never-ending tragicomedy of their lives. Laughter and tears have always gone hand in hand in that part of the world. It is important to understand that the communist system was not only cruel, domineering and blood-thirsty, but also ridiculous, paranoid and grotesque.

Before we start our journey, let me tell you about an extraordinary exhibition I attended in Leipzig, the second largest city of the former GDR. Called 'Tyranny and Banality', it was located in the former area headquarters of the Stasi, East Germany's fearsome secret police, which had 100,000 staff agents and 2 million 'freelance' informers (in the 17-million-strong GDR) on its payroll. It was near that circular grey building, ironically nicknamed 'Krumme Ecke' (Round Corner), that the 1989 anti-communist revolution began with a peaceful 'Candles against Violence' march.

Among the exhibits were:

- Stasi agents' spying aids: artificial beer-bellies, (real) capacious bras, and 'just-in-case' string shopping bags – all with in-built mini-cameras;
- a special device for steam-opening letters to and from the West (every post office in the GDR had a Stasi room, staffed with 'reader-agents');
- foreign postage stamps to replace the ones that were accidentally damaged by careless letter-opening;
- special optical devices allowing agents to look inside the parcels without opening them;
- a list of number-plates of the cars which were spotted parked near a church;
- a confiscated portrait of the communist dictator Erich Honecker, with his nose painted red by some local wit (a criminal investigation was launched to find the culprit);
- an agent's report, signed 'Gerhardt', on the out-rageous behaviour of a priest during a party: 'He drank a lot, smoked a lot, danced, and even kissed a woman.'
- a list of Western goods, unavailable in the East, in-advertently published by *Leipziger Volksgazette* and

sent to the Stasi, 'with socialist greetings' (!) by a facetious reader. To find the joker, the Stasi analysed fingerprints on the paper and conducted a highly sophisticated saliva test;

* an extract from an 'observation report' (not a joke!): 'Attention: the object has just raised his hand with a handkerchief in it and blew his nose, then he bent down and tied his shoe-laces.';

* a piece of cloth with the smell (!) of a dissident writer in a sealed glass can.

'We chose to laugh at them, to show how bizarre and banal a tyranny could be,' said Frau Perl, the exhibition's curator, whose husband, a well-known linguist, was imprisoned by the Stasi for 'contacts with foreigners' (*sic*), another act of the real-life tragicomedy of the former GDR – 'The German Democratic Republic': what a cynical misnomer!

'Laughing, mankind says good-bye to its past,' wrote Stanislaw Jerzy Lec, a Polish satirist. I wonder whether the same can be said about drinking?

It is an old Russian custom to pour the last shot of vodka before a departure on to the traveller's walking stick, hence the expression '*na pososhok*', a Russian equivalent of 'one for the road'. I won't commit such sacrilege, for which my drinking tutor, Evgeny Bulavin (whom you are going to meet many more times in this book), would never have forgiven me.

I: BEER LANDS

The Czech Republic, with a touch of East Germany

1 MY PINT OF VIEW

M y drinking guru, Evgeny Bulavin, didn't like beer. 'Chancellor von Bismarck used to say that beer makes you lazy and stupid,' he would observe thoughtfully, sipping a watery yellow liquid at Kharkov's Veterok (Little Wind) beer pub. Why he had to invoke the first German chancellor for such a trite statement, I don't know. He must have thought that a reference to Bismarck added intellectual weight to his inebriated pronouncements.

Veterok was unique, because beer was always (well, almost always) on sale there, although to call this urine-like drink 'beer' would have been an insult. To urine. Beer was one of the rarest commodities in the Soviet Union, and millions of thirsty (or hung-over) men all over the huge country used to start their mornings by scouring their neighbourhood shops and posing one sacramental question: '*Pivo yest?*' ('Do you have beer?'). Mind you, they were not asking for Courage, Guinness, Stella Artois or Pilzensky Prazdroy. Nor were they after the cannabis-flavoured Swiss beer Hanf, the Faroese brand Black Sheep, the Western Australian lager Red

Back (named after a venomous spider), or the Burundian beer Primus, famous for having triggered genocide in that remote African country. They were looking for any '*pivo*'* and the brand – the Soviet Union had two: Moskovskoye and Zhigulevskoye – didn't matter, because one couldn't buy it anyway.

The following episode from my time as a Moscow journalist serves as a good illustration of the beer situation in the USSR. In 1980, I was sent to Arkhangelsk, the city in the far north of Russia that was the destination of many of the wartime Arctic convoys. My task was to investigate the deplorable state of local hotels (there were only two in the town, so my mission did not look particularly burdensome). Here, it has to be said that at that time the Soviet Union, under the wise leadership of Leonid Brezhnev, was experiencing severe food shortages, and the Arkhangelsk region was one of the worst affected areas. Literally nothing was on sale in the town's permanently bare food shops. What made it worse, especially for children, was the total absence of milk, which was still fairly easy to get in Moscow. 'Milk is available only to the sick in possession of a doctor's prescription', ran the shocking handwritten signs in Arkhangelsk shop-windows (and they were the *only* things displayed there).

One morning I was recovering after an interview with the director of one of the two hotels whom I had started interviewing over a bottle of vodka at 6 p.m. and finished – at four the following morning – over a canister of pure alcohol, chased with sauerkraut, at his flat. My head was splitting, and my mouth felt as if it was full of cats' poo. There was only one thing that would cure me and allow me to face the director of the second hotel – a

---

* In the old Russian language '*pivo*' – from the verb '*pit*', to drink – denoted any liquid that could be drunk, whereas in Soviet Russia it came to mean one particular drink which couldn't be drunk as it was almost impossible to obtain.

job that promised to be as wearisome as the first, and possibly even more so, for the second director was a Georgian (and Georgians are notorious for their heavy drinking).

With my press card in my pocket, I joined the uneven ranks of the millions of suffering Soviet males trying to find beer on that particular morning. Having wandered along the town's wooden pavements for a couple of hours, I eventually stumbled upon a queue, although to call that enormous, disorderly crowd, consisting almost exclusively of red-faced and blue-nosed men, a queue was a gross understatement. All the male population of the Arkhangelsk region was probably there. And although I couldn't see what was on sale in the food shop they were boisterously queuing for (the entrance was several miles away), the answer was obvious: beer. Nothing else could have brought together so many Soviet men on an ordinary working morning (vodka was then sold from 2 p.m. only).

I was never in the habit of flashing my red press card in the face of sales people in an attempt to acquire some short-supplied goods, thus abusing my journalistic position. But on that particular day I was – literally – dying from hangover, and could only carry on with my work if I somehow managed to replace the cats' poo in my mouth with a hair of the dog.

I elbowed my way to the shop's back entrance and, having shown my press card to a drunken doorman, got inside. Blushing with embarrassment, I approached a buxom artificial blonde in a formerly white gown on top of her winter coat, probably the shop's manager. 'I only need a couple of bottles,' I pleaded. I didn't specify that it was beer that I was after: I thought it went without saying. 'Khorosho! [OK!]' she replied, having measured up my miserable, shaking figure with one quick professional glance. 'We might be able to help you. Wait outside.' It was not long before she emerged out of the back door. Looking around stealthily, she opened the flaps of her dirty gown, under which she was cradling two bottles of . . . milk.

The state of beer-drinking affairs was only slightly better in Moscow, which boasted a couple of seedy watering holes with beer-selling machines. The main problem was to get hold of an empty beer mug: glass mugs, unlike human (or rather semi-human) ones, were chronically scarce in those 'bars'. I remember standing on the dirty floor, which was covered with vomit and fish-bones, gulping my beer, while three or four unshaven and shaking types hovered over me, trying to grab my beer mug and droning every two seconds, 'Are you nearly finished, pal?'

No wonder Evgeny Bulavin didn't like beer. He and his numerous disciples (myself included) simply did not treat beer seriously: drunk on its own, it was not sufficiently intoxicating to lead you into the coveted oblivion – just a passable hangover cure, that's all. But adding some vodka to it was quite another matter. A hundred grams of vodka poured into a half-litre mug of beer produced a quick and staggering (in the true sense of the word) effect. This beer–vodka cocktail, known as a Ruff (after a prickly freshwater fish), was especially popular among students, always willing to get smashed as quickly and as cheaply as possible.

I remember that the country's first ever 'beer restaurant' Yantar (Amber), was opened in Kharkov in line with the umpteenth anti-alcoholism campaign. The idea behind Yantar was that of all alcoholic drinks beer *alone* would be served there. This noble concept was doomed from the start. Customers smuggled in *chekushka*s (small bottles of vodka) in their trouser pockets and busily made Ruffs behind the waiters' backs. 'How come you are all so drunk?' a worried manager lamented, running from one end of the restaurant hall to the other. In no time Yantar had won itself the hard-to-achieve reputation of the best boozing haunt in Kharkov. 'The way to hell is paved with good intentions, and the way to heaven – with bad ones,' as my friend Evgeny Bulavin used to say.

As a hack in London and in Australia, I could never come to grips with the so-called pub culture which most of my colleagues were so attached to. Standing for hours in a noisy, smoky room with a pint in your hand was not my idea of having fun. I discovered that even a modest half-pint had an adverse effect on my writing abilities (it did make me feel both lazy and stupid – *pace* Evgeny Bulavin and Chancellor Bismarck), whereas for some of my fellow-journalists it was the other way round: they were unable to write without fuelling themselves with beer first. One of the staff columnists on the Melbourne *Age*, where I worked in the early nineties, even moved his computer to a nearby pub and filed his copy from there.

As you must have guessed, I am not a keen beer-drinker, and as such I was not particularly looking forward to the beer part of my East Europe journey. But, like it or not, the job had to be done. For a start, I needed some background knowledge on the culture and history of civilised (as opposed to Soviet-style) beer-drinking and of beer as such.

I knew that beer is a fermented cereal beverage, made from malted barley, hops and yeast. I also knew that the difference between lagers and ales is that the former are fermented at lower temperatures than the latter and are usually lighter in colour. That was all.

As for the history of brewing, I had to trust Britain's biggest beer expert, Michael Jackson, who once wrote, 'Man's desire for beer, or perhaps woman's [*sic!*], may have been responsible for civilisation'. No less. The end of that very article by the politically correct beerologist was somewhat less inspiring: 'Some beers of the early civilisations in Africa and South and Central America were fermented with the aid of spittle or babies' faeces.' Remembering the taste of the beer served at the Veterok, the pub of my youth, I realised that they had managed to keep some of these ancient recipes alive in the Soviet Union.

In short, I was desperate for some more nitty-gritty on beer, and I was lucky: the annual Great British Beer Festival had just opened at Olympia. Having put on my bullet-ridden flak jacket (just in case), I took the Tube to Earls Court.

2 PLAYING IT BY BEER

The Grand Hall of the Olympia Exhibition Centre was buzzing and stirring like a hornets' nest sprayed with lager. Outside, cabs and buses were disgorging flocks of red-faced beer louts, many of whom were carrying their own personal beer mugs – for reasons of hygiene, I presume.

To get inside the hall, I had to negotiate several burly lads giving out leaflets to the entrants. The lads looked so ferocious that it was hard to ignore them (and their leaflets). 'Brussels Threatens Your Real Ale Choice', 'Great British Beer Drinkers Send Message to Brussels Eurocrats', screamed the leaflets. As I found out later, they were issued by CAMRA, the Campaign For Real Ale, an organisation campaigning for the preservation of traditional British beers and pubs.

Interestingly, among the leaflets forced on me at the entrance, there was one which had little to do with either pubs or beers: 'Only one party can free Britain from the Euro-Noose'. My first thought was that there was a misprint in the leaflet, which should have read 'Euro-Booze'. Having perused the text in full, however, I

realised that it had been issued by the UK Independence
Party, which didn't seem to mind European lagers but
said a firm 'No' to control of Britain by European
bureaucrats and to British surrender of her independence'.

After spending some time inside the hall, I came to
understand why the UK Independence Party had chosen
the Great British Beer Festival as a lucrative venue for
spreading its own anti-European propaganda. The
Festival patrons, most of whom looked and behaved like
football hooligans (they probably *were* football hooligans), were not just xenophobic and anti-lager; they
were anti-everything, except for the tepid bitter 'real ale'
and the grilled German sausages – the only part of the
European culture they were ready to embrace. The
crowd was 99 per cent male, and I thought that the event
could be renamed the Great British Beard Festival for the
profusion of facial hair.

The hall was like one enormous pub, the size of a
football pitch. In the middle, a brass band was playing
some noisy patriotic tunes from an elevated wooden
platform. Beer taps and bar stands were situated along
the perimeter. The stale air was filled with the clinking
of glasses, the hubbub of drunken voices and the
nauseating smell of chips, barbecued hamburgers and
burnt sausages. Numerous souvenir stalls were doing a
brisk trade in cheap T-shirts with dirty logos, cheap
CAMRA pins, cheap bottle-openers, cheap postcards with
pussy-cats, cheap (discounted) *Good Beer Guide*s, and
cheap back copies of *London Drinker*, *Loud Aler* and
Ale Mail magazines at from 10 to 30 pence each.
Everything about the place was *cheap* in every sense of
that word.

Having opened at random an issue of *Loud Aler*, the
organ of CAMRA's Surrey Branches, I read the following
under Local Brewery News: 'Firstly, apologies to those
who have been drinking Pilgrim Spring Bock thinking its
ABV was 4.5%. That's what we were told for the last

edition, but in fact it is somewhat stronger at 5.5%.' I thought that was inexcusable!

Standing there, in the middle of the Great British Beer Festival, which a London newspaper once called (in Saddam Hussein's inimitable style) 'the mother of all fests', I was reminded of a powerful, yet unwitting, indictment of beer culture by a beer-loving Hollywood film star, Clint Eastwood, who once remarked, 'My idea of a good evening is two beers in the front of the fireplace [in the case of an average British beer-addict, it would probably be 'ten beers in front of a TV set showing football']. I drink them. Squeeze the cans. It makes you feel kind of macho. You toss 'em in the waste-basket, you belch three times and go to bed . . .' What can I say? 'Those who drink beer – will think beer,' as William Warburton, Bishop of Gloucester, once remarked.

I was about to leave the Beer Festival, when, unexpectedly, I stumbled across a lonely espresso stall, bashfully tucked into one of the hall's darkest corners. The shock of this discovery was similar to that of spotting the world's most sophisticated chef and inventor of *nouvelle cuisine*, Alain Ducasse, stuffing himself with a hamburger in a seedy McDonald's outlet. A forlorn South African girl behind the stand was engrossed in a thick novel. 'You are my first customer in three days,' she noted, handing me a cup of steaming espresso.

'No wonder: beer and coffee do not mix,' I thought, sipping my beloved espresso and browsing through a *London Drinker* editorial: 'According to the latest printed statistics, Real Ale is on the retreat.' The last sentence of that rather disgruntled little article was: 'I think I'd better go down for a pint of Hop Back to cheer myself up!' There were two page 27s in that issue, which was probably put together when, having had their pints of Hop Back, the staff hopped back to the office. Brilliant journalism. I even felt like writing a fan letter to the editor and signing it 'Bibulously yours'.

The Great British Beer Festival convinced me that beer culture (or at least that particular manifestation of it) was not exactly my cup of tea, let alone coffee.

3 BABY AND BULLY

'Communists do not surrender,' said Comrade Stalin on learning that his son had been taken prisoner by the Nazis. Having spent a large chunk of my life rubbing shoulders with stubborn communists and having been once called a 'Communist for the *Guardian*' in an official letter from a not-too-literate London solicitor, I was not in the habit of giving up easily. My brief excursion to the Great British Beer Festival not having been particularly enriching, I decided to give it another try.

'If you really want to dip into beer culture, go to the Oktoberfest,' a beer-wise London friend advised. I started making enquiries and found out that the Oktoberfest was held in Munich and – surprisingly – started on 21 September. 'How come the October Festival starts in September?' I wondered, before remembering that the October revolution in Russia actually took place in November. These things do happen: obviously, some momentous October events had a tendency *not* to happen in October. Pondering this curious phenomenon, I even found an inverse connection between the Oktoberfest – the world's biggest celebration of beer-drinking – and the October revolution, which had led to the almost complete absence of beer in the world's largest country.

Some of the Oktoberfest statistics that I had managed to dig up were quite staggering: allegedly, in the course of the festival a million gallons (5 million litres) of beer were consumed, and the total length of the urinal 'troughs' for the men was 2,575 feet! The data on the length of the women's urinals (or toilets) were not available, the reason probably being the absence of an appropriate measuring unit.

On top of this, the insatiable 8 million visitors attending the Oktoberfest each year, reportedly gobbled up 725,000 roast chickens, 320,000 pairs of grilled sausages, 65,000 pork knuckles, and – as if that wasn't enough – 72 whole roasted oxen.

'Beware of Australians at Oktoberfest!' they told me at the German National Tourist Office in London. 'What's so dangerous about them?' I enquired, not disclosing the fact that I was an Australian myself (if only by passport). 'Well, they are a bit . . . er . . . rough' was the reply.

Here I have to say that during my seven years in the West I've developed a powerful spirit of contradiction: the moment I see a forbidding sign, a placard calling for this or that, or hear a warning, I feel an urge to disobey. An innocuous 'No Smoking' plate causes strong craving for a cigarette. A 'No Drinking or Eating on the Premises' triggers pangs of hunger and thirst. When I see a poster 'Vote Tory', I feel like voting Labour. A 'Vote Labour' political broadcast evokes strong Conservative sympathies, and Paddy Ashdown's fiery calls to vote Liberal Democrat never fail to discourage me from voting altogether and to remind me of the fact that as an Australian subject I don't have the right to vote in British elections anyway.

'The rougher the research, the better it is for a book,'

decided I. On an early September morning, having ignored the Tourist Office warning, I boarded a bus, full of young Bierfest-bound Australians, in Earls Court. The package, offered by a London-based Australian tour operator, included accommodation in tents near Munich, the Bierfest, a mysterious 'Frog Convention' in Austria, and Dachau concentration camp – as unlikely and bizarre a mixture as the infamous Ruff (beer plus vodka) of my Soviet youth.

The bus was to take us to Ramsgate, where we were to board a ferry to Ostende, the crossing to be followed by a fourteen-hour overnight drive to Munich.

I had no idea that I had embarked on the wildest journey of my entire life.

On the way to Ramsgate, I kept throwing furtive glances at my travel companions, none of whom seemed 'rough' or threatening. A lad behind me was telling his 'mate' how he had been backpacking from Sydney to Brisbane and suddenly 'saw a huge giraffe crossing the road'. A plump, freckled youth on the seat in front read a tabloid article with a long, heart-chilling headline: 'Baby Geoffrey suffocated when his boozed-up dad fell on him after a stag-night binge on beer and vodka'. For no apparent reason, I started feeling a bit uneasy.

A modest-looking girl sitting next to me was immersed in an Australian book, *Drinking Games*. I craned my neck and peeked over her shoulder: 'Contestants sit around a timekeeper, who allows them one minute to drink a film canister full of beer. The ultimate goal is to drink 100 canisters in 100 minutes, without a break to piss or puke. All bodily waste is eventually emptied on to a timekeeper, a voluntary position that is, unbelievably, highly sought after . . .'

This was the first clear sign of impending danger.

It was a crisp, misty morning. At times it felt as if we were driving inside a gigantic chilled beer glass. On the massive Belgian ferry, whose male crew members looked like secret paedophiles and child-molesters (this is what an excessively sensationalist media coverage sometimes does to your perception of foreigners), I didn't see much of my fellow-Aussies, whom I rejoined only after we docked in Ostende. A minor transformation had occurred in them: they were noisier and ruddier than before, and many were carrying crates of Stella Artois on their shoulders. 'What a strange thing to do,' I thought. Carrying beer to the Bierfest was on a par with carrying coals to Newcastle or water to the Thames. Only later did I realise that taking Stella Artois to Munich was not on my travel companions' agenda.

In Ostende our group was met by another bus with a Munich-based Australian driver, Mick, and a guide called Leonie, a diminutive Liverpudlian girl, who – from having to deal with too many Antipodeans – spoke English with a feline Aussie accent.

'No puking on the bus, mates!' announced Mick, starting the engine.

For the first half-hour or so everything was relatively quiet. Some of the Aussies were asleep, probably saving their strength for the impending battles. The girl next to me was now studying the rules of another – fairly innocuous – 'drinking game' called Balancing Act: '. . . requires ten cans of beer per player . . .'

Suddenly all hell broke loose. Everyone on the bus was drinking. The Aussies were frantically unpacking their crates of beer, and in no time all of them had tinnies glued to their lips. Those who had failed to bring their own supplies, were able to buy booze from the driver – with a surcharge for the service, of course.

'Our official attitude is no drinking on the bus, but since they are going to drink anyway, we had to introduce the policy of controlled drinking,' Leonie told me in confidence.

Meanwhile, 'controlled drinking' was slowly but surely getting out of control. Hiccups, burps and four-letter words sounded from all sides. They were soon joined by an uneven mix of singing and farting.

Discarded beer cans rattled on the bus floor like empty cartridges.

'Wanna beer, mate?' I was asked by the flabby red-headed youth whom I had seen reading a tabloid in the morning. His face was quickly acquiring the colour of his fiery hair. I nick-named him 'Baby'. He was sitting next to a burly, muscular youngster in dirty military fatigues who was trying to drink from two cans simultaneously. I christened him 'Bully'.

It was interesting to observe how beer was changing the behavioural pattern of these normal Australian kids. Their speech was faltering in direct proportion to the amount of alcohol they consumed. They were becoming boisterous and aggressive. Baby was now inserting f-curses not just before, but also after, every single word he uttered. The no-puking-on-the-bus regulation was violated every couple of minutes. The modest-looking girl, who had probably finished reading *Drinking Games* (her glassy eyes indicated that she had achieved 'the ultimate goal') was looking at me steadily. I moved aside lest she should take me for a 'timekeeper' – a position I hadn't sought.

It was getting dark outside the bus windows. The prospect of sleep seemed increasingly unlikely. My personal Bierfest started long before Munich.

'If you look at your right, you'll see the city of Brussels, the capital of Belgium, which is the country where we are now, by the way,' Leonie stated matter-of-factly. No one was listening. Somewhere near Liège, a truck with a load of pigs stopped next to our bus at traffic lights. The Australians suddenly went silent for a moment, probably struck by the uncanny resemblance. I noted that the pigs on the truck were much more orderly (and cleaner) than my human fellow-travellers.

Mick had to make frequent 'piss-stops' to allow his passengers to relieve themselves. 'Take it a bit easy. Remember there are six days of Bierfest ahead of you,' he pleaded from behind the wheel. His words fell on deaf ears. Neat Belgian forests were flooded with torrents of Antipodean urine.

'That was the longest piss of my life!' Baby announced proudly after one such stop.

The oldest person on the bus, I didn't want to be a party-pooper until Baby decided to sit on my head. I pushed his sweaty bulk away and returned to making some rickety notes on my memo pad.

'You, f—ing journo!' Baby screamed in a high-pitched falsetto. I grabbed him by the collar.

'Be civilised!' intervened Leonie.

'I am going to f—ing sleep,' declared Baby suddenly. Having wriggled his jelly-fish-like damp and fat body out of my grip, he switched off. In a second, he was snoring and farting in his sleep. His egg-shaped beer-saturated head bounced against the window like an elongated Aussie Rules football against the pitch.

Baby's role of ringleader was taken up by Bully. Pale and nearly fainting, he kept pumping himself with beer. 'Why do you torment yourself?' I asked him. 'And why n-not?' he belched.

The very beer culture that I thought I had fled by leaving Australia had come to haunt me in the European woods, through which we were now driving.

The din of drunken voices, let alone the stench, was unbearable. On top of it, Mick was playing some deafening rock music over the loudspeaker. 'Music helps drunken people to fall asleep,' he explained when I asked him to turn the radio down. It certainly didn't help me.

The sad Belgian moon, soaked with beer, was mooching about in the Guinness-coloured sky.

By 8 o'clock next morning, we had reached the suburbs of Munich. From there, as Mick explained, a shuttle to the Bierfest took only ten minutes – 'about two-thirds of a beer'. By that time, the bus had come to resemble a poorly kept pigsty on wheels.

Snow was lying on top of the tents at Campingplatz

Thalkirchen, where we were supposed to stay for six nights. It should have been called Camp Hangover instead. Freezing and shaking Aussies with sunken, faded eyes wandered around the camp grounds wrapped in blankets. Some of them were already drinking their first tinny of the day – in full accordance with a tested morning-after cure recommended by *TNT*, an Australian magazine published in London: 'Get stuck into the beer again when you wake up and drown the bugger!'

It was too much for me. Having made my apologies to Leonie, I headed for a nearby hotel, dreaming of a hot English breakfast. When I was leaving Camp Hangover, I got a glimpse of Baby and Bully queuing for the camp's only plywood shower shed. In their trembling fists, they were clutching white shower coupons with the German word '*Gas*' printed on them in big letters. I thought that they were two people I didn't particularly mind being gassed.

For the next several days I kept bumping into my travel companions in the streets of Munich and in the Bierfest grounds. I saw Baby and Bully, with Bavarian wooden clogs on their bare feet, thumping against the cobbles and chasing a group of unsuspecting Japanese tourists near the Hofbrau Keller, the beer hall where Hitler drank with his storm troopers on the eve of the so-called Beer Hall Putsch of 1923. I saw a young Australian bloke being loaded into an ambulance, while his drinking companion, his face covered in blood, was taken away in a police car. I saw another Australian youth writhing on the ground in an alcohol-induced epileptic fit amidst the cheerful Bavarian lederhosen-clad crowd (lederhosen struck me as the best possible attire to conceal a beer-belly).

I learnt that during every Bierfest several Aussies die of alcohol poisoning and many more end up at Munich hospitals. Is it really worth coming to Munich from the other end of the world only to get smashed? I kept thinking. And why do so many Australians tend to treat the rest of the world as an extension of their local pub, which down under they call a 'hotel'?

Leonie was standing on the steps of a bus parked near Marienplatz, a stunning Gothic square in the centre of Munich, and instructing another group of Aussies: 'Drunk or not drunk, throwing up or not, be here in time, like a Snow-white or whatever it was with a pumpkin!'

'Yesterday was a good day,' she told me. 'Only one throw-up on the bus, but plenty of vomiting in Bierfest grounds. And this morning one chap was run over by a car on the way to the Festival. He only survived because he was pissed.'

And I thought then that an excursion to Dachau concentration camp as part of the Bierfest package tour was not entirely irrelevant, for beer was not just a drink turning immature Australian 'babies' into aggressive bullies, and bullies into obstreperous and foul-mouthed adult babies. Beer culture was capable of triggering the worst forms of collective brutality. German Fascism as a movement started in Munich, with a beer-swilling coup at the Burgerbraukeller beer hall, which subsequently (and significantly) billed Hitler and his Nazi cronies for 143 steins (one-litre beer mugs), 80 glasses, 98 stools, two music stands – all of them smashed – and 148 stolen sets of cutlery. There's no need to tell you that the bill remained unpaid.

Dachau concentration camp was the ultimate example of what beer culture can lead to, if out of control.

4 PUB-CRAWLING IN PRAGUE

Some countries take a perverse pride in their beer-drinking statistics. The Germans maintain that they consume 251 pints per head a year, the Danes 225 pints, whereas the British average intake is a modest 180. The indisputable leadership here, however, is claimed by the Czechs, each of whom (including new-born babies and octogenarians), allegedly, gulps down a staggering 283 pints, or 150 litres, of beer annually. And although Bavarians assert that their per capita average consumption is 350 litres, we have to take into account Australian visitors to the Bierfest, whose contribution to the overall Bavarian figure, as witnessed by myself, must be close to 90 per cent.

I was looking forward to my time in the Czech Republic not so much because of its beer-drinking records, but rather because former Czechoslovakia was the first ever foreign country I visited while still living in the Soviet Union. The impressions of that trip in 1986 could be best described as shopping shock. I was stunned by the abundance of goods in the shops, by the fact that beer was always on sale and could be acquired easily – almost without queuing. I remember bringing proudly back to Moscow such flagrantly Western souvenirs as chewing gum, chocolate Easter eggs and strawberry-flavoured milk powder. For months after the trip, I was a welcome guest in many a Moscow flat on the condition that I shared with the hosts my impressions of the Czechoslovakian paradise and some of the milk powder, too.

Interestingly, a couple of my London friends who visited communist Czechoslovakia at approximately the same time, from the other side of the Berlin Wall, were genuinely appalled by 'near absence of everything' (in their words), unsmiling people and never-ending queues. What better proof of Einstein's theory of relativity?

An old Soviet joke makes the point even better than Einstein. An American and a Russian head off to Paris from their respective countries. By mistake, both end up in Prague (Warsaw, Budapest, East Berlin etc.), and both think that they have reached their destination.

Czechoslovakia had changed a lot since my last visit. After the KGB-inspired 'velvet revolution' of 1989, it was no longer communist; and after the 'velvet divorce' from Slovakia in 1993, it was no longer Czechoslovakia, but simply the Czech Republic.

If formerly I was advised not to speak Russian while in Prague (after the events of 1968, the locals were not exactly head over heels in love with Russians – and I didn't blame them), now a Prague-based Russian friend instructed me to speak exclusively Russian to taxi drivers as the best guarantee against being fleeced. 'If you speak Russian, they will think that you are a member of the Russian mafia and will be afraid to charge you a fortune,' he said. I did speak Russian to a glib taxi driver who picked me up at the station, but ended up being taken for a ride anyway. Having paid 350 crowns for a two-minute lift, I consoled myself that it was due to my total lack of resemblance to a Russian mafia gangster.

Post-communist Prague is a robber-city. Especially if you are a foreigner. They charge you 60 crowns (about $2) for a glass of watery orange juice or for a cup of decent coffee with an 'all-inclusive' hotel breakfast (the coffee that *is* included tastes like bad orange juice). They charge you extra for washing your hands at a public toilet. They make foreigners pay up to ten times the locals' fare for visiting the same tourist attractions. What's worse, they try to camouflage this injustice in a rather clumsy way.

Fluent in Russian and Ukrainian, I had no problem reading Czech street signs. I wished I had. Walking in Prague's Old Jewish Quarter, I spotted the following sign – in English and in Czech – near the entrance to the Old New Synagogue:

The Old New Synagogue –	adults – 150 kc
	children – 100 kc
Staronova Synagoga –	dospeli – zdarma
	deti – zdarma

As you have probably guessed, '*dospeli*' means 'adults', and '*deti*' means 'children'. What you might not have guessed is that '*zdarma*' means 'free'.

In other instances, they would indicate the foreigners' fare in figures (340 kc for 'entrance to the Jewish Quarter', say) and the locals' fare in Czech letters: '*padesat* kc' – fifty crowns for the same 'entrance'. A simple, yet pretty nasty, ruse.

Yes, in the ten years since my last visit, Prague had become an exemplary capitalist city, where everything was on sale, including human flesh. Every newspaper kiosk prominently displayed a glossy pinkish brochure, enticingly entitled *Prague Sex Guide*, in three languages, featuring photos of naked women with languorous raunchy eyes, and brothels with names like Club Apollon ('entrance includes a complimentary bottle of champagne'), Satanella ('designed to look like a hospital room, contains a chair with stirrups, and all the necessary tools for fantasy clinic sex') and Lotos Club ('if you wish to indulge, there are plenty of beautiful girls to choose from – the one you pick will take you to a tastefully decorated private room, the best of which is a jungle-theme room with a particularly large whirlpool bath'). To be on the safe side of AIDS, the *Sex Guide* provided potential clients of Prague brothels with such useful tips as 'A sore or chafed penis dramatically increases your risk of infection', and 'If you have any cuts on your fingers, don't insert them into your partner.' Nice and clear.

Don't get me wrong. Prague is still breathtakingly beautiful, and the new spirit of Western commercialism has added some entrepreneurial buzz to its narrow cobbled streets, lined with old baroque houses and churches. Baroque architecture, by the way, strikes me as somewhat beer-inspired: this extensive ornament-ation, this profusion of curved and interrupted lines, these heavy and solid – almost stout – façades, this beer-foam-like multitude of cupolas and turrets . . . And isn't it true that the best examples of baroque can be found in beer-loving countries? Please correct me if I am wrong (which I probably am).

Let's get back to beer, as Australians say. As a reluctant beer-drinker, I made sure I memorised one very useful Czech expression, 'Uz nepiju' ('I don't drink any more') before starting my pub-crawl. Saying that I didn't like beer in a Prague pub would have been tantamount to confessing to being impotent in a brothel.

Of course, my starting point had to be U Fleku, Prague's oldest and most famous beer hall, which has been brewing its own dark and strong brand Flekovsky Lezak since 1499. I am not sure about 1499, but when I came to U Fleku in 1986 during my first foreign trip from the beerless Soviet Union, I was seriously worried that they would run out of beer before I had time to be served. I also remember that the pub was full of swinging and mug-wielding East Germans.

U Fleku was easy to find. An uninterrupted line of neatly parked tourist buses led me to its entrance from Karlovo Namesti. Just as ten years before, the place was bursting with tourists, mostly Germans, although this time there were streaks of Americans and Japanese among them. A musician, dressed in the military uniform of the times of Good Soldier Svejk, was playing an accordion in one of the cavernous rooms. Just as I had ten years ago, I went out into the beer garden. It was cold outside, and the long wooden benches were half empty. Only some cold-resistant Scandinavians and several legless Germans were there. I sat next to a drunken German sugar daddy snogging his blonde and red-eyed young girlfriend. She was massive – Brünnhilde-like – and had a thick bovine neck. They both stank of beer.

Somewhere from above there came a voice 'Pivo?' ('Beer?'). It was the waiter, and I suddenly realised why in the Czech Republic and in Slovakia they call waiters 'Pan Vrchny' ('Mister Upper'). U Fleku's Mr Upper, sporting a short-sleeved white shirt under a black vest, was towering above me holding an enormous tray with several dozen beer mugs on it. His question was rather a rhetorical one: why on earth would someone come to U Fleku, if he didn't want beer? To play snooker? To board a flight to Bratislava? Or to scribble away in a W. H. Smith recycled notebook, as I did?

Thump! A weighty mug with dark brown liquid landed on the table in front of me. It was followed by Mr Upper's dexterous hand which made one quick notch on a piece of paper, stuck under my coaster. Before I could say 'Dekuji!' ('Thanks!'), another Mr Upper's hand was stretching towards me with a shot of Becherovka liqueur. But I was well prepared for the trick. Gently pushing his hand away, I told him resolutely 'Ne!' ('No!'), as the Pub Etiquette section of the *Prague Post* newspaper advised.

'Perchè?' Mr Upper asked in unexpected Italian.

'Because I don't want it!' I replied in English.

'But it is very good with beer,' the obstinate polyglot insisted.

'I don't think so. Take it away!'

The reason for Mr Upper's persistence was that they charged you 200 crowns (£5) for a shot, the price of a three-course meal (with beer) in a good Prague restaurant, whereas a 0.4 litre mug of beer at U Fleku was 'only' 39 crowns – by far the most expensive in the Czech Republic. Besides, contrary to Mr Upper's assurances, mixing the vomitingly sweet Becherovka with beer was like eating a pickled herring topped with raspberry jam. Ten years ago they didn't do this to unsuspecting tourists. Capitalism can sometimes be pushy.

I took a couple of sips from my mug and found the beer surprisingly pleasant. Its bitter-sweet taste reminded me of kvass, a drink of my Ukrainian childhood. Kvass is a mildly alcoholic (not stronger than yoghurt) drink made of yeast and black bread. It is the same dark brown and is – or used to be – sold by fat Ukrainian women from huge yellow tanks on every street corner. I stopped drinking kvass when one day I saw a tank break into two and all its contents pour out on to the asphalt: the streams of brown kvass were swarming with white intestinal worms . . .

Meanwhile, my neighbours were busily gulping their Becherovkas, washing them down with beer. Several happy Mr Uppers were hovering above them like butterflies, and the rows of pencilled 'notches' on their beer slips were as thick as hedges in Devon. A group of German students at the next table tried half-heartedly to swing, but quickly gave up. The sugar daddy was quarrelling with his bovine-necked Brünnhilde, whose face was by now pretty bovine, too.

The famous U Fleku, which claims to be the oldest beer pub in the world, was clearly no longer a place where one could find much local colour.

Not far from U Fleku, in Kaprova Street, I spotted a small pub called U Mestkiy Knihovni (At a Local Bookshop). What an ingenious name! Imagine an angry wife questioning her wayward husband: 'Where have you been all evening?' 'At a local bookshop,' he answers meekly. In Finland, by the way, they have gone even farther in pacifying angry wives: they have pubs called At My In-Laws and At My Brother's. The best pub name I have ever seen was in Scotland: The Why Not?

I didn't venture into A Local Bookshop, but through the window I could discern several fat, red-faced men drinking beer. And not a single book!

My next destination was U Pravdu, which translated as The Truth. My guidebook promised a nice beer garden and a convivial Svejk atmosphere. The beer garden was closed (it was too cold to sit in it anyway), the pub was totally empty, and this was the whole truth about The Truth.

I was luckier at U Cerneho Vola (At a Black Ox), although the name of this pub near Prague Castle would have been an immediate give-away for a beer-loving husband.

The atmosphere inside the pub was warm and brotherly: under low, beamed ceilings, the patrons were sitting next to each other on long dark-wood benches. They were drinking Kozel (Goat) beer and chasing it with traditional 'Pivni syr', a strong, spicy goat cheese. The balance, as I soon discovered, was perfect: my mouth was set on fire after each bite of the heavily peppered cheese, and the only way to put the flames out was to wash them down with a good gulp of Kozel. The man next to me had six notches on his slip already, and was thirstily approaching his seventh. A large mug of beer cost just 8.40 crowns (about 20p) – a big difference from U Fleku.

Through a small leaded window, I could see the palatial Foreign Ministry building across the road. It was there, in the courtyard, that the dead body of the country's democratically elected President Jan Masaryk was found beneath an open window on 10 March 1948. It was officially announced that he had killed himself by jumping to his death. Interestingly, the first doctor to arrive at the scene also committed suicide a fortnight later.

The death of Masaryk was the final episode in the communist takeover of Czechoslovakia. Rather than a suicide, it was the last (so far) case of a centuries-old Czech political tradition of defenestration (from the Classical Latin 'fenestra' – window), which means chucking an undesirable politician out of a window and making it look as if he has taken his own life. The first defenestration, a collective one, was in 1419, when several over-zealous Prague town councillors were hurled out of their office windows by a group of bullish religious reformers. Since then there have been three more (including the famous one during the Thirty Years War – uncannily similar to that of 1419 – and, of course, Masaryk's). In August 1996, the Czech news agency CTK reported that two Chinese men were tied up and thrown from the ninth floor of a block of flats in Prague, but both survived, which showed that the age-old defenestration tradition was very much alive.

Who is going to be the victim of the next great defenestration of Prague? It is hard to say, although when I was there many Czechs were inclined to believe it was likely to be Vaclav Havel, beer-loving former dissident, playwright and incumbent President of the Republic. Some time ago, he even won the honorary (if somewhat dubious) title of The-Most-Likely-to-be-Defenestrated Person in Prague.

After a mug of strong, pale Kozel, I started clearly seeing human bodies – in suits and ties – flying out, one by one, from the Foreign Ministry's windows. I needed a cup of coffee.

'What will happen if I order a coffee here?' I asked my

beer-swilling neighbour, who happened to speak some English.

'They will think that you are an alcoholic,' he replied, finishing off his tenth mug.

5 PROFESSOR OF BREWING

I could not believe my eyes: Vladimir Ilyich Lenin, the great leader and teacher of workers, peasants and executioners, was standing in front of me in the office of the Staropramen brewery in the central Prague area of Smichov. He was wearing his famous polka-dot tie, and his pseudo-intellectual social-democratic goatee trembled slightly when he spoke.

'The communists wanted to keep the Czech people quiet by giving them cheap beer,' he said. 'Beer was highly politicised. It was the country's main showcase, like ballet in Russia, and we never had shortages of it.'

Let me reassure you: my meeting with Lenin, who had been dead for 62 years (although in the Soviet Union we were always told that he was eternally alive and was always with us – hence the joke about triple marital beds), was not the result of several mugs of Kozel beer. Dr Pavel Ferkl, the 64-year-old former chief brewer of Staropramen, and now an adviser to the general manager, was the spitting image of Lenin, his complete lookalike. In post-communist Russia, he could have earned heaps of money by simply wandering around

Moscow and calling for the overthrow of the non-existing monarchy or by repeating Lenin's famous truism that communism was Soviet power plus electrification (or was it electrocution?) of the whole country. When he was showing me around the brewery, I half expected him to raise his hand suddenly and to cry out in a high-pitched, burred voice (Lenin could not pronounce 'r' and had to say 'g' instead), 'Comgades! The ggeat ghevolution has happened! Hoogay!!'

Except for this striking resemblance, there was not much in common between the first Soviet dictator, who had never had a proper job, and Prague's most respected beer expert, who had worked all his life at Staropramen and was also a professor of brewing at the Prague School of Food Technology, a member of the American Master Brewers Association, and so on. Dr Ferkl's brewing authority was so high that the communist government used to send him to the West as the ultimate ambassador of Czech beer. Now, the West had come to him, and Staropramen, the largest brewery in Prague, was partly owned by Bass, a British brewing giant, which had a 68 per cent stake in it.

'There are two secrets of Czech beer's success: ingredients – hops, barley and water, which are the best in the world – and tradition. Books on brewing have been written here since the sixteenth century,' Dr Ferkl said, as we passed by a huge fermentation tank. Flakes of greyish cotton-like foam in it did not look very appetising: they reminded me of the melting dirt-ridden Moscow snowdrifts at the end of March. In the next room stood four conical copper tanks, the so-called brew-kettles, in which the actual brewing process took place. These precious tanks – the pride of the brewery – were temporarily buried in Staropramen's spacious courtyard during the German occupation and thus survived the Second World War.

I was interested to see that the making of beer was not unlike the making of filter coffee: the mixture of malted grain and water was placed in vessels with sieve-like false bottoms through which the juices of the malt ran prior to being aromatised with hops, boiled and fermented.

'Our brewing technology remained unchanged for centuries,' Dr Ferkl continued. 'Communists did not intervene in technological matters, they only turned the Czech beer industry into a centralised military-type organisation and used it as a source of revenue. This is why Czech beer was less exposed to modernisation than German or American, which in itself was not so bad.'

I asked the avuncular Dr Ferkl about the ongoing Budweiser dispute, which has gained the same notoriety as the ancient argument between Poland and Russia as to the origins of vodka. That endless Czech–American squabble started in 1878, when a certain Augustus Buch registered the Budweiser name in the US, although a beer of the same name had been brewed by Czechs in the town of Ceske Budejovice (hence the name) for over a century. Nowadays, the American brewing giant produces more than a hundred cans and bottles of its light-flavoured, rice-based Budweiser for every bottle of dark, naturally brewed Budweiser Budvar and pays little heed to the Czechs' feeble demands to return the stolen name. The Americans even made a brazen attempt to buy the smallish Czech brewery and thus put an end to the dispute. When the Czechs refused to be bought, they were threatened with a court case, which the Americans were likely to win – not so much because of the qualities of their beer, but rather because of their deep pockets. The dispute looks set to continue for years.

'The Americans do not understand that Czech Budweiser is not for sale,' said the Professor. 'Budweiser is the last state-owned Czech brewery and it has to stay in Czech hands. As someone who has spent a long time in the US, I can tell you that they make the worst bread and the worst beer in the world. Their canned beer is but a totally fermented yellow water. They call us Czechs lucky people, because we allow beer to mature for a long time, whereas they, allegedly, can't afford it. They replace forty per cent of barley malt with corn, and the taste becomes bland and watery.'

Dr Ferkl was contemptuous of the very concept of canned beer, which, he asserted, had distorted the whole face of beer-making. He told me with pride that Czech beer was produced exclusively in returnable bottles, and it had become a popular Czech pastime to take crates of empty bottles back to shops on Saturdays. It was illegal (!) for the shops not to accept the bottles.

He also confided in me that, despite being the professor of brewing, he wasn't a big beer-drinker himself. I didn't see a contradiction there: one doesn't have to live on the moon to be a professor of astronomy.

From the colourful Staropramen brochure presented to me by Dr Ferkl, I learnt that one of the immediate results of the brewery's westernisation was that it now produced a politically correct 'diabetic beer' with reduced sugar and protein – and, I presume, beer – content.

The main thing I grasped from my visit to Prague's largest brewery was that the velvet revolution hadn't brought big changes to the Czech beer industry. The packaging and the labelling might have improved; the taste remained largely the same.

Walking back to my hotel past the unkempt houses of Smichov, decorated with bright Coca-Cola and Marlboro posters, I thought that – with some degree of certainty – the same conclusion could be applied to all the rest of the Czech Republic too.

6 STALIN'S EAR

Jerome K. Jerome, one of Britain's funniest writers of all time, in his book *Three Men on the Bummel*, published in 1900 and describing his hilarious bicycle journey across Europe in the company of his two friends George and Harris, warned visitors to Prague against 'getting too fond of Pilsener beer', which, in his words, 'is an insidious drink, especially in hot weather, but it does not do to imbibe too freely of it'. It was overindulgence in Czech beer that led George to believe that he saw one and the same equestrian statue in three different parts of Prague.

One morning I was walking along the embankment of the Vltava River admiring the magnificent view of Prague Castle on the opposite bank. I passed by the memorial plate to student Jan Palach, who set himself on fire and died on 16 January 1969 in protest against the Soviet invasion of Czechoslovakia. I saw some sad irony in the fact that '*palach*' is Czech for 'flame'.

Palach's suicide triggered a number of copycat acts, mostly by students, throughout the '60s and the '70s. It was on the powerful popular feeling spurred by these brave immolations that the communist authorities decided to play, when they provoked the 1989 revolution. Yes, as has been convincingly argued, the anti-communist uprising in Prague (and the similar events in other East European countries) was planned and organised by the pro-Soviet communist regime of Czechoslovakia on instructions from Moscow. It was part of the great KGB plot to overthrow simultaneously all aging East European dictators, replacing them with younger and somewhat more flexible 'Gorbachevites'. Interestingly, anti-communist demonstrations in Prague started with the alleged suicide of a Prague student, who, it turned out later, was an agent of the Czechoslovakian secret police (StB). Several years after the revolution, the 'student' was discovered to be alive and well, of course. The provocateurs' mistake was that they had greatly underestimated the degree of popular anger against the communist system which had made the initial KGB-inspired unrest irrevocable and quickly led to the system's complete demise.

Immersed in reverie, I trudged along the embankment with my head down, and when I eventually looked up . . . My first thought was that it was a beer-induced hallucination: a 30-metre-high statue of Stalin, which, I knew, had been removed from its pedestal in 1962, was towering over the steep bank of the Vltava. With his outstretched hand, the dictator was pointing upwards, to the bright Soviet-dominated future of Czechoslovakia, I presume. This monument, erected by the gratefully enslaved people of Prague in 1955, was the world's highest statue of Stalin, and the Czech communist apparatchiks used to take obsequious pride in this fact.

A popular Czech joke of that time illustrates the point.

'What nation has the largest cow in the world?'

'Czechoslovakia, of course.'

'Why?'

'Because its head is in Prague and it's milked in Moscow.'

When the statue was finally dismantled, bits and pieces of it were nicked by some entrepreneurial locals during the night, and now a Prague businessman proudly shows his guests one of Stalin's bronze ears which he had converted into a little swimming pool in his back garden!

If you ask me, I definitely wouldn't venture to swim in Stalin's ear (even if made of bronze), lest I should be mysteriously sucked into some dark inner depths of the cannibalistic dictator's body.

But how come the statue was there now, seven years after the downfall of communism? And both ears, as I could clearly see from the distance, were still in place. I pinched myself, but the mirage persisted.

'Bloody beer!' I thought, remembering Jerome K. Jerome. But in this case the explanation for the miraculous reappearance of Stalin's statue had nothing to do with the alleged hallucinogenic qualities of Czech beer, for my intake of it had been minimal throughout the trip, and on that particular morning I hadn't had a single drop.

Having come closer, I saw that it was not the statue of Stalin standing on its old, time-beaten pedestal. It was a 30-metre-high figure of the 'king of pop', the Great Friend of Children (especially boys) and the namesake of Britain's biggest beer connoisseur, Michael Jackson (or Wacko Jacko, as his fans call him).

I remembered reading in the papers that the beleaguered Jacko (alias Wacko) was undertaking a 'HIStory World Tour', during which he carried his own inflatable rubber statue with him. In Hungary, Romania and other former Soviet-bloc countries he placed it modestly on the vacant pedestals of the former communist leaders for the duration of his stay. I recalled seeing posters of Michael's forthcoming concert in Prague's Letna Park, and the *Prague Post* article, glumly predicting that on that day 130,000 fans of the self-ordained 'king' would descend on Prague.

Having thrown a last look at the blown-up figure of the dictator of bad taste and the great leader of all the dumb teenagers of the world (I was sorely tempted to puncture it with a blade of my Swiss Army knife), I walked away not knowing that a couple of hours later I was destined to see Wacko face to face. Well, almost (thank God).

Curiosity killed the cat, so they say. My natural inquisitiveness nearly led me to an untimely and un-dignified death.

I was enjoying an unhurried afternoon stroll along the narrow lanes of Prague's magnificent Old Town, when suddenly I heard some uneven, yet powerful, noise – not dissimilar to the hum of a big waterfall. I headed towards it, and soon found myself in a small square in front of the new Inter-Continental Hotel. Suddenly, I was surrounded by hundreds of yelling, shaking and periodically fainting teenagers, whose hungry stares were all fixed on a fourth-floor window of the hotel. There, in the company of five little boys and dressed in red, stood their formerly black idol, whose faded skin was now the colour of a freshly peeled orange. From time to time he stretched out his pinkish hand towards the crowd, after which the window was quickly shut: the health-crazy 'king of pop', who walked and slept with an oxygen mask, was obviously afraid of catching cold. His brisk and half-hearted greeting gesture invariably threw the crowd into a state that can be best described as a cross between Saint Vitus's dance and sleepwalking.

I climbed on to a bench to get a better view (of the crowd, not of Michael) and looked down. A little girl, having put two fingers into her mouth, was giving out deafening hooliganic whistles. Some teenagers held handwritten slogans: 'I love you, MJ!', 'Thanx [sic] for making us smile!' and even 'Michael! Moscow loves you!'

I was not so sure about Moscow, but I definitely did not like the scene. Especially when Jacko started hurling teddy bears, toy rabbits and 'I love you' notes, written in his childish lop-sided handwriting, at the crowd. The teenagers fought – cruelly, oblivious of all else – to get hold of them. They jumped up in the air, tearing at each other's hair and nearly scratching each other's eyes out, while Wacko watched their scuffles from behind the closed window with a sadistic-looking half-smile.

One of his crooked 'I love you' messages almost cost me my life.

Preoccupied with observing the teenagers, I didn't notice one folded sheet of paper, tossed out from the hotel window. Tumbling down like a falling autumn leaf, it was about to land right on my head. In a split second, the roaring mob of the Wacko-possessed children of the Prague Spring poured at me like the proverbial seventh wave at a tiny sinking boat. For a fleeting moment, I could clearly see their gaping, bellowing gullets, their ecstatic, bulging eyes, their sharp-clawed hands, stretching towards my head (or rather towards the note) and ready to tear me into thousands of little Vitalis.

I promptly jumped off the bench and took to my heels. I ran for all I was worth, my footsteps echoing loudly in the narrow streets of the Old Town. I was fleeing from the Western mass culture which had – unpredictably – caught up with me in the East.

It was a narrow escape. From the shelter of a doorway, I looked back. The pursuing crowd forgot about me the moment they took possession of the precious note. Having rolled themselves into an irregularly shaped human ball, the teenagers bit and scratched each other in futile attempts to grab the piece of paper, which quickly got shredded into hundreds of confetti-like bits.

I stopped to regain my breath only when I reached the Vltava. I had fled the teenagers, but there was no escape from Michael Jackson, whose rubber statue was still dominating the city-scape. Only this time, I was not as disgusted by it as before. 'New times have arrived, new names have arisen,' wrote Yevgeniy Yevtushenko, the favourite poet of my youth. No matter how weird and shallow the adoration of Michael Jackson might be, it was still incomparably better than the personality cult of Comrade Stalin which had cost humankind (and the Czech Republic, too) many millions of innocent lives.

It was wonderful to realise that Big Brother was no longer watching anyone. Nor was he listening, since his all-hearing ears have been severed and turned into swimming pools.

'Be it as it may, but Jackson is preferable to Dzhugashvili [Stalin's real name],' decided I, and I headed for a nearby pub. For the first time in years, I was desperate for a beer.

7 LIFE BEERAGE IN PLZEN

My beer-familiarisation trip to the Czech Republic wouldn't have been complete without a visit to the West Bohemian city of Plzen, the beer capital of the beer country and the birthplace of the world-famous Pilsner lager. For Czech beer-making Plzen is like Detroit for the US motoring industry, like Burgundy for French viticulture, and like Sellafield for Britain's environmental pollution.

The town's history is inseparable from beer. Plzen (or Pilsen) was founded in 1295, and in the same year King Vaclav II granted all its residents the right to brew. Two hundred and sixty smart burghers immediately took up this right, which also allowed them to sell beer in their houses, thus making them into the world's first off-licence shops. Beer was made 'in turn', meaning that each household would brew a fixed quantity once or twice a year at set times and would sell it throughout the town. In this way, many houses took turns acting as pubs, which was financially very lucrative. Once granted, the right to brew stayed with the holder indefinitely. It was also hereditary – a life beerage, so to speak.

It is interesting to note in passing that the first public library in Plzen opened only in 1876 – almost 600 years after the breweries.

The beer capital was a two-hour train-ride from Prague. On a Saturday morning I left my Soviet-style Olympik Garni Hotel (due to the erratic neon sign on the roof, after dark its name shrank to a somewhat Hebrew-like 'Olym arni'), and took the Metro to Prague's main railway station.

I liked the Prague Metro, whose capacious Soviet-made carriages and lushly decorated stations reminded me of Moscow. There was something aphrodisiac about it. On the train, I enjoyed listening to semi-orgasmic female voices announcing through the intercom, 'Kh-sh-sh-ee-zh-ee-ee-kova', as if verbally caressing your skin, and the fact that it was simply the name of the next station – Krzikova – did not matter. I liked watching young couples kissing on the steps of moving escalators which seemed natural in the city where five hundred years ago it was fashionable to make love in the streets (for this, the romantic Bohemians were duly chastised by the Pope – hence the origin of the word 'bohemian').

The main railway station, however, was far from aphrodisiac. It was swarming with stocky young men in leather jackets, who spent their time congregating in the middle of the station hall and keeping a vigilant eye on each of the several dozen money-exchange offices located inside the terminal. After every spotted transaction, one of them would knock peremptorily on the glass of the cash-window and would be – openly! – handed over a 'commission'. These were the gangs of Russian and Ukrainian racketeers who held the station and the whole surrounding area of Prague firmly under their control. The Czech policemen in their brand-new smart uniforms, designed, allegedly, by President Havel himself, tried not to look their way, preferring to harass the ubiquitous gypsy fortune-tellers instead. They were helpless against these leather-clad young men, the last envoys of the defunct evil empire, whose pockets were bulging with money and metal. Prague newspapers called the station Eastern Europe's main hotbed of crime, and they were right.

I had twenty minutes to spare before the train. For a while I walked among the flocks of racketeers, eavesdropping on their conversations. They were talking loudly, thinking that no one in Prague would be able to comprehend their Russian–Ukrainian street-wise vernacular. They didn't know that a street-wise Russian –Ukrainian was strolling right in their midst, pretending he was looking for a toilet. They talked about teaching somebody a f—ing lesson, about f—ing 'greens' (meaning 'f—ing US dollars'), f—ing Czech crowns and – interestingly – about some mysterious, but no-less-f—ing, 'common sense'.

I got quickly fed up with the gangsters (they were so 'f—ing' boring) and decided to have a cup of coffee. In the centre of the hall, I found a coffee stall and a table, covered with dirty oilcloth. The moment I sat down to sip a brownish watery liquid, which smelt like thin pea soup, a huge Alsatian, dragging its hapless owner behind it, materialised from nowhere and rammed the wobbly table with its muzzled elongated head. I dropped the steaming plastic cup of surrogate 'coffee', which landed on my lap and made me squeal with burning pain. The owner dragged his nosy pet away.

I went to the platform pondering over my extraordinary ability to have drinks spilt over myself, especially when I travel. If I don't spill orange juice on my suit on board a plane, a hostess does it for me. If I am on a train the spilling is performed by a travel companion or by a conductor. And at a station there's always an unruly child, or else a hyperactive Alsatian.

I was thirsty, but – to avoid further burns – I decided not to experiment with boiling-hot coffee any more and to buy myself a cold soft drink instead. A bottle with a colourful label in a platform kiosk attracted my desiccated attention. 'Vegetable Raspberry Lemonade', it said in Czech. Whatever it was, it was probably better (and safer) than 'coffee'.

My compartment was empty, except for a uniformed Czech soldier playing a pocket Nintendo. To while away the time, I sipped my mongrel 'lemonade' (it burned holes in the collapsible plastic table when spilled), and browsed through yesterday's issue of *Komsomolskaya Pravda*, a Moscow newspaper which I had bought at the station. The headlines in this formerly dull and tame herald of the Soviet Communist Youth Organisation were as follows: 'Talking Dog Gives Interview to This Paper', 'Why Did Tishkov's Mother Leave Singer Christian Ray for Millionaire Tennis-Player Kafelnikov?', 'Who Slept in Alla Pugacheva's Bed, Apart from Her Husband?', 'Is There Any Love in the Countryside?' and, to crown it all, 'Pigmies Grab Elephants by the Bowel'. It was clear that the paper was no longer tame or dull, although it still had a long way to go to catch up with the most ebullient Western rags, routinely carrying such electrifying headlines as 'Serial Killer's Brother Eaten by Peasants', which I once spotted in an Australian tabloid.

I looked through the window. The Czech countryside remained largely unchanged from ten years ago, apart from occasional Coca-Cola and Marlboro billboards. Clearly, there wasn't much love lost in it (*pace Komsomolskaya Pravda*). From a large roadside placard informing me that 'Plzen is the home of Skoda', I grasped that I was approaching my destination, where not only beer but also Skoda cars are produced in abundance.

Along with the tin-shaped East German Trabant, Skoda has won itself the reputation of the world's funniest car. With a top speed of 60mph, which it can reach in a mere thirty seconds, Skoda is the butt of numerous jokes, both in the West and in the East. I recalled reading a story in *The Times* about a Skoda, bought by the Suffolk police force not for the use of its regular officers or for responding to 999 calls, but for . . . taking off-duty constables to a market in the town of Bury St Edmunds.

I also remembered visiting a Bratislava-based friend who owned a Skoda. Once, I pulled its plastic door handle (both the handle and the door were made of plastic) a wee bit harder than was required, and the whole car fell apart.

The train screeched to a halt. The soldier pocketed his Nintendo and stood up abruptly, overturning my Vegetable Raspberry Lemonade bottle and spilling its unlikely contents all over my jacket.

Plzen was a real beer city. During my brisk fifteen-minute walk from the station to the town centre, I counted a dozen beer-selling points, from roofless street stalls to small supermarkets offering beer on tap.

I came to understand why the Czechs called Plzen 'an open town'. It was not just open, it was empty and windswept. The few pedestrians I came across reeked of beer, and I didn't blame them: there was nothing much else to do in Plzen on a dull Saturday morning.

The central town square, Namesti Republiky, was dominated by the spectacular sixteenth-century St. Bartholomew Church which boasted the country's tallest 121-metre-high steeple. The church's ornate façade was so heavily and hectically decorated that it looked covered with flakes of beer foam.

A small crowd was gathering at the entrance to the nearby Town Hall. This proved to be a wedding party waiting for the newly-weds to emerge. And here they were: a young man with a red carnation in his lapel, and a white-clad bride (most likely, already a wife). They were immediately given two large glasses, not of champagne but of beer! The young husband downed his glass in one long uninterrupted gulp, bringing applause from the crowd. The wife took a couple of bashful, yet substantial, sips before the husband lifted her from the ground and loaded her on to a small wooden cart, which he started pushing around the square. The cart was rattling against the cobbles. The wife was half screaming and half laughing. The guests were drinking beer.

I was reminded of a cartoon I saw in a Czech magazine. A happy beer-bellied bridegroom is standing at a bar. In his arms he is holding his happy, and also beer-bellied, bride in a wedding dress. 'A quick beer, please,' he says to the barman.

Beer seemed to accompany Czechs throughout their lives. Especially in Plzen. I wondered whether local women were offered a beer first thing after giving birth. Life beerage, indeed!

To my (not very great) dismay, Pilsner Urquell, the city's world-famous brewery, was closed. I had to confine myself to walking along its massive green fence and admiring its famous baroque entrance gate in the shape of a double arch. Through the gate I could see an old beacon-like water tower in the brewery's spacious courtyard.

As often happens, the appearance of Pilsner Urquell lager was the result of a technological mistake, made by a Bavarian guest maltster, Josef Croll, who was invited to Plzen to kick-start the new brewery in 1842. He probably wanted to brew some good old Bavarian brand, but while making the first trial batch he committed a boo-boo and came up with a totally different concoction. What sort of mistake it was remains a well-guarded mystery: the present-day brewers of Pilsner Urquell protect their 'secret recipe' no less vigilantly than the makers of Coca-Cola (although – for me at least – the latter is obvious: heaps of burnt sugar dissolved in caustic vinegary water). Whatever it was, it is reassuring to know that a human blunder can sometimes lead, if not exactly to a great scientific discovery, then at least to a new sort of beer.

Under communists, the taste of Pilsner Urquell was

practically unknown to the Czechs: the bulk of it was exported to the West to earn precious foreign currency, much needed by the rulers to finance their own plush life-styles. After the velvet revolution – in a truly democratic twist – Pilsner Urquell was made accessible to the locals, and as a formerly forbidden fruit it quickly became the country's best-selling brand.

From the closed famous brewery, I went to the city's Museum of Brewing, secretly hoping that it would be closed, too. But it wasn't.

The world's oldest brewery museum was situated in a one-time malthouse, later turned into a pub. I was the only visitor. For a couple of hours I wandered in solitude through semi-dark rooms with vaulted ceilings until I started hearing the muffled hubbub of all those boisterous medieval drinking parties which took place here in the days of yore. I could see the ghosts of drunken burghers and of careless and resourceful medieval brewers, who used to 'improve' spoiled brews with the bones of criminals, dogs' faeces, sawdust from old dug-up coffins and splinters from scaffolds – the unlikely ingredients (not unlike those of Vegetable Raspberry Lemonade, I presume) that must have eventually contributed to the uniqueness of Pilsner beer, and to my total loss of desire ever to taste it.

The oldest known scientific work on brewing was on display in one of the rooms. It was written in Latin by Tadeas Hajek, a Plzen 'beerologist', in 1588. Its title alone, *On Beer and the Methods of Its Preparation, Its Substance, Strengths and Effects* – as heavy and drawn-out as a pint of Guinness – made me yawn.

I examined the old brewers' certificates, collections of beer tags, beer taps and 'manual corking tools', a sculpture of 'Sir John Falstaff, the famous Shakespearean drunkard', and an icon showing Jesus Christ with a glass of beer in his hand and a crown of thorns, made of barley, on his head, which showed that beer was not just Plzen's life but its religion, too.

In a separate hall, there was a guest exhibition of Heineken – a sign of new capitalist times – which opened with a portrait of Mr Heineken himself. It provided a living illustration to the famous ad for Heineken beer which, allegedly, 'refreshes the parts that other beers cannot reach': it had certainly reached Plzen.

The exhibit that I liked best was a miniature model of a steam brewery which was fully operational and could produce thirty litres of beer in one cycle. I knew a lot of people (mostly hacks) in London and Melbourne who would kill to have a toy like that on their office desks.

In full accordance with the teachings of dialectical materialism, it was time to proceed (reluctantly) from theory to practice, i.e., drinking. I was hungry and was hoping for a good pub meal to combine business (beer) and pleasure (food).

I didn't have to go far. The Na Parcane pub was located in the same building as the brewery museum. It was a nondescript and cheap place with simple decor and simple food. I ordered *male pivo* ('small beer') and a big plate of goulash (a thin beef stew) with *knedli* (dumplings). Goulash is a Hungarian speciality borrow-ed by the Czechs, who, like the British, can hardly claim to have a cuisine of their own. Imitating the locals, I started dipping *knedli* into the spicy goulash and washing them down with beer. The meal was heavy, and I suddenly understood the reason for the beer bellies that many Czech males proudly sported. In reality, they were goulash-and-*knedli* bellies.

The pub menu said that goulash was served 'only before 3 p.m.' – the world's only case of 'goulash prohibition', even if partial.

How about the beer? Well, having learnt about some old ingredients of Pilsner Urquell, especially bones of criminals and dogs' faeces, I opted for another brand, Gambrinus, named after the medieval Czech King Jan I, or Jan Primus ('Gambrinus' being a distortion of his name and number), who was a part-time brewer himself. It was sort of OK, dark and bitter, but did little to quench my goulash-inspired thirst.

I couldn't leave Plzen without visiting its premier attraction, Na Spilce, the country's largest beer hall, capable of seating 580 people. Its fame grew considerably after Vaclav Havel popped in one day for a quick Pilsner Urquell with his American mate Bill Clinton and Bill's ageing auntie Madeleine Albright.

In a revealing photo of that historic occasion, which can now be found in every Pilsner Urquell promotional brochure, Clinton, his mouth stuffed with food, is chatting to Albright. Significantly, his beer seems untouched, whereas Havel, who is not taking part in the conversation, is greedily finishing his.

Vaclav Havel, the twice-imprisoned president of the Czech Republic, always had the reputation of being a chain-smoker (he gave up in 1996 prior to an operation on his lungs) and a heavy drinker. When still a dissident playwright, he used to spend long hours in Prague's Café Slavia, smoking, drinking and talking sedition with his maverick friends. It was there that he wooed his future wife, Olga, also a dissident, who died in 1995. One year after her death, the 60-year-old President Havel married a 43-year-old actress, Dagmar Veskrnova.

I first saw Havel in the flesh in Bratislava, at the funeral of Alexander Dubcek, one of Czechoslovakia's most controversial politicians, in November 1992. Walking behind Dubcek's coffin, he was visibly tipsy and had to be supported by his bodyguards, who almost carried him.

In the Czech Republic of the late nineties, Havel is bombarded with criticism, not only from his political adversaries, but also from his allies. He is routinely accused of having forgotten his old friends; of being a lousy playwright; of having swapped his modest 'ordinary' flat for a luxury villa in the Royal Garden, where kings and communist apparatchiks used to live; even of being a one-time secret police agent. Whereas most of these accusations might be true (except for the last one, I hope), they also show that Havel has achieved his main goal – making Czech society an open one.

Having an intellectual as a president is not always the best solution, but it is incomparably better than being ruled by a senile Brezhnev-type octogenarian who is unable to say a word on his own (a popular Soviet joke asserted that when the door bell rang in Brezhnev's flat, he would produce a piece of paper from his breast pocket and read slowly, 'Who . . . is . . . there?'). Havel writes his own speeches (over a beer?). 'I treat my speeches as literary works in their own right,' he once said. 'It is probably a relic of my past as a writer . . . I sometimes envy other presidents who get their speeches straight from their speech-writers or advisers, read them over, and are then able to play golf on weekends.'

One can't help respecting a president like that.

To my considerable disappointment, Clinton and Havel were no longer at Na Spilce (nor was Madeleine Albright, who had become US Secretary of State, and was probably somewhere in the Middle East negotiating yet another ill-fated peace deal). The enormous beer hall was empty except for a group of ubiquitous stone-faced German tourists. The moment I lowered myself on to a squeaky wooden chair, a Mr Upper brought me a beer (he lovingly called it '*pivecko*' – 'little beer' – although the mug was far from little) and a bunch of ten salty bagels. After the massive goulash at Na Parkane, I was not in the least hungry, but, having drunk some beer, I felt like a bagel, which, in turn, made me want more beer, and so on – a vicious beer-belly-forming circle!

I ended up consuming all ten bagels and having two beers – my record so far. Then, God knows why, I ordered beef soup with noodles, which I couldn't finish. I was full to the point of exploding, which also made me slow-witted and slightly aggressive. Beer culture was taking its toll. I felt like insulting somebody, but because

I didn't speak any German there was no one in the pub I could insult, apart from myself. Having called myself a silly beer-swilling idiot, I heavily stood up from my table and stumbled towards the exit.

I walked to the station along the deserted Americka Street, which was probably a former Lenin Street (each 'socialist' town was supposed to have at least one Lenin Street) renamed after the downfall of communism. American Street was lined with casually parked plastic Skodas.

I passed by a newly renovated windowless cottage with a pink marble façade. 'Pension Dallas' was written on a polished brass door-plate. Several cars with Estonian number plates were parked outside. It was a brothel, of course.

The town centre gave an impression of a protracted and potentially lethal coma. It was nearly dead. The only signs of activity could be observed around beer-selling kiosks. One thing was plain: this city started and finished with beer, and all its residents (not just the brewers) were firmly ensnared in the unending beerage of life.

I remembered a book I once saw on sale in America, *Near Death Experience Made Easy*. I didn't have a chance to open it, but now I was certain: it was a guide to Plzen on a Saturday.

8 U BRONKU

The Bohemians are a merry people. They are very fond of music, and they often carry little harps in their hands. They sing together as they return from their labours in the fields. They are very curious, and ask a great many questions. When they meet a stranger, they say, 'Where do you come from? Where are you going? What are the names of your friends?' and sometimes they get no answer ...

Near Home or Europe Described,
Longmans, Green, & Co., London, 1910

This small, unpretentious pub in the Prague district of Karlin was not mentioned in any guidebooks. It became my favourite because it was genuine and un-touristy. Sitting there over a Gambrinus beer, or over a slivovitz (plum vodka), which I had come to prefer, I could quietly observe the locals and the often confusing daily routine of post-communist Prague.

I would come to U Bronku for a morning cup of coffee to watch the first clients of the day fighting their hangover with a hair of the dog. Judging by the size of this 'hair', they must have all been bitten by the Hound of the Baskervilles the night before. These mornings patrons were often joined by the staff – waiters, chefs and doormen – who seemed to be suffering from the same problem and used the same trusted cure to treat it.

To understand a city one must be lonely there – at

least for a while. Unlike on some of my other East European journeys, I was alone in Prague, and soon the city itself became my constant companion and started opening up to me.

In the afternoon, I would order myself a traditional goulash with potato pancakes, or a mushroom-stuffed steak, held together by four wooden toothpicks, and an éclair for dessert. Éclairs in U Bronku were hollow tube-shaped pastries with some whipped cream on top. The menu, which, for some reason, indicated the exact weight of each portion in grams, listed a dish called Grizzly Bear's Ear, which I was tempted to try, but dared not order.

At about 4 p.m., a roly-poly red-faced chef in a checked apron would emerge from the kitchen. Within a minute, he would empty two large mugs of Gambrinus at the bar, wipe his mouth with the sleeve of his shirt and return to his steaming and sizzling workplace. It was probably beer that made him too lazy to stuff cream inside the éclairs.

The patrons in U Bronku were 90 per cent male. They all seemed to know one another and at times showed each other their family photos. This male domination was a common feature of Prague pubs, where women seemed to be rare and unlikely guests.

One afternoon I was joined at my table by a young blue-eyed Czech girl whose name was Zdenka. She had popped in for a quick coffee on the way to the station. Zdenka lived in Ostrava, an industrial coal-mining city in the north of the country, and came to Prague to buy . . . a map of Paris. A student of foreign languages at Ostrava University, she specialised in French.

Zdenka was a serious young woman. She spoke in curt, abrupt sentences and never smiled.

'I hate beer,' she told me, staring at the map of Paris, which she had spread on the table in front of her.

'But most Czech men seem to like it,' I said pointing at U Bronku's beer-swilling patrons.

'I hate Czech men.'

'You obviously prefer Frenchmen,' I noted wryly.

'Any men, but not Czechs.'

'What's so awful about them?'

'They are just . . . I don't know . . .'

Zdenka didn't know, but I thought that I could guess. It was hard not to notice a patronising and somewhat disdainful attitude of Czech men towards women, who, to my mind, were among the most attractive and good-natured in Europe. This attitude manifested itself not just in pubs but also in the streets, at parties and on public transport.

A fairly precise, down-to-earth description of this peculiarly Czech misogynism can be found in *Czechs and Balances*, a witty and clever book by Benjamin Kuras, a London-based Czech writer.

> . . . let's face it, boys. Where else do you find a beautifully feminine, gentle, sexy and caring female with a university degree who takes you lovingly into her home, gives you breakfast in bed, irons your shirts, goes off to work smartly dressed, comes home to you cheerful and unaffected by stress, cooks you dinner, massages you from head to toe, bonks you blind, blows you back for another round when you thought you were finished for a week, does not get tired, does not fake orgasm, keeps telling you how wonderful you are, and does not want to change you – and manages to be all that on an average income of 200 dollars a month?

Czech males tended to treat the members of the fair sex like a valuable, yet easily disposable, commodity similar to a beer: if it tastes good, you swallow it; if not, you spit it out and order yourself a different brand. A Czech male's scale of values would probably read beer, food, women – in that order. How else can one explain the extraordinary (even by Western standards) pro-fusion of ridiculous and often humiliating (for the contenders) beauty contests in the post-communist Czech Republic?

The posters advertising these contests were displayed in pubs, at railway stations, on park fences and in public toilets. In 1996 alone, apart from the fairly conventional Miss Czech Republic, the following national beauty pageants were staged: Miss Long Hair, Miss Mini Miss (less than 160 centimetres tall), Miss (or Mrs) Mum, Miss Mensa, Miss Witch, Miss Press, Miss Sales, Miss Doll (for toddler girls), Miss Long Hair–Long Brain (I wonder whether a 'long brain' testifies to being smart, having a long memory, or suffering from cretinism?), Miss Exotica, Miss Model 96, Miss Secondary School, Miss Kindergarten, Miss Milk (for 9–11-year-olds), Miss Summer, Miss Fitness, Radio Crocodile Babe or Miss Queen of Clubs, Miss Gypsy and Miss Chastity. The last was held at Prague's Police Museum during an exhibition of security systems. The winner was a 19-year-old peroxide blonde who appeared on stage naked but for her winner's sash and a chastity belt – complete with shiny padlock.

Significantly, one contest they didn't have was Miss Beer. Feminism and beer culture were obviously far from ideal bedfellows.

At U Bronku, I often noticed small groups of dark-skinned men, who would enter the pub hesitantly and indecisively. They would look around worriedly, as if constantly expecting a blow from behind their backs, and always sat in the darkest corner. The waiters openly snubbed them and made them wait for their beers for ages, while other customers sneered at them and scornfully called them 'the blacks'. I knew who these people were. They belonged to the Czech Republic's largest ethnic minority, the gypsies (or, as they call themselves, Romany), of whom there are over 300,000.

Travelling around the country, I often had to pass through derelict vermin-infested shanty-towns, where gypsies lived in terrifying poverty and filth. In the cities, I saw them hanging around the streets aimlessly. The unemployment among the Romany was close to 90 per cent (as opposed to the overall Czech figure of 3 per cent). They were meticulously oppressed, abused and humiliated. In 1993, the so-called 'Romany Clause' passed by the Czech parliament stripped 100,000 gypsies of citizenship rights – Europe's first act of mass disenfranchisement since the Second World War. In 1996, the Republican Party chief, Miroslav Sladek, declared he wanted to send the gypsies to Spain or to the gas chamber, while Liana Janaczkova of the Citizens' Democratic Party proposed that they be given free tickets to Canada.

Instead of going to Spain or Canada, sixty families of Czech and Slovak gypsies chose to come to Britain and ask for political asylum in October 1997; they had been duped by a Czech television documentary on the happy life of a gypsy family in Dover. After several weeks of parliamentary debates, vitriolic abuse by the tabloids and demonstrations of protest, all of them were branded 'economic migrants' and deported back to their countries of origin (I wanted to say 'home countries', but couldn't: the gypsies never felt at home in the Czech Republic, in Slovakia, or in any other country where they had chosen to settle).

The Romany, who left India over six hundred years ago, have been persecuted through the centuries. In 1725 Friedrich Wilhelm of Prussia decreed that any gypsy older than 18 should be hanged. In Silesia and Moravia (part of the present-day Czech Republic) there used to be a law by which the left ear of every gypsy woman had to be cut off. Hitler exterminated half a million gypsies; only six hundred Czech Romany survived the war. And now the Czech Republic, Slovakia, Hungary, Romania, Russia, Ukraine and others are making a considerable contribution to this age-old history of terror and oppression.

Sadly, by thoughtlessly deporting the desperate Romany, Britain sided with the gypsy-hating countries. I wish those British officials who took the disgraceful decision could read a poignant letter which was published in October 1996 by the *Prague Post*, an English-language weekly, staffed by expatriate Americans.

The letter was written by an American female computer technician of Indian descent who came to live and work in Prague. Because of her dark skin, many locals took her for a Romany.

I was asked to leave the first youth hostel I stayed in. The staff ladies used to spit whenever they saw me. I was taken for a prostitute . . . I had an encounter with skinheads . . . I've been stared at, glared at, spat upon, cursed, ordered out of a building where my friends live . . . Women move their handbags when I sit near them . . . All because I look Romany . . . I have seen a Czech store owner set his dogs on the Romany kids who entered his store. I am from the American town where Ku Klux Klan still exists. My state keeps electing Jesse Helms as senator. But I have never seen a white store owner in America set his dogs on black kids . . . I am scared . . . I have started carrying around an English-language paperback book wherever I go. I pretend to read it. This is especially useful on trams. When people discover that I am a foreigner, the tension immediately evaporates . . . A Czech friend tried to comfort me by saying, 'Oh, not you. You are Indian, not Romany; that makes you my equal.' I am not comforted. Could I respect myself if I were? . . . My experience here has been an education many white Americans could benefit from. There is nothing like getting spat on by a bunch of teenagers to change a girl's laissez-faire attitude about race relations . . . Still, I am pretty lucky. When I get off the plane at JFK Airport in New York, I am suddenly a white girl again.

Unlike feminism, racism seems to go well with beer. Like a salty bagel, I would say. Only the shiny crystals of salt on this bagel are condensed tears of the millions of victims of the most hideous and repugnant human legacy: racial and nationalistic prejudice.

I have finished my beer, I have licked my goulash plate clean, I have just put into my mouth the last bit of the éclair. It is time to go back to my 'Olym arni' hotel, which is just a stone's throw from U Bronku.

I look forward to the Spartan comfort of my hotel room, which makes me feel almost at home. My bags are unpacked, my pyjamas are neatly spread on my bed, my toothbrush and razor are in a plastic cup in the bathroom. My scanty 'valuables' (passport and a couple of credit cards) are safely locked in a hotel safe, and the key is in my wallet. As a bonus of post-communist times, I can now receive CNN in my room. What else does a traveller need? I know what's in stock for me – at least for tonight.

And, thank God, I am neither a Czech woman, nor a gypsy.

9 THE INGLORIOUS END OF BOHUMIL SOL, THE FATHER OF SEMTEX

In June 1997, I read in a London newspaper about a suicide of a 63-year-old Czech by the name of Bohumil Sol. He chose an unusual way to die: by blowing himself up in a psychiatric sanatorium where he lived. The reason? The hospital personnel tried to stop him firing off rockets that scared his fellow patients and aggravated their condition.

Who was he? A jingoistic arsonist? A suicidal madman? An infantile pyromaniac with a crazy hobby of blasting holes in the frozen Labe river? Yes, he was all these – and more. Bohumil Sol, the former Czechoslovakia's leading explosives expert, was also known as 'the father of Semtex'.

I don't have to explain what Semtex means: every British (and especially Northern Irish) schoolboy has this word at his fingertips. Just a couple of reminders to refresh your memory.

The favoured plastic explosive of terrorists worldwide, including the IRA, Semtex has always been produced exclusively by the Synthesia (formerly Explosia) factory in the East Bohemian city of Pardubice, about a hundred miles east of Prague. Along with Pilsner Urquell and Budvar lagers, Semtex remains one of the best-known Czech trade marks and export items. Unlike the famed beer capable (allegedly) of reaching the remotest parts of human body, Semtex is capable of blowing this very body apart. The PanAm flight over Lockerbie was destroyed by Semtex, of which more than a thousand tons were sold to Libya in the late 1980s. Thousands of tons went to Iraq and North Korea. It was used in many IRA bombs on the territory of Britain and has taken hundreds of innocent lives. Not much is needed. Experts say a piece of Semtex the size of a fist would blow a hole in the side of an aircraft.

In 1991, Synthesia was forced to add to the explosive a chemical almond-like 'smell' that can be detected by airport security machines, but, miraculously, the stocks in terrorist hands remain odourless, and their Semtex caches do not seem to be suffering from shortages.

I can hear you saying: wait a moment, this book is supposed to be about drinks, not about explosives. I agonised over how to tie up Semtex to drinks, but this time the capricious luck of a travel writer was on my side.

'TIME FOR ENERGY DRINK. SEMTEX FORTE' was written on a billboard I spotted in Prague's Argentinska Street.

Yes, Semtex, the Italian-made fizzy drink, had blasted into Prague. The billboard showed a young woman blissfully tasting the explosive drink in front of a KLM airline poster. Was there some hidden meaning there? Whatever it was, I doubted that either KLM or CSA, the Czech national airline, was likely to offer Semtex to passengers on its flights. It also occurred to me that Synthesia, the manufacturers of the solid, not liquid, Semtex, must have been pretty annoyed by such flippant abuse of their awe-inspiring trade mark.

Callers to a popular Prague radio show unanimously concluded that the new Semtex soft drink was tasteless (not half as much as the billboard, I am sure). But for my

purposes this didn't matter. The much-needed link between Semtex and drinks had been found! There was
only one little thing left: to visit Synthesia. As far as I
knew, no Western journalist had ever been allowed to
do so.

I decided to be persistent. My rationale was simple: if
indeed, as Synthesia kept publicly asserting, the
production of Semtex had been wrapped up since 1991
and they had nothing to hide any longer, why couldn't
they show me round – as they did at, say, Staropramen,
Prague's largest brewery?

'Hopeless. Forget about it!' I was rebuffed at the
offices of the *Prague Post*, where I popped in one day in
search of advice. 'We have tried it many times, but
they've never allowed us to come close to Synthesia. The
only thing they were willing to give us was their glossy
brochure on environmental protection – and even that
only by post. Communism or free market, Synthesia's
policy remains unchanged: strictly no press visits.'

The journalists also assured me that if I phoned
Synthesia myself they would feign inability to communicate in English. But, having dealt in the past with the
Soviet mafia and the KGB, I was not easily discouraged.
I asked a Czech acquaintance, a respected Prague businessman, to make the initial contact with Synthesia. 'Let
them try and pretend they don't speak Czech,' I thought
venomously.

Next morning the following fax message from my go-
between was waiting for me at my hotel: '*Regarding
your visit to the Semtex producer, I was trying to
arrange a meeting for you, but the notice was very short
for some people, and others are just not available at the
time you were suggesting. However, should you still be
interested in contacting them, they are ready to handle
your questions at least.*' A phone number and the name
of a 'contact person' – a certain Mr Mokren – followed.
Not bad for a start.

My call was answered by a woman ('Pani Misova')

whose English was limited to just two words: 'not possible'. Remembering an old bureaucratic dictum – 'If you can't convince them, confuse them' – I switched to Russian. Pani Misova's Russian was only marginally better, just good enough to convey that Mr Mokren was unavailable. Having lost patience, I decided to take advantage of our lack of a lingua franca and told her clearly in English that I was leaving the Czech Republic the day after next (which was true) and that I would be coming to Pardubice the following day. 'Call us tomorrow morning,' she replied in unexpectedly correct English.

Next morning I dialled the same number. 'Can you call me back in a month?' Pani Misova asked nonchalantly.

'Look, I am taking a train to Pardubice in half an hour,' I told her firmly. 'Would you be so kind as to pick me up at the station?' The line went dead for a while. 'Not possible,' she mumbled after a long pause. 'OK, I will take a taxi,' I said, and hung up. I decided that I had managed to confuse Pani Misova, if only a little.

Two hours later I was shifting from one foot to the other on the cobbled station square of Pardubice. It was raining. I had a cold. My nose was running, but taxis weren't: there were none in sight. The unknown town around me was bleak and uninviting. The people looked bleak and uninviting too, quite a contrast to the bubbling and bustling Prague.

I was hoping to flag down a private car (a normal thing anywhere in Eastern Europe), but had to give up the idea after fifteen minutes of fruitless hand-waving. Having returned to the station building, I found a public telephone and dialled the Synthesia number. This time I was lucky enough to get Mr Mokren himself on the line. His English was much better than Pani Misova's. 'I am sorry, the working day is over,' he told me curtly.

'So this is your famous Czech hospitality!' I exploded, Semtex-like. I was fed up with their ridiculous cat-and-mouse game. 'Here I am in Pardubice, having come all the way from London to ask you a couple of simple questions, and you are telling me off!'

'OK, I shall be with you in seven minutes,' said Mr Mokren all of a sudden. He obviously didn't want to appear inhospitable.

Ten minutes later, a battered Lada stopped in the far end of the square. A round-faced young man wearing a suit and tie got out and angrily paced towards me. In his hand he was clutching a glossy pamphlet, probably a brochure on environmental protection.

'You must go back to Prague now,' said Mr Mokren, giving me the brochure (it *was* on environmental protection) and his business card which said simply: 'Ales Mokren, Manager'.

'You can't do this to me!' I insisted, flashing my press card in his moon-like dispassionate face. 'Your factory is not protected by any official secrecy acts, and as a member of the press in a free democratic country, which you now claim to be, I am entitled to see it. Besides, the next train to Prague leaves only in two hours.'

My last statement was an outright lie, but, fortunately for me, Mr Mokren was not too familiar with train schedules. He scrutinised me carefully for a couple of minutes. Soaking wet and shivering in the wind, I must have looked pitiful enough to inspire some trust. 'All right,' he said finally. 'I shall take you to Synthesia for half an hour, but you won't see anything, because the working day is over.' From the expression on his face it was plain that he couldn't wait to get rid of me.

Promptly (before he had time to change his mind) I climbed into his Lada. Mr Mokren took out a map of Pardubice. 'Synthesia is here,' he said, pointing to an unmarked blank area at the map's edge. 'We'll be there in ten minutes.'

We drove past smoking chimneys, naked pipelines and shabby houses, dotted here and there with Marlboro and Coca-Cola signs, a familiar city-scape of post-communist Eastern Europe.

'I am sorry,' said Mr Mokren from behind the wheel. 'We have to be careful with journalists. In all our history, only a couple of local ones have been allowed into the factory.'

'Why such secrecy?' I enquired.

'Terrorism,' he said gravely. 'We are a chemical factory, you know.'

He went on to explain that Semtex was only one of their hundreds of products and he couldn't understand why everybody was so interested in it. 'We stopped shipments of Semtex to Libya in 1981, and that was the end of the matter.

'We are now a joint-stock company with thousands of shareholders,' he babbled on. 'Privatisation of the factory was completed in 1995.'

I couldn't care less about privatisation.

We were already driving across Synthesia's territory. Contrary to my escort's assurances, the factory didn't give the impression that the working day was over. Chimneys were belching out clouds of yellow smoke into the uncomplaining Bohemian skies. Cargo trains were rattling along the viaducts, criss-crossing on several levels above our heads. Trucks and tanker-lorries were driving in and out of the gates, guarded by security men in grey uniforms. Business was clearly booming at the world's only Semtex factory.

'We are the largest industrial enterprise in eastern Bohemia,' Mr Mokren commented in a guide-like manner. 'The factory consists of a thousand buildings connected by two hundred kilometres of road and sixty kilometres of rail tracks. We employ seven thousand workers.' There was genuine pride in his voice.

We stopped near an unmarked red-brick house, overgrown with acacias. Mr Mokren opened the front door with his own key. It was probably an administrative building. Its long, dark, Soviet-style corridors were lined with anonymous plate-less doors.

'This is my office,' said Mr Mokren letting me into a spacious room with an oblong table in the middle and bookshelves along the walls.

'I'll ask my secretary to make us coffee,' he said and went out.

So his secretary was still at work, despite the 'end of his working day'.

Left alone in Mr Mokren's office, I picked up a couple of brochures from a shelf. One was the company's annual report for 1995. On page 18 I found a 'Production of Explosives' section with parallel texts in Czech and stilted English:

> Despite of a continuing decrease of sales in the sector of military production, the sales of explosives show a steady increase of sales. This was contributed by an increase in sales of nitrocellulose and also owing to the sales of explosives and smokeless powders. The assortment of the latter products was innovated and their production modernised. In the division of explosives the export-oriented sales amount to nearly 65%.

On the following page, there were some tables and diagrams. One of the latter – 'Export of products by the Sectors' – showed a steady growth in the export of explosives, from 9.8% in 1993 to 14.0% in 1995. 'The most significant increase was recorded in the sales of organic substances and explosives,' ran the caption. Another diagram – 'The most significant export destinations' – listed, among others, Great Britain (3.8%), Italy (8.5%), Austria (3.3%) and 'Other Countries', to which unnamed destination 12.1% of Synthesia's export products were dispatched.

The second pamphlet was a 1996 edition of the factory's list of products. It included several different types of Semtex: Semtex 1A, Semtex 1AP, Semtex 2P and Semtex 2PN, all described as 'plastic explosives for special blasting operations'.

The secretary brought in a coffee tray. I hastily replaced the brochures. Mr Mokren returned and sat down behind his desk looking at me with impatience.

'To which countries do you export Semtex these days?' I asked him.

'I don't know,' he said briskly, and he looked at his watch. 'The only thing I can say is that our export of explosives keeps going down.'

'Not according to the annual report,' I thought.

'Do you have many incidents of theft at your explosives department?'

'Not many. One or two a year.'

'And who are the thieves?'

'Workers. We have recently cut our workforce by three hundred people.'

'What do you export to Britain?'

'Everything.'

'Including Semtex?'

No reply.

I looked at the smoking chimneys behind the window. 'Is it possible to see a Semtex production line?'

'Out of the question. You have to go back to the station now.'

There was no point in continuing this fruitless verbal exchange.

'Can I take a couple of your brochures?' I asked. Unexpectedly, Mr Mokren nodded. I took the annual report and the list of products and stuffed them hurriedly into my shoulder-bag.

'I am sorry I was unable to tell you much,' said Mr Mokren as we shook hands near the station. 'I am not an expert in explosives.'

'What are your areas of expertise?' I asked.

'Well, I am not a chemist,' he replied enigmatically and went back to his Lada.

On the train back to Prague, I tried to make some sense out of my impromptu visit to Synthesia.

It was obvious they hadn't wanted me to go to

Pardubice in the first instance. It was no less clear that when I did get to Pardubice they hadn't wanted me to see the factory, an abnormal attitude for a freshly privatised 'joint-stock' company which, theoretically, should grab every opportunity for media exposure.

It was also evident that the facts and figures in their brochures, targeting prospective buyers, were in stark contradiction of what Mr Mokren was prepared to tell a visiting 'member of the press'.

Or could it be that Mr Mokren – in defiance of his bosses (whoever they were), or for some other unknown reason – actually *wanted* me to visit Synthesia and to see the brochures?

One thing was certain: Semtex, the deadly substance invented by Bohumil Sol, was being produced in huge quantities at Synthesia, and the bulk of it was exported to countries which the factory was not willing to reveal.

A week later, police in London seized a cache of Semtex destined to be used in IRA attacks on British targets.

Now you will understand why I wasn't inclined to shed any tears over the inglorious death of Bohumil Sol, the father of Semtex, who blasted himself to smithereens in a psychiatric asylum near Pardubice.

10 THE LAST FEW DROPS OF BEER

Before I started my East European travels, I was determined to include East Germany in the Beer Lands part of this book. But after spending some time there, I realised that it wouldn't qualify. Having suffered more ideological pressure than any other Soviet-bloc country, East Germany has practically lost its age-old beer-drinking tradition. East Germans used to (and still do) prefer much stronger drinks, usually mixtures of several unlikely ingredients, to get away from the all-seeing eye of the Stasi and the all-permeating Soviet propaganda. They showed a good deal of truly German inventiveness and ingenuity in concocting these hard-hitting 'cocktails'.

Not that East Germans have given up beer completely. In the pubs of East Berlin you can still order a drink called Berliner Weisser, a top-fermented white beer mixed with . . . raspberry syrup. You are supposed to drink it through a straw. Never in my life have I had anything so disgusting and so conducive to making you feel like throwing up. Try to eat a pickled cucumber with cream custard, or dip a Mars bar into ketchup, and you will get a similar taste and effect.

Berliners themselves seem to realise the absurdity of this combination (which is probably why they often add schnapps to Berliner Weisser and call the resulting drink a 'small liaison'). But, with perseverance better known as obstinacy – another truly German trait – they keep drinking it.

Mixing beer with spirits was a purely East German way of 'obliterating communist reality', in the words of my old friend Nigel, a British hack who has lived in Berlin for many years. He likes remembering how once, when the Berlin Wall was still in place, he got smashed in an East Berlin pub with a local truck driver: 'We drank the so-called "*kleiner Feigling*" [little coward] – fig schnapps – and washed it down with beer. After a couple of hours I got so pissed that I don't remember how I went through the heavily guarded Wall back to West Berlin where I lived. I woke up in my bed next morning – and only then I got really frightened.'

The 'little coward' with beer, an equivalent of my student days' Ruff, was clearly capable of turning you into a real daredevil, impregnable to the bullets of East German border-guards.

In short, Berliner Weisser and other East German beer-based concoctions struck me as resembling post-communist eastern Germany itself, a land, resplendent with seemingly incompatible, even mutually contradictory – and yet somehow co-existing – phenomena.

I discovered a similar tendency in Slovakia, where they brew lots of good beers, but the favourite drink is the so-called 'Slovakian combination': beer mixed with gin or liqueur.

On the other hand, Poland – a traditional vodka land, whose beers have always been sneered at by everyone, including Poles themselves – is now showing a considerable increase in beer consumption, which signifies the progress of the country's democratic reforms (Poland is the great success story of Eastern Europe) and hence the subsiding need for the 'obliteration of reality'.

To sum up, it is the Czech Republic that remains the real beer land of Eastern Europe, for Czechs still prefer beer to any other drink. Poor sods.

II: SPIRITS LANDS

Poland and Slovakia, with a dash of East Germany

11 AQUA VITAE – EAST AND WEST

You must not imagine that we English are always wiser or better than other people. You may meet with danger in places where you least expect it. You may find many things that are very dangerous though they look very pleasant. They are like the draught of sparkling water from a poisoned well: it looks innocent and wholesome, but it brings death to the drinker . . .

Near Home or Europe Described,
Longmans, Green, & Co., London, 1910

Few East European phenomena are so distorted and misunderstood in the West as vodka.

In *Golden Eye*, one of the latest James Bond movies, I was appalled to see Robbie Coltrane in the role of a Russian mafioso, sipping vodka and holding it in his mouth before swallowing. And the Russian General Arumov (I forget who played him) took little swigs of vodka from a pocket flask. At least he did not swig it from a bottle, as has been the case with every portrayal of a Russian alcoholic in Western movies, which testifies to a lack of understanding of both vodka's qualities as a drink and its social significance.

To begin with, vodka first appeared in Poland (and then in Russia) as a medicine. As far back as the eighth century, it was noticed that water in wine or beer left outside in winter would freeze and leave a higher-strength alcohol residue. People started using this residue as a lotion for washing the chin and the cheeks after shaving, and, later, as an ointment for aching joints. When mass production of vodka began in Poland in the fifteenth century, it started (at long last) to be used internally as a cold-prevention and stomach-fixing medicine and was taken in spoonfuls. Vodka was the only alcoholic drink that did not freeze in sub-zero temperatures – no wonder it first appeared in Poland and Russia, Europe's coldest countries.

It was only in the eighteenth century that vodka began to be drunk for pleasure, rather than for purely medical reasons, but even then it retained such medicinal properties as an unpleasant smell and a lack of definite taste. This did not bother vodka-drinkers who consumed it not so much for its bouquet as for its after-effects. When you take cough mixture or a prescribed liquid medication to ease indigestion, you don't particularly care about its taste or smell, do you? What you do care about is whether or not it will relieve unpleasant symptoms. This is why you would be unlikely to sit and to savour it. You would rather swallow it in one gulp, wash it down with juice or water, and wait for its healing effect to set in. And this is the whole truth about the nature of vodka-drinking, which has remained largely unchanged since the fifteenth century, even if the range of ailments this liquid medicine is used against has broadened and now includes such purely psychological and spiritual conditions such as inability to cope with oppressive reality, desire for a brief escape from the hardships of life, failure to relax in a social situation, and so on. That is exactly how people (especially those who lived under totalitarian regimes with few other opportunities of escape) started abusing this potent liquid drug, which also proved addictive: my drinking tutor Evgeny Bulavin always asserted that the real healing effects of vodka began only after the second bottle.

Now, the issue of purity. As a thoroughly filtered product of distillation, a good vodka is designed to be the purest alcoholic drink on earth. Any additives, even ice cubes, immediately ruin its balance and character turning it into a foul-smelling mildly alcoholic wish-wash. Flavoured vodkas, which are getting increasingly popular in the West, are a corruption of the drink's very nature, a fact which even such connoisseurs as the late Jeffrey Bernard, who used – disgracefully – to mix his vodka with lime, fail to recognise.

Whenever I see London pub patrons cheerfully mixing vodka with lime, orange juice, Coca-Cola or even milk (I knew a London woman who could drink vodka only in conjunction with milk – and milk only if accompanied by vodka), it makes my heart ache.

A few words about the importance of a glass. The same medicinal principle applies here. Would you endeavour to swig cough mixture from the bottle? Would you think of sipping your anti-indigestion (or anti-constipation) potion from a flask? I doubt it. You need a proper glass, which makes it easier, faster and less unpleasant. Again, the process of consuming vodka (like any other liquid medicine) is not supposed to be a feast for your taste-buds: it is the after-effect that makes it worthwhile. Therefore, the faster the better.

A Russian (or Polish) vodka-drinker will give any-thing for a glass. Even the most degraded of alcoholics wouldn't drink vodka from a bottle, for this would be like severing his last remaining connection with the breed of civilised humans. I don't know whose sick fantasy created the stereotype of a Russian (or a Pole) smashing his vodka glass against a wall after emptying it. A glass is too precious a commodity to be disposed of in such a barbaric way.

Here are a couple of real-life illustrations.

Once, waiting for a train at a Moscow railway station I got talking with a man who had just been freed from a labour camp, where he had served an eleven-year stretch for murder. At that time, I was researching an article about the appalling conditions in Soviet labour camps, and the ex-convict was an invaluable source. He happened to have a bottle of vodka on him, and he insisted we drank together as a precondition of a conversation. The only problem was where to drink it: we were in the midst of the Gorbachev-induced anti-alcoholism campaign when drinking in any public place could (if you were caught) lead to a hefty fine with subsequent loss of one's job. For my ex-convict friend this would almost certainly mean returning to the labour camp, a scenario to which he did not particularly look forward.

After a quick reconnaissance, it was decided that the safest place would be a stretch of railway track behind a stationary cargo train. We were about to uncork the bottle when a derelict red-nosed type, with two weeks' stubble on his hollow cheeks, materialised in front of us. 'Are you planning to have a drink, guys?' he enquired, hypnotising our bottle with his faded yellowish eyes. We mumbled something incoherent. 'You are not going to drink vodka from the bottle, like savages, are you?' he asked us, and without waiting for a reply to this largely rhetorical question, added, 'Give me one rouble, and I shall provide you with a glass!'

And although the type did not inspire the slightest degree of trust, although the ex-convict, who had had to imbibe glue and glass-cleaning fluid during his eleven-year incarceration, was clearly not a proponent of civilised drinking, we gave the type a rouble. Drinking tepid vodka from the bottle was out of the question, and the bottle was there waiting to be emptied. We didn't have a choice.

The type took the rouble and disappeared like greased lightning, having told us to wait. We waited for an hour, suspecting that he wouldn't come back. And he didn't, of course. The ex-convict blurted out a prolonged and hard-hitting burst of sophisticated underworld curses aimed at the unshaven liar (which would have definitely brought the crook to his knees had he been around), after which we said goodbye to each other and split up. The vodka remained undrunk, and the conversation never took place. What else could we do? We couldn't drink vodka from the bottle like uncultured brutes, could we?

The second incident took place at about the same time in Byelorussia, where I was sent by the satirical magazine *Krokodil* to write a 'rosy' piece glorifying the republic's achievements in procuring some food for its population at a time when the rest of the country was literally starving.

There was indeed some food in Byelorussia's shops (I remember being particularly impressed by the availability of two different sorts of cheese, whereas the shops in Moscow remained totally cheese-less). Throughout my trip, I was accompanied by the republic's minister of agriculture, who had kindly offered to let me travel in his chauffeured black Volga limo.

On the last day of our trip, the minister was visibly restless and agitated. He was looking around like a troubled bird, and kept winking at me conspiratorially from the front seat of the Volga. At last, after a visit to a collective farm near the town of Orsha, he leant towards me and whispered, 'Vitali Vladimirovich, do you feel like having a rest?'

I knew this was a euphemism for having a drink. On my journalistic missions I had to be careful not to fall into the trap of drinking with potential heroes of my satirical pieces who were only waiting for a chance to compromise me and to ruin my credibility. I remember one bureaucrat in the Zaporozhie region following me with a string bag full of booze wherever I went for three days. 'Let's have a drink, Vitali Vladimirovich,' he kept whining. Of course, I refused to be provoked: a written denunciation, substantiated with the photos of me drinking with a potential target of the article, would have reached Moscow before I did.

But this case was different: the article was to be a positive one. There was no immediate harm in drinking with the minister, except for the danger of being caught doing so in a public place (restaurants included), in which case even he would have lost his ministerial job before he could say '*Vashe Zdorovie!*' ('To your health!')

A popular joke of those times was about a director preparing to make love to his secretary on a sofa in his office. 'Have you closed the door?' she asks him. 'What for? We aren't drinking, are we?' he replies.

I agreed to have a drink with the hospitable minister and suggested that we should do this in the privacy of my hotel room. 'Are you mad or what?' the minister objected. He told me that several voluntary stooges were constantly on duty near the hotel. When they spotted a group of men with carefully wrapped parcels entering the building, they would wait for half an hour, and then burst into the newcomers' room without knocking. If they saw the men drinking, they would blackmail them: pay us a hundred roubles, or we shall report you to the management. Normally people paid the blackmailers off rather than risk exposure: alongside non-alcoholic restaurants (they were *all* non-alcoholic under Gorby), a hotel room was classified as a public place, too.

Having stuffed the Volga boot with booze and drink, on the minister's recommendation we headed for a nearby forest, which he thought was the safest place. It was late November. For a good hour we drove along a narrow forest path in complete darkness, with wild rabbits jumping from under the mud-covered wheels of our car. The forests are thick in Byelorussia. During the Second World War, they gave excellent shelter to the partisans, and the Nazis were scared of entering them. But we were neither Nazis nor partisans. We simply wanted to have a drink.

'Can't we stop here? It looks perfectly safe,' I said from time to time, like a tired child in the back of the car who keeps pestering his parents with the question. 'Are we nearly there?' 'No, it's not safe enough,' the minister would reply. For some reason, we communicated only in whispers.

Eventually, we reached the end of the forest path. The car could not go any farther. It was a real no-man's-land, and we could hear wolves howling somewhere close by, behind the bushes.

'It's OK,' the minister said to his driver. We climbed out of the car. The driver switched on the headlights and started laying food and vodka on the top of the boot. When everything was ready and we were about to 'have a rest', it turned out that we had forgotten the glasses.

On the way back, none of us uttered a word. We could hear the unopened vodka bottles clinking merrily in the boot, as if they were giggling at us.

Western misconceptions about vodka do not stop there. Let's look at the names given to some popular Western brands.

In any London off-licence you can find cheap locally made vodkas with names like Vladivar, Imperial Commissar, or even Tolstoy.

Vladivar would have been a fine name for a beer ('var' from the verb 'varit' – to brew), but for vodka, which is distilled not brewed, it sounds ridiculous. Imperial Commissar is a contradiction in itself, like a four-angled triangle, or a 'royal proletarian'. As for poor Leo Tolstoy, a convinced teetotaller, vegetarian and tireless propagandist for abstention, to name a vodka after him is like naming a Jewish school after Adolf Hitler. If the author of *War and Peace* knew that he had a vodka named after him, he would turn face down in his coffin.

And how about the vodkas Kirov (Stalin's henchman, not the popular ballet), Chekov (which should be spelt 'Chekhov'; he, by the way, preferred champagne), and

Gorbachov (a German brand, aptly commemorating the politician who made buying a bottle of vodka in Russia almost as difficult as becoming the Communist Party general secretary)?

If you ask me, I would not touch them with a barge pole. I would rather go for the obscure Luxembourg-made brand Black Death, or for the Danish liqueur North Sea Oil. At least their makers are being honest.

12 PRE-DRINKING EXALTATION IN KRAKOW

Prussia is rich – Poland is poor. Prussia is prosperous –
Poland is unhappy. Prussia is free – Poland is conquered
. . . Poor Poland has no king of her own.
Near Home or Europe Described,
Longmans, Green, & Co., London, 1910

Several hundred people huddled at the LOT (Polish national airline) Gatwick–Krakow flight check-in point. The airline's name was more than appropriate: there were a LOT of people at the check-in and they were making a LOT of fuss, but our LOT was an unlucky one: the LOT flight to Krakow was being delayed a LOT.

I was about to embark on what promised to be the most exciting part of my East European travels: a trip to the motherland of vodka. As a reformed vodka drinker, I was well aware of all the dangers involved. Although vodka is the drink least likely to give you a hangover and make you feel woozy the morning after, I carried a considerable supply of Resolve in my shoulder-bag (just in case). I also carried a tape-recorder, for on this trip I was supposed to record a travel feature for BBC Radio 4's *Breakaway*, thus killing two birds with one (vodka) shot, so to speak.

My travel companion was Susy Atkins, a young

London wine critic whom I was expected to convert to drinking vodka as part of the scenario suggested by a resourceful *Breakaway* producer. The task was formidable.

'I know nothing about vodka,' Susy said. 'I have a full palate, but an empty mind.'

'Never mind your mind. We'll fill it with vodka soon,' I promised.

It was easier said than done. After several years of nearly total abstention, I had largely lost the vodka-drinking skills instilled in me by the unforgettable Evgeny Bulavin. I had some catching up to do.

'Learn in Italy, clothe yourself in Germany, flirt in France, banquet in Poland,' runs an old Polish proverb. My previous visits to Poland had led me to conclude that this particular folk wisdom was right. I am not so sure about banqueting, but as regards drinking and smoking Poland is in the very top bracket of European nations – a natural thing for a country with a strong national identity and a schizophrenic history of being a geo-political sandwich-filling between the constantly warring giants, Russia and Germany. It was in Poland that vodka was pioneered first as a medicine and later as a drink. The staggering statistics of more recent times classified Poland as the world's heaviest smoking country (according to the WHO, each Pole over 15 smokes on average 3620 cigarettes a year). As for the notorious Polish drinking, it had shown a 40 per cent increase since the collapse of communism: in 1992 each Pole drank three gallons of alcohol (in pure spirits), as opposed to two gallons in 1989.

In short, post-communist Poland sounded like my sort of place.

When we finally found ourselves on board the LOT flight, I was shocked to discover that it was a fully non-smoking one. What could I say? Poland *must* be changing, after all! Susy, who sat next to me, kept loudly extolling the miraculous healing effects of drinking three glasses of red wine a day. One or two were not enough and four were excessive, she insisted. I only shrugged: after all, it was I who was supposed to convert her, not the other way round.

Looking through the onboard newspapers, I realised that our Polish trip had fallen between two great natural calamities, the previously unseen floods and the Polish parliamentary elections.

The floods, which affected not just Poland but most of Eastern and Central Europe in the summer of 1997, had, allegedly, brought Polish political life to a near standstill. They had drowned the political ambitions of all twenty-five competing parties, they had exposed the country's multiple problems, of which there were heaps, despite the so-called 'Polish economic miracle' making Poland the only country in Eastern Europe that had managed to achieve economic growth in the few years after the end of the Cold War. The flooded streets of Wroclaw, the worst-affected Polish city, were infested with legions of brown rats, rodents of extreme biological viability, whose females took just twenty-four days to come to term. The response of the rats, once they had saved themselves from the torrents, was to mate, and therefore their numbers were growing by the day.

From the informative and vivacious newspaper *Warsaw Voice*, I grasped that it was not only the rats that had become promiscuous as a result of the floods. The owner of one of the three Wroclaw brothels that stayed in business throughout the flooding was quoted as saying, 'We had to expand our services to provide safe docking for clients' boats and rafts.' Speaking about the flood's impact on his department, Colonel Jan Pyrcak, deputy director of Wroclaw's prison services, claimed that in one Wroclaw prison, guards had to go to work in kayaks.

It was obvious that in toughness and viability (let alone promiscuity) the Poles could compete successfully with brown rats.

Seriously speaking, there was something really spooky about this sudden wave of floods in Germany, Poland, the Czech Republic and all over Eastern Europe – floods which had washed away political borders (borders up!) and brought about a number of disasters. One senior Russian MP even claimed that this calamity was the work of the dead Soviet dictator Joseph Stalin: Stalin's revenge on those former Soviet-bloc countries which had been planning to join NATO. 'There will be more floods if the NATO talks continue,' he said.

What the paranormal Russian MP did not know (and I did) was that on top of the floods of water, post-communist Eastern Europe (and especially Poland) was flooded with equally unheard-of torrents of alcohol and was busily drinking itself into a stupor.

For the purposes of my would-be book the timing of my Polish escapade was not so bad, after all.

Armed Polish soldiers met our plane at Krakow airport – an old communist habit which seems to be dying hard. On the bright side, there were no longer ceiling mirrors at passport control. These oblong and dusty overhead mirrors used to be part and parcel of every Soviet-bloc immigration point. Their exact purpose had always been a mystery to me. Were they designed to enable the officer to scrutinise the crown of your head for signs of a wig, or, maybe, to monitor your dissident thoughts? Or were they simply supposed to make every visitor feel like a trespasser?

A little black box was attached to the control panel of a taxi which took us to the hotel. The driver explained that it was a special Polish device to neutralise police speed cameras: electro-magnetic waves emitted by the box made the cameras go haywire and unable to read the car's exact speed. A very East European device. I thought that it could have been successfully patented in Britain.

Our hotel was in an old castle on top of a hill. 'Paul

McCartney Square', read the street sign on its façade. I wondered what the square had been called before. General Yaruzelski Square? Karl Marx Square? Renaming streets and squares was a good thing. Sometimes, however, it went a bit too far. In Leipzig, in a door-plate-changing frenzy after the collapse of the Berlin Wall, they even renamed Spartacus Street Manhattan Street. What was the link between the rebellious Roman gladiator and Stalinist oppression? I wish I knew. They have probably branded poor Spartacus a revolutionary and therefore – automatically – a communist.

The hotel was owned by Poland's biggest independent radio station, Wolnosc (Liberty). I had never stayed in a hotel like that. To begin with, it was called Hotel FM. The rooms had frequencies, instead of numbers, on the doors. My room number – sorry, frequency – was 95.3 FM, but no matter how hard I tried to tune myself to it, reception remained poor.

Before visiting Krakow's Polmos vodka distillery, we were in for a quick tour of the city. Our guide Barbara, a busty young woman with a malachite cross nestling in her cleavage, was waiting for us at Reception. She started the tour with a Polish proverb (they do like their proverbs in Poland): 'The money is in Warsaw, but the heart of Poland is in Krakow.' I asked her whether she had heard another Polish proverb: 'There aren't any ugly women, only too little vodka.' Barbara was upset (I think Susy was upset, too). 'Vodka is not romantic, it is a social problem,' she said, wrinkling her nose. She was a serious girl and was studying to be a lawyer.

I asked her whether it was true that in Krakow the florists charged you for sniffing their flowers (as my guidebook assured me). She got even more upset. 'It is not true! Flowers are so romantic!' 'Romantic' was clearly her favourite word.

Krakow owes its name to the ancient Polish King Krak, who, in his turn, was named after a raven's croak (this is probably why Poles spell it 'Cracow'). It was a slow city, only slightly touched by the post-communist economic boom in the form of numerous Coca-Cola signs, and the moronic face of Mr Bean (Pan Fasola in Polish) scowling from billboards, Bermuda travel agencies (were they offering trips on which tourists disappear without a trace?) and a chain of shoe-shops called Athlete's Foot.

'Yak,' commented Susy. 'The next thing on the agenda is probably a chain of Thrush lingerie stores.'

On the way to the centre, we passed a newly built apartment block called Acropolis. Fresh memories of the world's most famous ruin (I had just come back from Greece) made me think that the Krakowians needed some help with naming their new capitalist ventures properly.

When Barbara was showing us the imposing St Mary's Church in the Main Market Square, I noticed several rusty metallic shackles on one of its walls and asked her what their purpose was.

'In the Middle Ages, adulterous spouses were chained to them on Sundays for everyone to view,' she explained with a wry smile. 'Poland is a good Catholic country, but we are also very romantic people.'

'And you are also sure that romance can only be found outside marriage,' I wanted to say, remembering the heroic clients of Wroclaw's flooded brothels, but thought better of it – so as not to upset her (and Susy) even further.

We dutifully examined the Gothic building of Krakow's 630-year-old Jagiellonian University, where Nicolaus Copernicus, Marie Curie and Pope John Paul II studied at different times (the Pope was a bit of a hero in Krakow, where he was archbishop before his promotion to the papacy) and where Barbara was doing her law degree now. We looked at the impressive dome of the Church of the Assumption of Our Lady, commissioned by King Sigismund in the first half of the sixteenth century. It used to be the most expensive dome in Europe; now it is presumably the second most expensive one, after Mandelson's Millennium Dome in Greenwich.

At midday, we suddenly heard a clear and melodious trumpet solo above our heads. The sound came from the top of St Mary's Church. It was one of the famous Krakow bugle-call trumpeters who have inhabited the Church's Guard Tower for the last six hundred years. There were six of them, all members of the Krakow fire brigade, working in pairs twenty-four hours a day. Every hour they sound their bugle-call, which is broadcast live on Polish national radio, rather like the chimes of Big Ben in Britain. Barbara told us that the trumpeters had a cosy little room on top of the tower with a bed, a TV set, a fridge and a stove. I wondered whether it was possible to climb up and pay them a visit. 'It is only the trumpeters who are allowed up there,' she said. 'How come you know they have a bed in their duty room, then?' I wanted to ask, but, again, stopped short of doing so out of respect for her innate romanticism.

At that very moment we were approached by an unshaven type with darting eyes who offered us access to the tower, if we paid him 20 zlotys (£3.50). Before I could say '*Tak*' ('Yes'), Barbara shooed him away. To me, the sight of this shabby character was strangely reassuring: he was living, unshaven proof of the fact that some aspects of Eastern Europe, where not so long ago 'nothing was allowed but everything was possible', remained unchanged – there was always a way round an official ban.

Barbara told us that on some Mondays the trumpeters, following an old custom (and probably bored out of their minds), poured down a few bucketfuls of water on to the unsuspecting passers-by. Before she had time to say how romantic it was to be splashed with water from a church tower, I suggested that we should move on, despite the fact that it was Friday. You never know what crazy idea may occur to someone stuck in a tiny room eighty-one metres above the ground for twenty-four hours a day.

We proceeded to Wawel Hill to have a look at the old Wawel Castle. Looking down from one of its bastions, I saw a metallic sculpture of a dragon on the bank of the River Vistula. The beast stood on its hind legs and looked fairly unsteady, as if drunk. From time to time, flames came out of its open gullet. I wondered (this time aloud) whether the fire-spitting dragon had something to do with vodka. In response, Barbara told us the following legend.

'Once upon a time there lived a terrible beast in Krakow. It took its lodging in a cave at the foot of Wavel Hill and would devour pretty girls and young lads for breakfast. Krakowians lived in constant fear, since they never knew who would be the dragon's next victim. One day a young shoemaker's apprentice came to King Krak and promised to free the town from the frightful monster. He decided to play a trick on the dragon and left a sheepskin stuffed with sulphur near its cave. The dragon pounced on it and devoured it greedily. Then it crawled to the nearby Vistula to quench its thirst. It drank and drank for two days until it swelled up and burst.'

This jolly 'legend' reminded me of the purpose of our visit to Krakow. It was already past midday, and the dragon was already enjoying itself and impersonating a flame-thrower, whereas we were still sober like bastards – a favourite simile of Evgeny Bulavin. The exotic Polish beer soup with cheese that we had consumed for lunch in a café with the not particularly appetising name of Chimera (another Krakow misnomer) did not count. It was time for us to quench *our* thirst. We flagged down a cab and went to the vodka factory.

Both Susy and myself were in a state which Evgeny Bulavin would have described as 'pre-drinking exaltation'.

13 VODKA 'AUSCHWITZ'

More Jews live in Poland than in any other country. You might once have known them in a moment by their long black muslin gowns and their long black shining beards. They have eyes like the hawk, and noses like its beak . . . The Jews are not indolent like the Poles, but try in every way to get money . . . Some of the Jews are very troublesome to travellers. They follow them about, offering to help them, and will not go away when they are told . . . The Poles often speak rudely to the Jews, and think themselves much better than they; but the Jews bear this with great patience, because they are accustomed to be ill-treated.

Near Home or Europe Described,
Longmans, Green, & Co., London, 1910

The Holy Virgin, her sad, wide-open eyes full of reproach, looked down from the wall at the endless procession of clinking vodka bottles on the conveyor belt. The bottling line of Polmos distillery was working non-stop. It was staffed exclusively by women in white gowns and with plastic plugs in their ears (had men been employed here, they would have probably had mouth-plugs, too). From time to time, one of them would pick up a defective bottle from the conveyor and toss it into a rubbish bin, where it broke with a brief, submissive thump.

Most of the roly-poly bottles on the line had one and

the same label – Cymes Kosher Vodka – on their tummies. The label showed a red-nosed Orthodox Jew in a wide-brimmed hat clicking his fingers in a well-known Jewish gesture of appreciation.*

On a smaller conveyer, Fiddler Kosher Vodka was being bottled. A woman was topping each bottle with a tiny plastic 'rabbi's hat', taking the 'hats' one by one from a cardboard box at her feet. The sight of hundreds of them in the box was somehow disturbing.

'What is the different in production methods between an ordinary vodka and a kosher one?' I asked Maria Wojciechovska, the distillery's marketing manager.

'The only difference is that a rabbi comes in at the beginning of the process and blesses the production line,' she said.

'Does he come here every day?'

'No. Once a year, maybe,' she smiled.

A serious breach of kosher regulations was evident: I knew that an unfinished kosher product was not supposed to be touched or overseen by women. I also doubted that the blessing of the vodka took place at all: there were only two rabbis left in Poland, and they had more pressing things on their minds than blessing kosher vodka production lines on a daily – or even a yearly – basis.

Later, we were sitting at Ms Wojciechovska's office and tasting kosher (Jankiel, Rachela, Tevie, Fiddler, Herszl etc.) and other vodkas, washing them down with kosher mineral water (!), also produced by Polmos. I asked our hosts about the production of Zmiyovska vodka, with a pickled (or was it plastered?) small black adder resting on the bottom of every bottle – I had heard that this peculiar vodka was made in Krakow. 'We had

---

* The Yiddish word *Cymes* originally denoted a traditional Jewish delicacy of carrots, plums and honey boiled together and added to food as a dressing, but in the course of time it came to mean anything yummy.

to stop manufacturing Zmiyovska because of the shortage of black adders, which had become a protected species' was the reply. I wanted to ask why they hadn't started importing the snakes from Russia, where, as far as I knew, they were still plentiful.

At the end of the tasting we were given a promotion leaflet for Cymes vodka which said, 'Jewish tradition was always present in Cracow [*sic*]. Both cultures – Polish and Jewish – evolved together through the centuries in a kind of symbiosis . . .' And so on.

Whatever the present-day state of Polish–Jewish relationships can be called, their sad history can hardly be characterised as 'symbiosis', for whereas Polish culture has indeed 'evolved through the centuries', Jewish culture in Poland has been continuously and meticulously eradicated, especially during the last sixty-odd years. Thanks to the concerted Polish–German effort, there are now fewer than 7000 Jews left in the country, which at the turn of the century was home to 3.3 million of them. As for Krakow, which had 68,000 Jews before the Second World War, it now counts no more than 200. Indeed, thirty brands of kosher vodka are on sale, but there are not many Jews left to drink it (Jewish people were never big drinkers, anyway).

Despite the near-absence of Jews, Polish anti-Semitism is alive and *kike*-ing, so to speak. Politicians and religious leaders regularly make anti-Semitic pronouncements. Jewish graves are desecrated. Walls are covered with anti-Semitic graffiti.

The prevailing view among the Poles is that in reality there are many more Jews in the country than the 'official' 7000. During my previous visit to Poland in 1994, one Warsaw intellectual kept assuring me that there were still millions of 'hidden' Jews around. Even the serious and 'romantic' Barbara, our Krakow guide, was adamant in asserting that there were 'many more' Jews in Krakow than the number stated by the official statistics. To me, it looked like national-scale paranoia, triggered by a combination of hatred and guilt. How else can one describe a situation in which anti-Semitic feeling keeps growing in inverse proportion to the number of Jews left in the country?

The only Orthodox Jew I was able to spot in post-communist Poland was a visiting American rabbi on the train from Krakow to Gdansk.

Speaking of the Holocaust, it was not by chance that the Nazis built dozens of concentration camps on Polish territory – many more than in any other occupied country. As to the Nazi extermination camps, *all six of them* were in Poland. They obviously had reason to count on if not the support, at least the silent in-difference of the locals. And they proved right: when the remaining handful of the heroic Warsaw ghetto uprising fighters, who had been resisting the Nazis for eight months, pleaded with the Polish anti-fascist under-ground for assistance, they received no reply.

One month before my vodka trip an interesting development occurred in Poland. Polish public television banned a documentary on one of the most terrible episodes in Polish history. Shortly after the Second World War a shoesmith in Warsaw claimed that his son, Henryk, had been kidnapped by Jews, when in fact he had sent the boy to live in the country, out of harm's way, for the duration of the war. This malicious falsehood quickly spread through the local community, helped by spurious confirmation from the Polish secret police. A furious anti-Semitic mob tracked down and murdered forty-two Jews, all survivors of the Holocaust, during a night of terror. The film featured Henryk himself, now in his sixties, who had finally – after fifty years – decided to come forward and speak the truth about his 'abduction', a gruesome truth which Poland, it appeared, was not ready to face. And although excerpts from the film's script were published by Warsaw's *Gazeta Wyborcza*, edited by my good friend Adam

Michnik (who is Jewish himself, by the way), the documentary was never shown.

After the tasting (which Susy very much enjoyed), we were shown a publicity video about the distillery. A tipsy, winking rabbi kept appearing in different corners of the screen throughout the film, to the accompaniment of a symphony by Tchaikovsky.

For me, drinking vodka without food was torture. We were both hungry, so we stopped short of tasting all seventy vodka brands produced by this particular distillery, one of thirty independent Polmos factories throughout Poland. On Barbara's suggestion, we headed for Kaziemierz, the Jewish area of Krakow, in the hope of having a well-deserved meal.

Kaziemierz was eerie. It looked like a cross between the dead Ukrainian town of Pripyat, evacuated after the explosion of the Chernobyl nuclear reactor, and the tacky Leather Lane street market in London. Most of the houses were empty and unkempt, their frameless windows gaping like the dark and hollow eye-sockets of a skeleton. 'We are waiting for the original owners to return and claim them as part of restitution,' explained Barbara. I thought that they would be waiting for ever, for the 'former owners' either had perished in Auschwitz, or (less likely) had fled to America or Australia, and were not planning to come back.

All eight synagogues stood half ruined (except for one which now housed a bank): the remaining two hundred Jews had little use for them. Pigeons were cooing in a small square, in the centre of which several souvenir stalls were doing a brisk trade in Jewish paraphernalia, although 'memorabilia' would have been a more appropriate word for all those crudely made trinkets: cheap menorahs and mezuzahs, wooden figurines of bearded rabbis, photos of the pre-war 'happy' Jewish life in Kaziemierz, and bottles of kosher vodka, of course. The buyers were flocks of American tourists,

whose buses were parked near by. The very history of
the extinct Krakow Jews had been made into a knick-
knack and put on sale in the former Jewish quarter,
which had now become a Spielberg-style theme park
(several scenes of *Schindler's List* were filmed there).

We had *karp po zydowski* (carp Jewish-style) in a
newly restored Menorah café. Martin, a young barman,
was one of the remaining two hundred Krakow Jews.
He didn't speak a word of either Yiddish or Hebrew. He
was also a teetotaller – the only purely Jewish trait he
had managed to preserve. 'People now drink more than
before. I don't know why,' he said, pouring us another
shot of kosher vodka. Centuries of Jewish suffering were
reflected in his sad brown eyes. 'Sometimes tourists
come in just to gape at me, as if I am an ET,' he
complained, but added, 'But it's OK. It's good for the
business.'

'Welcome! We are going to Auschwitz!' a cheerful
young guide greeted us the next morning as we boarded
a tourist bus with 'Auschwitz–Birkenau' written on its
side.

Before coming to Krakow we had agreed that we
would give Auschwitz a miss since it had little to do with
the purpose of our vodka familiarisation trip, or so we
thought. But the visit to Kaziemierz convinced us that
we had to go.

'How amazing! I haven't got a hangover,' said Susy as
the bus was making its way through the suburbs of
Krakow: Auschwitz was just a forty-minute drive away.

'What did I tell you?' I noted contentedly. 'If you stick
to vodka during the evening, a hangover is extremely
unlikely.'

Our jolly mood evaporated the moment we reached
Auschwitz. Fast-food stalls at the entrance were selling
meat pies, crisps and borscht in plastic cups. There had
been plans to build a supermarket and a McDonald's
outlet there, and only public outrage in the West had

stopped Polish developers from carrying out their plans.

How shall I describe what we saw in Auschwitz? And should I? A few details were firmly imprinted in my memory. Japanese tourists taking photos of themselves near the 'death wall' and at the camp's entrance gate under the words *Arbeit Macht Frei* ('Work brings freedom') – probably the world's most cynical sign. A withdrawn female guide, who kept repeating that it was not just Jews but also Poles and Russians who were killed in Auschwitz (in fact, 95 per cent of the victims were Jewish). Empty cans of Cyclone-B gas (each can was enough to kill a thousand people) neatly stacked near a gas chamber camouflaged as a shower room. And, displayed under glass, piles – no, mountains – of spectacles, crutches, artificial limbs, shoes, suitcases, toothbrushes and children's dolls, all sorted and arranged in a purely German orderly way. I suddenly realised why I had been disturbed by the sight of hundreds of plastic rabbi's 'hats', piled together in the cardboard box at the vodka factory.

In one window there were stacks of human hair that had all gone grey with time, or was it from shame and sadness at our striking inability to learn from the past? 'The one who doesn't remember history, is bound to live through it again,' said George Santayana. Wasn't something similar happening in post-communist Poland, where anti-Semitism was still rife, despite the thirty brands of kosher vodka with joyful tipsy rabbis on the labels?

There were no joyful Jews left in Poland – they had all been murdered in the gas chambers of Auschwitz. No seas of kosher vodka would be enough to drown the grief of their few surviving relatives and loved ones. Contrary to what was stated in the colourful promotional leaflets, Cymes and other vodkas, made to old Jewish recipes, were not doing much to revive the exterminated Jewish culture in Poland. They were rather an insult to the traditions of that long-suffering – and still ruthlessly persecuted – race, whose tragic plight had been turned into a money-making commodity and a tourist attraction.

The faces of the dead looked at us blankly from thousands of photos on the barracks walls. I could see reproach in their eyes, the same reproach that I had spotted in the eyes of the Holy Virgin at Krakow's vodka factory.

I wouldn't be particularly surprised if one day they produced a new brand of kosher vodka: Vodka 'Auschwitz'.

14 A DEER IN BLUE UNDERWEAR

With Yacek and Adam, we were sitting in a Krakow café, Herbaciarnia Number 1. '*Herbaciarnia*' means 'tea-house' in Polish, but, although tea was also on its menu, most of the patrons were happily imbibing pure vodka and different vodka cocktails: Flag (vodka with raspberry juice – the Polish national flag is red and white), Takanka (vodka with apple juice), Bomb (50 grams of vodka added to beer. There were some 'Westernised' drinks on the menu, too: Heaven So Sweet (vodka plus whisky), Alexander's Sister (gin plus smetana, a thick Polish soured cream) and even Dirty White Mother (smetana plus cognac with coffee liqueur). The most frequent orders, however, were for Sivukha, a 60 per cent proof moonshine, made of potatoes, which many drank from beer glasses.

Yacek and Adam, both in their early forties, were old Solidarity mates. They were both intellectuals, former dissidents and newly made businessmen. Adam, an ex-journalist, now owned the Chimera café, where we had lunched on beer soup a couple of days before. Yacek, an Oxford-educated philosopher and a musician, was the happy proprietor of Herbaciarnia Number 1. Dissidents turned restaurateurs seemed to be a popular human metamorphosis in post-communist Poland.

'When I drink vodka, I start seeing a deer in blue underwear after a couple of glasses,' Yacek said, blissfully drowning his umpteenth thimbleful of Wyborowa. 'Drinking vodka is like listening to music in moonlight, as Somerset Maugham used to say,' he added, having probably thought that a blue deer was not a strong enough argument in favour of vodka-drinking.

'Vodka has killed many of my friends in the anti-communist underground,' objected Adam, who was sipping one of the café's unlikely concoctions, probably a Dirty White Mother. 'Under communism, many Poles chose vodka as an escape, whereas now they drink out of confusion.'

I asked Adam why he had left Solidarity.

'They have become a bit power-drunk,' he explained.

'Whatever you say, I like drinking vodka with Vitali, because he is a nice man, who knows our part of the world,' said Yacek. 'We can talk with him about music, politics, literature and lots of other things.'

Susy was listening to our verbal exchange with fascination.

'The number of times I've been drunk or hung over, traipsing round Moscow from one end to the other, and I've never once seen the Kremlin.' Yacek was quoting from the novel *Moscow – Petushki* by Venedict Yerofeyev, an alcoholic Russian writer, who died in 1990 of throat cancer. The novel was banned in the Soviet Union, and I first read it in Russian samizdat (an underground typewritten edition). So did Yacek, who had learnt Russian to read samizdat books, whereas I tried to learn some basic Polish to be able to read Stanislaw Lem, a brilliant Krakow-based science fiction writer, and a number of Western authors who were banned in the Soviet Union but were published in Poland. A curious symmetry of oppression.

'Under communism, drinking was one of the few things which were allowed,' continued Adam. 'A Pole will never confess to being a drunkard. He will always find heaps of reasons to justify himself.'

'And we are not drunkards!' exclaimed Yacek, not realising that by saying that he was confirming Adam's words. 'It was the policy of the communist government to make people drunk, so we were forced to drink a lot!'

We parted with Adam and Yacek shortly before midnight, after half an hour of handshakes, hugs and friendly kisses. We exchanged addresses and promises to stay in touch. Each of us realised that we would never see each other, or hear from each other, again. We knew that if we bumped into each other in the street the following morning, we wouldn't recognise one another, and, even if we did, there wouldn't be much to talk about. Another peculiar East European custom.

'I've had a wonderful evening,' Susy told me in the cab. 'Lovely people! And what a conversation! Nothing like our silly English small talk.'

'Wine and beer are for small talk, and vodka is reserved for big issues,' I said gravely.

Susy was learning fast. She was clearly getting hooked by vodka culture. Maybe she was hearing some music in the moonlight, like Somerset Maugham. Or, maybe, like Yacek, she could even see a scantily dressed deer after a couple of glasses of vodka. As for me, after a long non-drinking interval, vodka made me feel slow and heavy-headed, and I couldn't see much, except, perhaps, for my Abbey National bank book with a huge overdraft in it.

The elusive deer in blue underwear had escaped me so far.

We couldn't possibly leave Krakow without visiting its premier tourist attraction, the Wieliczka salt mine. I also had to do some more recording for the radio feature, and the salt mine was bound to have interesting acoustics (if nothing else).

Connecting the mine to vodka was not a problem after I remembered an old Russian recipe for fixing an unsettled stomach: a glass of vodka with salt. I was once saved by this unsophisticated combination after getting badly poisoned by *chal* (camel's milk) in Turkmenistan.

'This is your last chance to sit down,' Andrzej, our guide, said with a smirk. We were about to descend 378 stairs into the salt mine's shaft. Besides Andrzej, our group was escorted (for security reasons?) by a uniformed miner in a white helmet: the Wieliczka salt mine was still a working (and a recently privatised) industrial enterprise.

'If anyone is going to survive, it will be him,' said Andrzej, pointing at the miner, as we made our way down the stairs into the shaft. Our guide had a penchant for black, tacky jokes. Listening to him, I remembered what Leo Tolstoy once wrote about Leonid Andreyev, a turn-of-the-century Russian author with a passion for gruesome symbolism: 'He tries to scare us, but I am not frightened.'

On the way down, we dutifully learnt that the excavation of salt in Wieliczka started around year 3500 BC; that it had 2040 chambers, over 200 kilometres of galleries and 26 surface shafts. We were supposed to cover a meagre 2 kilometres of the mine's underground territory.

The walls of the dimly lit corridors along which we walked were covered with graffiti in all imaginable languages. Cauliflower-like layers of salt hung precariously from the ceilings. Soon we entered the first chamber, which contained a life-size sculpture of the Polish astronomer Nicolaus Copernicus. The sculpture was made of salt. The ornate chandeliers above it were made of salt, too.

'Unbelievable!' shouted an elderly American in our group. He and his wife were both wearing baseball caps with crosses embroidered on them. They probably belonged to some obscure religious sect, of which there are plenty in the US.

Next on our route was St Anthony's chapel. The pews, the pulpit and all three altars in it were hewn by hand from the salt, as were the floor and a pinkish sculpture of Baby Jesus.

'You can get married here,' Andrzej said matter-of-factly.

'Incredible!' screamed the American. 'Just imagine: to be married in a salt mine!' His wife looked at him with disapproval. She obviously didn't fancy the idea, whereas I thought that there was some sense in it: as they say in Russia, really to know someone, you have to eat a pound of salt together.

'We have lots of accidents in the mine,' Andrzej informed us cheerfully. 'Before the ceilings collapse, there comes a crackling noise. We can't hear it now which can mean two things: either everything is safe, or it is too late. So we'd better move on.' His comments had to be taken with a grain of salt, too.

The very idea of this salty underground town struck me at first as rather zany. But then I remembered a restaurant made of ice, which I once saw in Sweden (its obvious advantage was that Absolut vodka, which they served there, didn't need to be chilled), and decided that the mine was worth its salt, after all.

I was quite taken by the so-called Chamber of the Dwarfs, in which there were eight sculptures (made of salt, of course) of *solilubki* ('salt-lovers') – the dwarfs, who were, allegedly, there to protect the mine and to warn the miners of any impending danger. Their leader, called Bieliczka ('Whitehand'), was a female, also known as the never-ageing Salt Lady. The beard of one of the male dwarfs was missing. Andrzej explained that it had been licked off by generations of visiting women, for according to legend, a woman had to lick the beard if she wanted to get married.

We had been moving around in semi-darkness for about an hour. Having turned the corner into another dark cave, we were suddenly blinded and deafened. Blinded by the flood of lights which came on as we approached. Deafened by the live brass band which burst into a noisy military march the moment the lights went on. The band was hiding in a dark cave above the small underground Lake of Weimar. The musicians all wore red plumes on top of their hats. They had been sitting there – in pitch darkness – for hours waiting for unsuspecting groups of tourists, in order to scare them to death with their noisy trumpets and cymbals (a brass band was not something one would expect to come across in an old salt mine 100 metres below ground).

Having finished playing, the musicians took off their miners' caps and asked to be paid. Relieved by the dead silence which made our teeth ache, we started tossing worthless Polish coins into their caps. Busking inside an old Polish mine was even more ridiculous than getting married in an underground church made of salt.

Eventually, we reached the very last gallery on our route, the Vistula Chamber, which contained a shopping centre, a post office, a basketball field (?) and a cafeteria selling hamburgers and hot dogs! Even deep under the ground, there was no escape from junk food. The staff of the cafeteria looked like vampires. They were all sombre and pale-faced from having to spend too much time in the dark, I presume. When we walked past, the catering creatures of darkness bent forward behind their counters, as if ready to pounce at us.

We had had enough of this salty hell. Besides, I was dying for a cigarette. 'No smoking if you want to survive,' noted Andrzej when he saw me fumbling for a fag. The escorting miner probably didn't care a pneumatic drill about his survival, for he was puffing away for all he was worth.

When we were about to enter the lift which was supposed to take us back into daylight, Andrzej decided to finish us off. 'The last lift left five minutes ago, so we have to climb up, unless you want to wait until tomorrow morning,' he announced through his clenched, nicotine-stained teeth.

'This is unbelievable!' cried the gullible American couple. 'We want to get out of here!'

Of course, this was just another sick joke. Luckily, it was the last one.

The Polish swear word '*psy*' (dogs) was carved on the inside of the lift's wooden door. For once, I didn't mind it.

One thing was clear: the Wieliczka salt mine deserved to be on the list of the world's tackiest museums: the Museum of Worms, not far from Melbourne, where you can take a walk through a worm's intestinal tract enlarged to the size of a school corridor ('Attention, you are now inside the worm!' says the sign at the worm's entrance); the Museum of the History of Toilets in Leicester; the Footwear Museum in Canada, displaying, among other things, a pair of Napoleon's black silk socks, bought at Sotheby's for £2900; and a permanent presentation in Trier, run by the local Committee for the Preservation of Anti-capitalist Artefacts (no kidding) and exhibiting a pair of longjohns once worn by Karl Marx and preserved for posterity (or is it for the posterior?) by Helena Demuth, one-time maid of the Marx household, who was made pregnant by her master – possibly with these very longjohns down his ankles (no wonder they were of great sentimental value to her).

'You know what, I feel like a vodka,' Susy said when we were back in the real world. 'I, too, want to see a deer.'

It was her last evening in Krakow. Next morning she was returning to London, whereas I was in for a long train journey (across the whole of Poland) to Gdansk.

With a bottle of Starka ('old vodka' aged in oak barrels), we were standing on top of the hill next to our

Hotel FM and looking down on the flickering lights of Krakow. Of course, we had glasses and some food. We were drinking vodka in a true East European way.

I was admiring Susy, who did everything precisely as I had taught her: she breathed out before downing her vodka and chased it promptly with a pickle. The drink went down her throat as cheerfully and as naturally as kids go to school (Evgeny Bulavin's metaphor).

'I am converted!' she announced after the third glass. 'You were right: pure vodka is the best. Adding flavours to it is like violating a virgin!'

'Can you see a blue deer?' I asked her, shamefully choking on my Starka.

'Yes, yes! There he is!'

I looked down. There, peeping from behind a bush half-way down the hill, stood the Deer. His blue luminescent underwear glowed in the dark.

'Can you buy a bottle of vodka and deliver it to number sixteen, Krowoderska Street? The client will pay you. Over.'

It was 6 a.m. I was in a taxi on the way to Krakow railway station. Sitting next to the driver, I could hear every word of his radio communications with the dispatcher. And again I thanked God for my knowledge of Russian and Ukrainian, which allowed me to get by in any East European country, apart from Hungary.

'Roger. I am going to drop this passenger at the station and then I shall do the job. Over.'

The driver was not at all surprised by such an unusual morning order. It was probably a routine thing in Poland to ask a taxi driver to bring home a bottle of vodka first thing in the morning.

The empty streets of Krakow were flashing past the cab window. The town was still fast asleep. But someone in one of those sleeping houses was already willing to see a Deer in Blue Underwear.

15 'LIBIDO' HOTEL

My train from Krakow to Gdansk was called the Malopolska Express. The journey across the whole of Poland was to take seven hours, and I was not particularly looking forward to it. My new Krakow friends (Barbara, Yacek, Adam etc.) had inundated me with frightening stories about careless travellers who were either robbed or killed or both (first robbed and then killed, or vice versa) on the sinister Malopolska Express. 'Don't go to sleep, not even for a moment,' they warned me. 'Watch your luggage constantly. And under no circumstances should you agree to drink with fellow-passengers: they add drugs to vodka, you fall asleep, and when you come to – your luggage is gone.'

I got very upset when I saw that my carriage was a *Wagon dla Nepalyacich*, that is, a non-smoking one. Bracing myself for seven hours of extreme nicotine deficiency, I entered the carriage and immediately smelt the beautiful stale stench of burnt tobacco. Half the passengers were smoking. This made me realise again that in Poland things are often poles apart from what you expect them to be. As I could clearly see several hours later, this includes rumours, too: it was the safest journey I had had in Eastern Europe, with not even a hint of devilishly cunning robbers waiting to pump you with poisoned vodka, so as to nick your shoulder-bag containing your most precious possession, the *Lonely Planet Guide to Eastern Europe*.

The most 'dangerous' moment of the journey was when an angry-faced 5-year-old Serbian beggar peeped into my compartment and tugged me by the sleeve, asking for money. He was followed by a moustachioed young Pole with an English sign on his chest: 'Good morning! My name is Yarek. I am hungry.' 'So am I,' I was tempted to say. I wondered whether he carried with him several different chest-signs for different times of the day. At midday he would probably replace the 'Good morning' sign with a 'Good afternoon' one, and so on.

My neighbours were a young Polish couple: an effeminate youngster who spoke in a falsetto voice and was reading the memoirs of Pope John Paul II, and his girlfriend (or sister), immersed in the Polish edition of *Hello!* magazine. In frequent intervals between reading, they ate (in Eastern Europe people like eating on trains). I was salivating, unable to abandon my suitcase to go for lunch at a restaurant car until hunger took the upper hand. Having returned from lunch, I was surprised to discover that my suitcase was still safely in its place on the luggage rack.

In Gdansk I was met by a fussy official of the local branch of the Polish Tourism Promotion Agency. 'We have decided to put you up at one of our new hotels as a sort of . . . er . . . experiment,' he chuckled. I never enjoy being a guinea-pig, but there wasn't much choice.

The hotel was just five minutes' walk from the station. It was an unremarkable freshly painted two-storey building. 'Lido. Restaurant – Night Club' ran a bright pink sign on its roof. Two burly security guards with square shoulders and broken noses blocked my way. I tried to explain that I had a booking, but they kept pushing me away from the door.

A huge gorilla-like man ran out of the building. He threw the guards aside with a brisk wave of his hairy left hand (he was twice as thick and robust as either of them) and – simultaneously – extended his right palm, the size of an excavator's digging bucket. 'Maciek, the hotel owner,' he introduced himself in Russian. 'You are our very first guest. Welcome.'

We climbed a narrow, dark staircase and found ourselves in a small room, lit with a treacherous pink light. An empty bar stand was in the corner. There were no spirits or wines on the shelves above, only bottles with mineral water and . . . an impressive selection of condoms. 'This is our Reception,' said Maciek.

A stunning long-haired blonde, wearing a transparent blouse and such a short mini that one could be forgiven for thinking that she had forgotten her skirt at home, materialised from one of the room's dark corners. 'This is Angela, our receptionist,' explained Maciek.

The sight of my dog-eared Australian passport, which I had dutifully produced for registering, made Angela all gooey-eyed. 'Ah, Australia. It is my dream!' she sang in passable English.

Maciek told me that they had six rooms in the hotel, and as the special first-ever guest of honour I was assigned the best luxury suite, which he (Maciek) normally used himself.

The 'suite' consisted of two rooms, a lounge with an old, squeaky sofa covered with cigarette burns, and a bedroom. The furniture was drab and battered. The TV set was firmly tuned to one channel showing an erotic movie in German. The menu on the coffee table informed me that the nightclub downstairs was open from 1 a.m. to 6 a.m., which didn't bode well for a good night's sleep. It also listed several alcoholic drinks and basic Polish dishes, with blank spaces instead of prices. To make a phone call, I had to give a number to Angela, who would dial it for me from the Reception and then transfer the call to my room. There was no fax.

I have seen many hotels in my life, but I was nevertheless puzzled in the extreme. Pondering the mystery of the Lido, I sat on the bed and— Some unknown force suddenly pushed me on to my back, then threw me up in the air and – after a brief levitation – deposited me on the floor. I felt like a hapless American cowboy trying to harness an obnoxious wild mustang on the prairie.

Rubbing a fresh lump on my head, I crawled to the offensive bed on my knees and cautiously, as if I were testing the temperature of bath water to make sure it was not boiling hot, touched the mattress with my index finger. The mattress recoiled and began rocking up and down, as if it was riding a sea-wave.

'Do you like your water-bed?' Maciek's voice sounded from behind my back. He had entered the room without knocking.

'I think it's fine for anything – except sleeping,' I replied.

'Nonsense! You will sleep like a baby,' he said. 'Our ex-president Lech Walesa has six water-beds in his Gdansk home.'

'That is probably why he lost the last elections,' I muttered.

Maciek then told me to beware of muggers and pickpockets while I was in Gdansk and suggested that I should leave all my valuables at the Lido. I was not sure whether the hotel's wild-looking security guards (to say nothing of the owner himself) were less dangerous than street muggers and mumbled something incoherent in response.

'As you wish,' Maciek said before leaving. He paused near the door and added gravely, 'But remember: Gdansk is not London.'

And it certainly wasn't. The centre of Gdansk was one huge flea market: it was the time of the annual St Dominic's Trade Fair. The innumerable street stalls selling souvenirs made of amber blocked out the sights of this pretty Hanseatic town, which looked more German or Scandinavian than Polish. Indeed, for many years it was known by its German name of Danzig and was prominent in the Hanseatic League, a medieval commercial union of north German and Baltic towns. In the fourteenth and fifteenth centuries it even rivalled Lübeck, the capital of the Hanseatic League, in size and richness.

In more recent times, Gdansk became famous for two momentous beginnings. It was there that the Second World War broke out at 4.45 a.m. on 1 September 1939, when a unit of 210 Polish soldiers was fired on by the German battleship *Schleswig-Holstein* cruising near the Westerplatte peninsula. Thirty-one years later, in December 1970, the Solidarity movement, which triggered the destruction of the communist system all over Eastern Europe nineteen years later still, was born at the Gdansk Shipyard. One of its leaders, a modest shipyard electrician called Lech Walesa, was eventually catapulted to international stardom and became the first democratically elected president of Poland and one of the world's most charismatic politicians, who forged unlikely friendships with the Queen and with the Pope.

In an ironic twist of fate and fortune, by the mid-1990s Walesa had fallen into political disfavour. Having been voted out of office, he was replaced by the reformed communist Alexander Kwasniewski in December 1995. Walesa then returned to Gdansk, where he reportedly resumed his employment as an electrician at the money-starved shipyard. His life had turned full circle, although certain things were never going to be the same. First, his work at the shipyard was a media hoax, for he spent all his time running the so-called Walesa Foundation, whose headquarters were just a stone's throw from my Lido Hotel, and fighting with the authorities over the tax from the $1,000,000 dollars he had received from Hollywood (for a film about his life) which he refused to pay, claiming that 'it was a gift'. Second, the house where he lived was a far cry from his former electrician's abode, and not just because of its (allegedly) plush six-water-bed interior. Situated in Oliva, one of Gdansk's most prestigious areas, it was a well-maintained cottage which stood in a spacious garden surrounded by a security fence with video cameras and barbed wire on top. The low-built, stocky cottage looked very much like its podgy, broad-shouldered post-presidential owner. To complete the simile, the thick rows of barbed wire along the perimeter of the fence could easily pass for Walesa's famous long and droopy moustache.

There was nothing much left in Gdansk to remind the visitor of the heroic times of Solidarity, except for a tacky avant-garde monument on the shipyard's territory and Solidarna vodka on shop shelves. The latter reminded me of the main purpose of my trip to Gdansk, which, like Krakow, is one of Poland's oldest centres of vodka-making. The famous Zlota Woda (Golden Water) and Srebrenik Gdanski (Gdansk Silver Vodka, with flakes of real silver) are produced by the Polmos distillery in the town of Starogard, about 80 kilometres from Gdansk. It was getting late, and I decided to go to Starogard first thing the following morning.

Before retiring for the night, I went to the nearby seaside town of Sopot, which together with Gdansk and Gdynia constitutes a three-city agglomeration called Trojmiasto. There I had a quiet dinner in a totally empty (it was too expensive for the locals) John Bull, The Real English Pub, which looked the spitting image of a pub almost anywhere in England. The only difference was that one could get Polish borscht (beetroot soup with soured cream) there (which I did). It is probably the world's only English pub where they serve this peculiar East European delicacy.

Shortly before midnight I got out of a taxi near the Lido Hotel. And again my way was blocked by the security guards, who let me inside only after I showed them the key to my 'luxury suite'. A different, yet equally skirtless, receptionist stood behind the bar. I asked her whether it was possible to make a phone call to London. She said that it wasn't, but for me she would try.

The prospect of spending the night on the undulating water-mattress was not particularly enticing. Having taken a sleeping pill, I carefully approached my bed and lowered myself on to it gently. I tried my best not to stir or make any sharp movements, but whenever I turned over, the obnoxious bed would give me a kick in the ribs before tossing me up in the air, and it would take several minutes for the rolling and pitching to subside. Finally, having found a more or less quiet corner (or should I say haven?), I dozed off.

I was awoken by deafening music, played somewhere underneath. The sound was so loud that it filled my 'luxury suite' to the brim and rocked my water-bed. I looked at my watch. It was past 1 a.m., the time when the basement nightclub was due to open. In the short intervals between the blasts of music, other noises reached me from the hotel's corridor: doors slamming, women screaming playfully. I thought I could even hear a dog barking. From the street there was the distinctive clap-clap of multiple gunshots: the vigilant security guards were probably reasoning with some pushy late-comers.

At the bottom of my bag, I found several cotton-wool balls which I stuck into my ears. The moment I lay down there came a phone call: the skirtless girl had managed to put me through to London.

Soon I had to give up all hope of falling asleep and I started leafing through the hotel's glossy brochure, which had probably been brought to my room in my absence by the hospitable Maciek. I learnt that the hotel's nightclub offered 'erotic show, striptease, women mud and oil wrestling, sexy excitement, charming company of beautiful hostesses, pig's feet with beer, and pig's feet with shaved [*sic*] horseradish'.

My last doubts as to the nature of the Lido evaporated: it was a brothel, thinly camouflaged as a hotel. I thought that it would have been more appropriate to rename it the Libido.

At 6 a.m. the music at the nightclub suddenly stopped and I was able to steal a short nap on the floor, next to the water-bed.

Angela – as skirtless as the day before – was back at her post behind the bar. 'Did you have a good sleep?' she asked me with a sadistic smile before presenting me with a bill for my three-minute phone call to London. A Polish friend told me later that the sum amounted to her total phone bill for six months. I paid it, consoling myself with the thought that by doing so I was contributing a further boost to the growing Polish economy, although in this case it was most likely the black economy which would benefit from it (brothels are illegal in Poland, hence the desire to disguise the Libido as a hotel).

Angela was very surprised when I asked whether I could have breakfast. 'It is too early for breakfast,' she muttered. It was almost 10 a.m.

'And what's on your breakfast menu? Shaved radishes? Oily hostesses? Condoms with eggs? And what's your tart of the day?' I asked. Without waiting for her reply, I ran down the stairs and out into the street.

I thought that the experiment of my Gdansk hosts, who had put me up at a brothel, was probably a success. From their point of view, that is.

PS: You won't believe it, but when I first tried to print this chapter out, it came out in pink letters. It so happened that my printer had run out of black ink. The only ink that remained was red, but, because there wasn't a lot of that either, the text became all pink!

16 HOW ANGELS PUKE

The main store-house of the Starogard distillery resembled the engine room of a huge merchant ship. It contained several dozen stainless-steel storage vats, with 1,246,700 litres of pure alcohol (in potato and grain spirits) in each. Evgeny Bulavin would have loved the sight and been keen to spend the rest of his life there. It was mind-boggling to think that all that limitless ocean of spirit was destined to end up inside submissive human stomachs and was bound to cause millions of heated conversations, silly arguments, hysterical laughs, tears, hangovers, family scandals, split-ups, date rapes and liver cirrhoses. How many momentary escapes it was going to provide. How many life-long traps it was going to set up.

Next to the vats stood several smaller tanks – the so-called rectification columns, in which spirits were purified from fusel oil, the very stuff that gives you morning-after headaches. Several distillery workers were walking sleepily among them. From the look of the workers it was clear that they did not stick to tea during their twice-daily tea-breaks, the schedule of which was pinned up to a notice-board. Their puffy faces and fiery eyes gave meaning to a somewhat mysterious placard on one of the walls: 'Workers do not have friends but Vodka does!'. They certainly didn't look like people one would want to make friends with.

In the control room next door, several technicians in white gowns were staring at devices resembling electric cardiographs, which, in this case, helped to monitor volume, pressure and other parameters in each storage vat. Judging from the 'cardiograms' the devices were drawing, everything was fine with the vats, and their liquid hearts were beating with a steady rhythm, like those of trained marathon runners during the first mile of a race.

The distillery's tasting room consisted of several cubicles, separated by plywood partitions. 'We have to isolate the tasters from each other,' Jerzy Jakubus, the managing director, told me. Was it because vodka might make them aggressive? I wondered.

'In the '70s vodka was rationed in Poland,' Mr Jakubus told me in his office. He showed me an old vodka ration card made of several square coupons, each entitling the holder to buy one bottle. After the purchase, a saleswoman would cut the relevant square out with scissors. I saw similar ration cards for butter, sugar and meat in the Soviet Union. But vodka-rationing was new to me.

'Under communism, shops were bare. Only vinegar and vodka were on the shelves. You could buy as much vinegar as you wanted, but vodka sales were limited,' the manager continued. 'Now we have abundance, but less money. The unemployed can only afford cheap Russian brands. As for the new rich, they prefer Smirnoff and other Western varieties as status symbols. On top of this, we have to compete with bootleggers and with other Polmos factories – this is why we were forced to cut our staff by twenty-five per cent and to keep inventing new brands.'

I asked him about Zlota Voda.

'Vodka with gold flakes is an original Gdansk recipe, although now we have to import gold from Switzerland. It is a good catalyst for digestion.'

'How about Zmiyovska, the snake vodka?' I enquired with hope. 'Some people say that they saw it but never tried it, others that they have tried it but never saw it, and so on. Does it exist?'

'We first thought of making Zmiyovska after a visit of Korean vodka-makers, who brought us a similar drink as a gift. We analysed it and replaced the Korean snake with our Polish black adder. The brand became so popular that soon we ran out of snakes and had to wrap up its production.'

My hopes of ever trying the evasive Black Adder vodka evaporated like pure alcohol left overnight in an uncovered glass.

Mr Jakubus told me lots of interesting things. He complained that vodka advertising was banned in Poland as a result of the pressure from the government and the Catholic Church. Only cryptic advertising was possible, which was not sufficient in the highly competitive Polish vodka environment, with thirty-odd factories and a thousand different brands vying for the fleeting attention of the confused post-communist consumer.

He also told me that August had recently been proclaimed National Abstinence Month by the Polish government. For me, this triggered memories of the ill-fated Gorbachev's near-prohibition in the Soviet Union in 1986–9, when buying any alcoholic drink was not much easier than getting a drinking audience with Gorby himself. Countless Sobriety societies, which every working person was forced to join (fees were simply deducted from salaries), sprang up like mushrooms after a good July rain. The Sobriety societies were staffed for the most part by carefully vetted bureaucrats from the uneven ranks of heavy drinkers and chronic alcoholics.

They did nothing, apart from getting their salaries and organising politically correct 'sober' birthday parties and wedding ceremonies, during which vodka was covertly poured from samovars and tea-kettles. Anything with an alcohol content (no matter how mild) was swept out of shops and pharmacies in no time. Vodka-deprived blotters happily gulped shampoos, glues, perfumes, insect repellents and glass-cleaning fluids.

In a Moscow park, I once witnessed three drunks boiling tooth-powder in a tin can on top of a bonfire. They boiled it for five hours (so they claimed), then carefully removed the accumulated alcohol from the top with tablespoons, drank it – and immediately started vomiting. Looking at the white foamy liquid spurting out of their mouths, a passer-by noted, 'This is probably how angels puke.'

I told the managing director the story of puking angels, and we both had a good laugh. 'That's what our hypocritical sobriety enthusiasts are like – puking angels,' he concluded.

Before I left the Starogard distillery, Mr Jakubus invited me to attend the official opening of a new factory-owned vodka shop in the town of Elblag the following morning.

That evening my Gdansk contacts took me to a countryside party to celebrate the purchase of a *dworek*. What is a *dworek*? The best explanation I could find is in the book *The Polish House* by a young Polish journalist and politician, Radek Sikorski.

I had always wanted to live in a 'dworek'. Every Pole does. An expatriate Englishman may dream of returning to a Georgian Old Rectory in the home counties. An Irish-American may long to go back to a mythical little white cottage. A German or a Frenchman may dream of retiring to a stone farmhouse in Bavaria or Provence. A Pole sees himself as the proud resident of a 'dwor', a manor house, or 'dworek', a little manor house. A classic 'dworek' is eighteenth- or early nineteenth-century, neo-classical, and falls halfway between an aristocratic palace and a prosperous peasant house, with an obligatory white porch, pillars, and at least a hint of park. It need not be grand – most used to be wooden – and in England an average 'dworek' would qualify as little more than a spacious cottage. Thousands used to dot the length and breadth of Poland . . .

The happy new owners of that particular *dworek* outside Gdansk were the family of a doctor called Marek. They were very proud of their acquisition. Marek showed me around the property, explaining what he was planning to build and where.

The house was overgrown with acacias. It stood near the fields, with limitless blue sky above it. Invisible cicadas were chirping in the grass as we sat outside, around a crude wooden table, and drank vodka.

'Piemo? [Shall we drink?]' Marek asked rhetorically from time to time after raising his glass. 'Piemo! [Yes, we shall!]' we all echoed in chorus before downing ours. This reminded me of a peculiar pre-drinking ritual invented by Evgeny Bulavin. When a vodka bottle was put on the table, one of the party was supposed to read its label aloud, from the first word to the last, while the rest sat quietly and listened. Then the reader was supposed to ask, 'So, maybe we shouldn't drink it but just pour it out?' to which, after an awesomely titillating pause, we would all scream in chorus, 'Hey, let's do it just for once!' and the top would fly off.

I was sitting next to a slim and youthful granny, who kept telling me how Russians had destroyed everything in Gdansk during the war. She spoke with bitterness, but with no spite.

We talked about Russia and about Poland, about literature and the arts – a normal East European conversation. I felt very much at home with these proud and heavy-drinking, yet very intelligent and gentle,

Europeans, and I could feel that they were enjoying our conversation as much as I was.

The illusion of having gone back in time persisted until Marek's son Yacek, a bright 12-year-old anglophile, asked me (in English, which he studied at school) whether it was OK to 'kill a bobby in London'. I suddenly realised that for him, curiously enough, I was a representative of Britain, whereas in Britain I was for ever pigeonholed as a 'Russian'. This made me wonder what, if anything, I did represent in my trans-continental peripatetic life – Russia, Ukraine, Britain, Australia, or Europe as a whole? I could not find an answer and, out of frustration ('You can't sort it out without a bottle of vodka,' as we used to say in Russia when faced with a dilemma), I poured myself another glass of Zubrovka, a Polish vodka made of bison grass.

A couple of merrily puking angels were hovering above my head.

The stars appeared like pimples on the dark skin of the night sky. Cicadas kept screaming deafeningly. For a fleeting moment, it felt as if I was back in Ukraine, the country of my childhood, whose nature was so similar to that of Poland . . . I realised that I was getting drunk and – reluctantly – asked my hosts to take me back to the Lido Hotel.

'Is that the Mafia-frequented brothel near the station which was recently raided by the police?' asked Marek. 'What a bizarre place to stay at.' It was obvious that his respect for me had dwindled considerably.

Before the knowledge-hungry Yacek could ask me what exactly 'a brothel' meant, I jumped into a car, and was driven away.

That night I slept well on my unsleepable water-bed. Undisturbed by the loud music from downstairs, I dreamt of floods, earthquakes and puking angels. I finally discovered that being drunk was the only way to cope with the night-time noise of the Libido and with my precarious liquid mattress. It was a rather belated awareness, for I was to leave Gdansk the following afternoon.

Next morning I made my way to Elblag under torrential rain. On the way, I passed through a village called Stare Babki (Old Hags) and through another village called Zle Mieso (Bad Meat). I nearly threw up (angel-like?) at the sight of the latter's name on a road-sign: my hangover, which resulted from mixing vodka with *samogon* (moonshine) the night before, was taking its toll.

The brand-new vodka shop was ready for the opening. Hundreds of vodka bottles winked temptingly at me from the shelves. They looked like soldiers lined up for a military parade in their dress uniforms. Among them were the politically correct Solidarna; the controversial Chopin Vodka, which the protectors of the Polish cultural heritage had been trying to ban, regarding it as an insult to the memory of Poland's great composer; Piolunovka – the pride of the Starogard distillery – made to a 300-year-old recipe from the town of Lviv; and many, many others.

Mr Jakubus arrived in almost presidential fashion, under a huge umbrella, which was held above him by a seemingly waterproof factotum. He cut the ribbon with a pair of scissors from a tray held by another rain-resistant factotum, and made a brief speech. 'Vodka is a wonderful drink,' he said. 'It is good with food, before food and after food.'

'How about instead of food?' I wanted to ask, but restrained myself.

The director also spoke about the dangers of kitsch in vodka-making (did he mean Chopin Vodka?) and the importance of choice. In the end, he offered a toast to the success of the new shop, downed his glass of vodka and staunchly refused an orange-juice chaser, obsequiously offered to him by the umbrella-holding serf. 'I never wash down a good vodka with anything!' he said.

He was a brilliant PR man, Mr Jakubus.

The opening ceremony was followed by a lunchtime banquet in a side-room of a local restaurant – a leftover from communist times. In the Soviet Union, every restaurant and every canteen had a side-room, which was firmly reserved for important visiting bureaucrats and local party apparatchiks. No matter how inedible the food in the filthy canteen itself might be, the side-room tables were covered with starched tablecloths, the food was always plentiful, and vodka was constantly on offer, even in the most rigidly anti-drinking times, when alcohol was officially banned from all places of 'public eating'.

In Elblag, I felt fine sitting in the restaurant side-room and eating Polish borscht with *kolduni* (dumplings). The atmosphere was relaxed, although I noticed that everyone at the table (apart from me) was waiting for Mr Jakubus to start each course first, and only then dug hungrily into it – another old communist custom.

I was sitting next to a chemical engineer from Starogard distillery called Agnieszka, a long-legged young woman, who confided in me that she adored *Monty Python*. When I shared with her my casual observations on the deathless communist mannerisms, she put down her fork and said angrily, 'I hate communists!' She told me that her father had been in a labour camp under Stalin and again in 1980, when pro-democracy demonstrations rocked the core of the 'People's Republic of Poland', as the country used to be known under the communists. During his second prison term, he suffered brain damage and lost his power of speech.

There was a lot of vodka talk at the banquet. Someone was complaining of the American Food and Drugs Administration which demanded that one of the herbal components be removed from Zubrovka as a pre-condition of exporting it to the US; someone else spoke about the necessity to change the distillery's name from Polmos to Gdansk Vodkas, which would cost the factory a real fortune.

'Churchill cigars' were offered for dessert, but I had no time to smoke them: I had to return to Gdansk to catch the train to Warsaw.

Two security guards were smoking sullenly near the bar at the Libido when I popped in to fetch my suitcase on the way to the station. A brand-new fax machine was sitting on top of the bar. 'We have bought it for you,' Angela, the skirtless receptionist, announced with a grin. 'Would you like to send a fax to London?'

The memories of the phone-bill robbery to which I had been subjected a couple of days earlier were still too fresh.

'Look,' I said. 'I know that Poland has a huge foreign debt and is desperately looking for someone to pay it off. I also know that you have chosen me to help your country out. Had I been Bill Gates or George Soros, I would have been happy to oblige. But I am not. That is why I am going to say a firm "no" to your kind offer to send a fax to London. I would rather go and buy myself a nice *dworek* on the outskirts of Gdansk, which would probably cost me much less.'

Having finished my tirade, I picked up my suitcase and left the Libido, never to return.

17 POLISH SCRABBLE

In Poland, the men shave their heads . . .
Near Home or Europe Described,
Longmans, Green, & Co., London, 1910

At Gdansk station, which was swarming with drunks, tramps and crippled beggars demonstrating their stumps, I bought a dozen Polish newspapers and magazines to while away my travel time to Warsaw.

I had no problem understanding the bulk of spoken Polish, which sounded similar to Russian and Ukrainian. But reading was much harder. To help you comprehend what the difficulty was, here's a popular Polish tongue-twister: '*W Szczebrzeszynie chrzaszcz brzmi w trzcinie*', which, in our melodious and beautifully simple English language, means 'In Szczebrzezyn [a small Polish town], a beetle is heard in the reeds.'*

Thank God, I didn't have to live in Szczebrzezyn (it took me half an hour to type this word on my computer) or, say, in Krakow in 1312, when the Polish Duke

---

* To facilitate the printers' – and my own – task, while reproducing Polish and other East European words in this book, I decided to stick to the 26 letters of the English alphabet, ignoring innumerable dots, apostrophes, crosses and hooks, with which local orthographies are resplendent.

Lokietek retook the city in his campaign to reunite the country after the Tatar invasions. In a sure (if somewhat cruel) test of patriotism, Krakow residents were rounded up and asked to repeat Polish tongue-twisters. Those who failed to do so were promptly beheaded. I don't know about you, but I would have been headless several times over.

Reading Polish newspapers, a foreigner can be forgiven for thinking that Polish spelling was invented by someone who was either dead drunk or else severely dyslexic (or both). At times, it feels as if half a litre of vodka would be an essential prop for deciphering these unpronounceable combinations of hissing and spitting consonants: cz, dz, rz, sz, and the most awful-looking szcz, pronounced like 'shch' in 'fresh cheese'. In the Polish version of Scrabble (if any), the letter 'z' should not be worth very much, for they seem to stick it into words in an obsessive and illogical fashion – like sultanas into a rich English fruit pudding. In a Gdansk restaurant, I once dined on *barszcz and kaczka with kasza* which turned out to be simply beetroot soup and roast duck with a sort of porridge.

I was musing over the mysteries of Polish spelling and pronunciation, when the train came to a stop at a station whose name was a living illustration of the baffling topic: 'Tczew' (pronounced 'Chev').

After a couple of hours of painstaking perusal of the Polish press, I had a feeling that all the curious ups and downs of the country's political and social life were similar to a giant game of Polish Scrabble, in which invisible players went out of their way to construct words out of a handful of seemingly meaningless (and often superfluous) letters, or, in plain language, to make some sense out of chaos.

Apart from the ongoing floods, the lead story in almost all newspapers was a double controversy in the fairly unremarkable Polish town of Torun, known mostly as the birthplace of Copernicus and the country's

biggest manufacturer of gingerbread. The first controversy had flared up when the local authorities decided
to get rid of a memorial to the Soviet Army soldiers who
liberated the city in 1945. This decision sparked
powerful protests from Russian authorities and from
some Torun residents, whose argument was that 'this
concrete monstrosity was becoming a local attraction'.
To aggravate the situation, the removal of the monument proved impossible, for it staunchly resisted all
attempts to pull it down or blow it up. The authorities
tried to knock it over with a ram, but the memorial,
conscientiously built by German prisoners of war,
refused to budge. Since toppling the obnoxious 150-ton
obelisk was impossible, it was decided to cut it into slices
with a diamond-tipped saw. The cutting was interrupted
by a thunderstorm passing over Torun, which prompted
some senior town residents to comment that it was an
'evil omen from heaven', while others sarcastically
called the rain 'Lenin's tears'. Getting rid of the past
proved a difficult task.

During my travels around Poland, I often encountered
a certain ambivalence towards the innumerable monuments to Soviet soldiers which adorned the streets of
Polish towns and villages. A taxi driver in Krakow was
displeased with the demolition of the monument to
Soviet Marshel Konev, whose army drove out the Nazis
early in 1945 – mere hours before the planned
demolition of the city's historic centre was due to go
ahead. On the other hand, many Poles justifiably felt
humiliated by the profusion of memorials to those
whom they regarded as invaders and aggressors. In
actual fact, the so-called liberation of Poland quickly
turned into a killing, looting and raping spree, evidence
of which was carefully suppressed by the Allies,
unwilling to irritate Big Stalinist Brother.

In a small second-hand bookshop in Warsaw, I dug
out a faded little booklet entitled *The Situation in
Poland*. Published in Glasgow in September 1945, it was

marked 'For Private Circulation Only'. It cited thousands of cases of atrocities towards the civil population of Poland committed by the 'liberating' Soviet soldiers. Here is a quote from just one page (45) of this blood-chilling ninety-page chronicle of Soviet brutalities.

On July 9th 1945, a group of Cossacks visited the local vodka distillery at Wierzchoviny, to obtain some alcohol. After getting what they wanted, on their way to Chelm, the Cossacks encountered a lonely woman and decided to hold a shooting contest. As a result – the woman was killed and the same fate met two small boys returning to their village from Chelm at the time.

A public meeting was organised at Jasnow Lubelski, in the course of which three people were shot (two men and a woman). The victims were brought in with their mouths gagged and the execution was held in public in the town square. It was supervised by General Zajkovski and a number of Soviet officers.

Soviet soldiers behave like savages as regards sexual matters and are continually committing outrages against women. In some of the Polish villages and small towns women dress and make themselves up to look much older than their actual age, so as not to attract the attention of the utterly demoralised Soviet soldiers.

A band of Cossacks arrived at the village of Horodyszcze on July 14th, 1945, in search of girls and young women. The girls and women, having been warned beforehand, succeeded in escaping in time, but out of vengeance the Cossacks dragged out an old woman of 70 and raped her . . . A large proportion of the Soviet soldiers suffer from venereal disease which they are spreading over the country.

Even from this brief account it is clear why there has never been much love lost between the Red Army and ordinary Poles.

The second Torun controversy was triggered by a

billboard advertisement promoting the use of condoms. This fairly innocent poster, which appeared in many Polish cities, including Torun, featured a pink condom on a huge raised thumb. 'It's OK. Don't blow it. Condoms protect you from AIDS,' it read.

Members of the Torun clergy came out against the ad and demanded its total ban from the town. 'The ad is too modern – it encourages infidelity,' one of the activists of the Guardians of Morality civil group said in a newspaper interview. At the same time, anti-AIDS campaigners were in favour of the ad and insisted on keeping it. The town's authorities found themselves between a rock and a hard place. After several weeks of shilly-shallying, they came up with the following judgement of Solomon: wherever the billboard was placed on communal buildings, it was to be torn down, whereas in other places it was allowed to stay. Some of the country's newspapers called this decision 'the first attempt to return to censorship in Poland', while one unidentified Polish film director went even further, claiming that 'having lost the communist enemy, the church is now looking for a new one – in people's pants and under their skirts'. To counterbalance the Torun authorities' restrictive decision, a factory in Czarnovo announced the start of an intensive nationwide marketing campaign of its new product: an emergency kit for travellers containing four tins of meat and a condom!

To my mind, the best definition of all sorts of small-town upheavals, into which category both the condoms billboard scandal and the Soviet memorial saga fell, was coined by the nineteenth-century Russian satirist Nikolai Gogol: 'the idiocy of provincial life'.

After my narrow escape from the fans of the king of pop, Michael Jackson, in Prague, I was hoping that Poland, with her conservatism and strong Roman Catholic tradition, would be a Wacko-free zone. Tough luck!

Several newspapers ran stories about the pop star's visit to Warsaw; he had announced his decision to buy a castle in Poland and open an amusement park there. After a helicopter tour of the Polish capital and a whirlwind visit to three historic castles and palaces to survey possible sites, the Great Friend of Children (especially boys) made the following statement: 'My dream of returning to the world of childhood has become real in Poland.' I wondered whether he had ever left that world in the first place.*

To give credit to the Poles, not all of them were prepared to embrace Michael Jackson, who, to my mind, is one of the main banes of Western civilisation, together with Coca-Cola and McDonald's restaurants. When Professor Marek Kwiatkowski, director of Warsaw's Lazienki Royal Park (which was on Jacko's shopping list, too) was asked to pose for photos in the jacket given to him by the king of pop, he refused point-blank and said, 'I won't make a buffoon of myself!' Good on yer, Professor, as they say in Australia.

Reading the papers, I was surprised that road rage, one of the newest and ugliest creations of consumerist Western society, had come to Poland too, albeit in a rather primitive public-transport form. A reader's letter to one newspaper, written by a visitor from America, complained that in Poland motorists 'violated every civilised rule of driving' and had a penchant for 'driving on the sidewalk'. This was in line with an accident in Gdansk, when the newly appointed head of the province administration, who had run over a boy and didn't bother to stop and help the victim, gave the following explanation of his behaviour: 'The boy's lively movements assured me that everything was all right.'

---

* In the end, the king of pop bought a former Soviet military airport in the Warsaw suburb of Bemovo with the aim of creating a $500-million 'World of Childhood' amusement park on its site.

There was also a story about a Krakow cyclist who got angered by an overtaking city bus, climbed aboard at the next stop and began a row with the driver, during which he beat the driver up, broke his nose and, as if that were not enough, bit him in the genitals. In Warsaw, a female stowaway, detained by the conductor and frog-marched out of tram number 25, picked up a rock from the ground and hit the conductor on the head. She was obviously a kind woman, for she didn't try to throw him under the wheels of the moving tram.

Naturally, I took particular interest in stories about drinks and drinking, of which there was no shortage in the Polish press. I had mixed feelings about the news that a former Soviet military base outside Warsaw had been turned into another vodka distillery.

Many papers reported the success of the new chain of road-side Non-Stop Drinking Bars for motorists, where a passenger (or a driver) could have a drink at any time of day or night – just the thing to improve the chaotic nature of Polish driving.

The dispute on whether to ban or not to ban Chopin Vodka was running rampant. Zdislaw Podkanski, Poland's minister of culture, spoke in favour of outlawing the offending drink. Such a move would, in his words, 'help to protect the memory of our great compatriot'. From the opposite side of the fence, Andrzej Sawczuk, the sales and marketing director of Polmos, Chopin's beleaguered manufacturer, tried to protect the trade name: 'Take Austria. There, everything is called Mozart, and no one makes a fuss about it.' Drawing examples from the West in an attempt to justify one's point of view had always been popular in Eastern Europe. To be fair, however, I have never heard of an Austrian-made schnapps called Mozart or Strauss.

In yet another drinking development, a tipsy Polish woman, identified only as Iolanta G., was arrested in Ostrow Wielkopolski after eating a church's supply of

communion wafers and washing them down with
sacramental wine – another proof of the well-known
fact that most Poles always remain devout Roman
Catholics. Even when drunk.

Most, but not all, as was shown by the story of a 32-
year-old Krakow resident who came close to sharing
John Wayne Bobbit's fate. One evening, the man, whom
the papers discreetly named as Robert B., had a drinking
party in his apartment to which, among others, two of
his live-in partner's female friends were invited. Around
11 p.m., B. decided to call it a night because drunken
guests prevented his three young children from sleeping.
He kept asking his guests to leave, but they were having
such a ball they didn't feel like going home. B. had to
raise his voice, which provoked his female guests. The
three women (his girlfriend included) pounced on him,
threw him on the floor and pinned him beneath their
bodies, after which his drunken girlfriend ripped off his
pants and sank her teeth into his penis, nearly biting it
off. After a short struggle, B. managed to get the women
off him and hid in the bathroom. When the women
finally left, he called the police.

'Robert B. can't qualify as a Polish Bobbit because his
lover only bit into his penis,' said a female CID inspector
assigned to the case. 'He was taken to a hospital, where
doctors dressed his wound and sent him home.'

The following day, B. dumped his biting girlfriend
and moved out of his apartment, even though it
belonged to him. His disappointment was understand-
able: had his girlfriend bitten a bit harder, he could have
become world-famous and possibly, like Bobbit, even a
millionaire movie star. As it was, her bark proved to be
much worse than her bite.

Crime was another popular subject in the Polish press.
The papers reported the sadistic murder of 24-year-old
Agnieszka Kotlarska, a former Miss Poland (who had
narrowly missed death once before, when she cancelled
her booking for the ill-fated TWA flight 800, which

exploded in mid-air off Long Island, New York); the arrest of a gang of Ukrainian bandits, who had attacked cars with Western numberplates, robbed the passengers and tied them to trees; the discovery of the severed hand of a mobster killed by a bomb blast which was identified by an expensive watch on the wrist; and so on.

Burglaries were also on the rise, although some of them ended badly for the perpetrators. When two burglars blew open a safe in Warsaw, the whole building collapsed: the safe contained dynamite, instead of money. Police found the robbers still dazed in the rubble. One of the 'stars' of the Polish underworld, the experienced robber Torge Czar, was less lucky. His wily plan to burgle Warsaw jewellers involved tunnelling through a wall and into a safe on the other side. A minute miscalculation took him into a next-door food factory, where he fell out into a vat of spinach and drowned. Serves him right! Next time he will think twice before drilling through someone else's walls.

There was no end to the tragicomic idiosyncrasies of post-communist Poland.

One paper carried a report about an unemployed man, who got so fed up with his wife's nagging about his alleged 'parasitism' that he tried to get himself registered as a prostitute. He expressed readiness to pay taxes and estimated his would-be earnings at around 300 zlotys (£60) a day, 100 zlotys from each of the three clients he was prepared to serve daily. After he was denied registration, the aspiring 'gentleman of the night' appealed to Poland's Supreme Court.

A farmer from the town of Pisz tried to remove an ugly stump in his garden with a spade. When he failed, he put a small stick of dynamite along its roots. But directly beneath the stump was an unexploded Second World War bomb which blew up, destroying not just the stump but the farmer's garden and house.

Police in the central Poland town of Nowy Dwor told people to avoid contact with two kangaroos missing from a circus, saying that both were skilled boxers and could turn violent. 'The animals can be dangerous because they are not friendly to people and have been taught to box,' a Polish news agency quoted a police duty officer as saying. 'Anyone meeting them should not try to come close.' The Russian-trained kangaroos, named Gin and Tonic (!), were stolen from a travelling circus when it stopped in Nowy Dwor.

Panic broke out on a Warsaw-bound BA flight when a python slithered over the seats of an American couple. It had escaped from the duffel bag of a fellow-passenger, who was taking it back to Poland as a pet.

This last story reminded me of the travelling exhibitions of snakes, scorpions and tarantula, which I had seen advertised everywhere in Poland. Why this sudden nationwide obsession with creepy-crawlies? There must have been a solid sociological reason for it. But since I was no sociologist, it remained one of the unsolved mysteries of the tongue-breaking and mind-boggling Scrabble of Polish life.

From the Warsaw-based *Zycie* ('Life') newspaper I learnt that, after fifty-odd years of broadcasting, the Polish service of the formerly Munich- and now Prague-based Radio Free Europe had been closed down. After a couple of hours in the company of the Polish press, the closure made perfect sense to me: there was no more need for anti-communist propaganda in the country, where on the same day several national newspapers could run the following ad: 'Married couple, teachers, seeking work plus apartment in non-communist environment.'

I'd like to end this scrabbled chapter with my favourite Polish newspaper story of all time. Although I could have easily pretended that I had read it on the train from Gdansk to Warsaw (as was the case with all the above ones), I have to confess that I came across it several years before.

One day, a group of entrepreneurial Poles decided to make a quick buck by organising bear-hunting for adrenalin-hungry Western money-bags. They advertised their venture in a couple of Western newspapers, and one gullible merchant banker swallowed the bait. The immediate problem for the Poles was where to get the bears, which (along with black adders, I presume) had become extremely scarce in the country's polluted forests. The only possible solution was to borrow one from a circus, which they did. The adventurous banker was given a rifle and was instructed to climb a roadside tree and wait. Meanwhile, the tame bear was pushed out of a circus van (which was not easy, since the poor animal didn't feel like leaving it) on to the road. At this particular moment, a local village boy was riding past on his bike. The bear, which was nearing retirement age after a long circus career during which he had been trained – among other tricks – to ride a bicycle, leapt on top of the unsuspecting cyclist, pushed him aside, and, having mounted on to the saddle, paddled away purposefully. When the banker spotted the happily cycling bear from the top of the tree, he fell down and broke his leg.

As an old Russian proverb goes, do not share the skin of a bear while he is still at large in the forest. Especially if the bear is a cyclist, I'd like to add.

18 MY GRANDAD'S TRAVELLING-BAG

This is the capital of Poland. It is full of soldiers. They are Russians, sent by the Emperor to keep the poor Poles in order. The palace is still there, but there is no longer any king to live in it. Houses, where lords once lived, stand empty . . .'

Near Home or Europe Described,
Longmans, Green, & Co., London, 1910

The former House of Soviet Culture in Warsaw's Foksal Street was a weird place. Built in the fifties in the inimitable architectural style of the Soviet Empire, also known as Stalin Gothic, with turrets on the roof and massive columns at the front entrance, it was grim, empty and echoing inside. The Soviet Empire was no more, and there was nothing left in the House of Soviet Culture except a couple of second-hand bookshops with the most unlikely selection of old Russian books – from a turn-of-the-century description of Turkestan railways (with the portrait of the ill-fated last Russian tsar on the title page) to a collection of political jokes from post-communist Russia compiled by the famous circus clown Yuri Nikulin.

I spent hours in these bookshops, in which – as in the Welsh book village of Hay-on-Wye – you never knew what literary treasure (or literary trash) you were going to find. I remember coming across a stack of dust-covered tourist maps of the Kharkov region of Ukraine, where I was born.

On another shelf, I saw the familiar brown cover of an *Atlas of the World*, published in Moscow in 1964. As a junior schoolboy in Kharkov I had exactly the same atlas, given to me as a gift by my grandad Misha, who died in 1968.

The atlas reminded me of some indeterminate connection that existed between my grandfather and Warsaw. Then it came to me. My grandad had never mentioned the subject himself, but his Warsaw adventures in the early 1920s were recounted to me by my granny and, later, by my mother.

Like many of his young contemporaries, duped by the nice-sounding Leninist slogans of equality and fraternity, Grandfather Misha took an active part in the Bolshevik Revolution of 1917. During the civil war of 1918–21, he was a soldier with the Red Army. In 1919 he was captured by the 'White' Poles, and spent several months in a Polish prison camp, where he contracted typhoid and nearly died. He was saved by a young Polish nurse who took a liking to him. After his release, he returned to his Ukrainian home town of Khorol – much to his family's consternation: they were sure that he had been killed.

Soon my grandad was contacted by some big shots from the Communist Party Central Committee. They decided to send him on a secret mission to Poland. After a crash training course, he was supplied with a (false) passport, a lump sum of (real) Polish money, and the (real) outfit of a Western gentleman in the early 1920s: flannels, bowler hat, cane and a leather travelling-bag with a false bottom. Disguised as a first-guild merchant, he was supposed to spread Bolshevik propaganda among Warsaw workers.

He was nearly captured by Polish border-guards, as he tried to cross illegally into Poland, and had to hide in a haystack. While in Warsaw, he was expected to lead a posh and seemingly care-free existence, to frequent restaurants and theatres, and also to visit his contacts from Poland's communist underground and to leave the subversive pamphlets at secret drops and in dead-letter boxes.

It was not long before the Polish secret police tailed him wherever he went. His businessman's cover was blown, and he had to return to the Soviet Union.

Right up to his death, my grandad's secret mission to Poland was supposed to be hushed up so as 'not to spoil the friendly relations between the two countries'. By the end of his days, he was profoundly disillusioned with the Bolshevik cause, and his eyes had acquired that peculiarly painful expression best described as belated awareness.

My grandad's old travelling-bag with its false bottom – a souvenir of his Polish escapade – was kept in our flat's tiny loft. It was my favourite toy. Its leather interior smelt of adventures and spycraft. As often happens with old, quality things, it had outlived its owner and was eventually thrown out, when my parents moved house.

Such was the sudden flashback that I experienced in Warsaw's former House of Soviet Culture which now housed two second-hand bookshops. It was good to think that there was nothing much left from the former 'Evil Empire', except a pile of old books.

That last statement is not entirely true, for the whole of the former Soviet Union in miniature could also be found at the main arena of the Central Stadium in Warsaw, which had become home to Europe's largest flea market. Russians and Ukrainians, Chechens and Armenians, Yakuts and Georgians were all there to do a brisk trade in smuggled goods: icons, amber, watches, clothes, firearms. Bruised Russian prostitutes and leather-clad racketeers were swarming all around the stadium's circular terraces, making them look like the proverbial vicious circle which had come to life.

'Hey, *pan*, take some more of these fine watches, I've only got twenty left and I am tired,' a Ukrainian woman was saying in broken Polish to an indifferent second-hand wholesale dealer. In front of me, a shabbily dressed Russian lady, with dark shadows under her eyes, sold an excellent eighteenth-century Russian icon to a Polish dealer for just 200 zlotys (about £40). The dealer hid the icon under the rags piled on his squeaky trolley, and hurried away.

There was something spooky about a former empire selling its odds and ends to a former satellite state at a stadium turned into a flea market. My grandad Misha wouldn't have liked this scene, proving beyond a shadow of doubt that his courageous mission to spread Bolshevik propaganda in Poland had resulted in a complete failure seventy-five years on.

The Warsaw of the late nineties reminded me of my grandad's old travelling-bag with a false bottom: there was much more to it than met the eye. Formerly one of the gloomiest cities in the world, with the wedding-cake skyscraper of the Palace of Science and Culture (a gift to the Polish people from Comrade Stalin himself) towering above the crumbling apartment blocks, food queues and unwashed teenage boys begging the passengers of international trains for empty Coke cans at the Central Station, Warsaw was now bubbling with life and commercialism. In spirit, it has become unmistakably Western, a cooler version of Hong Kong, with people making money on every street corner, whereas its façades remained largely unchanged, if not to count colourful Western ads, one of which – a billboard advertising card phones – struck me as brilliant. It featured a huge and painfully familiar food ration card of the communist times and a public telephone. 'At last – telephones on cards!' was written in big letters across the billboard.

The other obvious difference was the profusion of

McDonald's and other fast-food restaurants, whose density in Warsaw is probably one of the world's highest. The ill-famed Palace of Science and Culture (now without stars on its turrets and spires) was surrounded by them, like a newly discovered dinosaur skeleton by scruffily dressed archaeologists.

My main destination in Warsaw was Agros, Poland's sole vodka-exporting agency, but, out of respect to my hosts, I had to have a quick look at the city sights. Also, I wanted to catch up with my old friend Adam Michnik, a former dissident and one of the founders of Solidarity, who was now editor-in-chief of Poland's biggest newspaper, *Gazeta Wyborcza*.

I was accommodated at Dom Chlopa (Peasant's House), a Soviet-style hotel which was under reconstruction. Some of the rooms had armour-plated doors, and security guards with walkie-talkies patrolled the lobby round the clock. The hotel's restaurant was closed, and for breakfast I had to go to another hotel across the empty windswept square covered with piles of construction debris.

My hosts assigned me a personal guide, a 21-year-old graduate of the Polish School of Tourism, whose name was Wanda. She was an extraordinary young woman.

I was Wanda's first 'live' job in her capacity as a qualified tourist guide. Obviously, she was nervous and kept blushing and apologising all the time. On the other hand, like most Poles, she was naïve, opinionated and emotional, not to say sentimental. In the first several minutes of our first guided tour she told me about her late grandfather and cried, then showed me a photo of her newborn niece – and cried again. She assured me that the Egyptian pyramids were all fakes, forbade me to use taxis ('we have the mafia here'), told me that I reminded her of the devil, who 'also had blue eyes' (it was meant as a compliment), recounted the latest joke about a 'Polish parachute which opens automatically on touching the ground' and assured me that she was prepared to stay with me 'until tomorrow morning', only she had to telephone her parents and tell them that she would spend the night with her sister (I politely refused this kind offer).

She took me for lunch to a new 'French' restaurant in the former House of Journalists, where all the dishes on the menu, except for one, contained snails. The only snail-less dish was pike with crayfish, which we both ordered. On seeing the miniature crayfish on her plate (it was so scrawny and tiny that I was sure it had died of malnutrition), Wanda burst into tears. 'Poor thing,' she moaned (meaning the crayfish, I presume) and dashed to the toilet, where she threw up, as she dutifully informed me halfway through lunch.

Of all the Warsaw attractions I toured with Wanda, I was most impressed by two: the Royal Castle in the Old Town, and Wanda herself. I learnt that, on top of her other amazing qualities, Wanda couldn't stand heights and fainted in lifts (I witnessed her doing so more than once); that she wanted to open her own travel agency; that she was religious and went on annual pilgrimages to Centstochova (the place where the most sacred Polish icon is kept); that she hated 'one woman' at her office, 'because she is blonde'; that she confused 'restoration' with 'restitution' and called a fireplace 'a chimney'; and that her favourite answer to my questions was a slightly coquettish 'I don't know.' Like a miniature human bulldozer, she dragged me around Warsaw, pushing her way through tourist crowds with a blissful smile on her face.

The most interesting thing I learnt inside the magnificent Royal Castle was that Poles were always reluctant to give absolute power to their kings, and this was why from the fourteenth century Polish kings were democratically elected. The elected kings were for the most part intellectuals rather than warriors, and as such they always had difficulties with taking decisions and reaching agreements with the Seim (parliament), which, sadly,

eventually led to the collapse of the excessively democratic Polish kingdom. Monarchies have always stood
on ruthlessness and unquestioning obedience rather
than on intellectual debate.

The last elected Polish monarch, King Stanislaus
Augustus Poniatowski (1765–94) was an erudite and a
bookworm; he had read thousands of books. He
conducted weekly salon meetings called Thursday
Dinners with Warsaw fellow-intellectuals. He also
incurred many debts. What a lovely character! No
wonder that under his soft rule Poland fell under the
authoritarian Russian tsars, who hadn't read many
books and had never been elected. Obviously, democracy wasn't (and isn't) the best way to run an East
European state.

The vodka department of Agros was situated on the
twenty-eighth floor of a brand-new skyscraper near the
Central Station. Wanda dutifully fainted in the lift. She
had to be carried into the Agros offices and put on a
couch in the corridor. She recovered after a couple of
hours – only to faint again on the way down.

Luckily, I didn't need an interpreter at Agros, because
two executive and matronly ladies, who received me,
both spoke excellent English.

One of the ladies was Lidia Kulesza, whose official
business title was Alcoholic Beverages Division
Director. My old drinking friend Evgeny Bulavin
would have died to hold a post like this, even if for a
day or so. The second lady's name was Wanda
Moscicka, and her business card, which she had
solemnly handed over to me, modestly described her as
'Deputy Manager of Vodka Department'. I think that –
all things considered – Evgeny would have agreed to
this position as well.

I was offered a cup of coffee, whereas the vodka ladies
were drinking orange juice. Our conversation concerned
one subject only: Polish vodka.

'Westerners were not prepared to drink vodka neat several years ago. It is good to see that now the attitude is changing: more and more people are drinking it straight – as they should have done from the start,' Mrs Moscicka noted with content. For me, it was pleasing to think that my age-long crusade for proper vodka-drinking might have played a role in this momentous change.

'We are having big problems with advertising,' complained Mrs Kulesza. 'Only between-the-lines advertising is allowed. As to the photos of bottles, they can only be used in professional trade magazines.'

The ladies told me that it was not allowed to open vodka shops near schools or churches. 'But there are so many churches in Poland,' they sighed.

This reminded me of similar regulations which existed in pre-revolutionary Russia, where it was illegal to consume vodka within a distance of 100 yards from a vodka shop. A French traveller who visited Moscow in 1905 recounted how Moscow cabbies, notorious for heavy drinking, used to pace a hundred steps away from the shop in a straight line, then stop abruptly, pour a bottle of vodka down their throats of cast iron and return to their cabs – all within a couple of minutes.

Agros Trading Co. Ltd. specialised in exporting two Polish vodka brands, Wyborowa – the 'Chosen' vodka, and Zubrowka – the bison vodka.

The ladies explained that Wyborowa was one of Poland's best-selling brands. It was the only vodka in the world produced exclusively from rye grain. Its production process was based on the so-called 'triple three' formula which meant 'triple cleaned, triple distilled and triple filtered'. I wondered whether it was also supposed to be 'triple drunk': in the Soviet Union it was customary among hard-up alcoholics to seek volunteers (among total strangers) to split the cost of a bottle among three drinkers. For some reason, it was the third party who was always hard to find. '*Tret'im budesh?*' ['Will you be the third one?']: such was the sacramental question one could hear frequently near (and inside) vodka shops. Having quickly consumed a bottle in a dirty gateway, the trio would have a short yap-yap about politics or women (a jabber was an obligatory part of the ritual) and split up, never to see each other again.

This peculiar Soviet custom can be illustrated by the following joke. A bespectacled 'intellectual', clutching a rouble in his hand, goes to a food shop to buy some yoghurt. He is stopped by two drunks. 'Give us your rouble,' they demand. The frightened 'intellectual' obeys. One of the drunks disappears into the shop and immediately returns with a bottle of vodka and a dirty glass. 'Drink fast! We only have one glass!' he commands. The 'intellectual' obeys, downs the glass and tries to run away. The drunks run after him.

'Stop! Where are you running to?' they scream.

'What do you want from me, guys? Haven't I given you the rouble?'

'Yes, you have.'

'Haven't I drunk vodka with you?'

'Yes, you have.'

'What else do you want then?'

'How about a chat?'

Zubrowka, the bison vodka, so the vodka ladies from Agros assured me, was flavoured with bison grass, a rare plant growing in the Bialowieza forest, where bison grazed on it. The correct Latin name for the grass which, allegedly, gave bisons their strength, was *Hierochloe odorata* or *Hierochloe australis*. It gave vodka a delicate herbal aroma and a distinctive yellowish tinge (as if these mattered).

Talking about vodkas without tasting them was like reading *Delia Smith's Complete Cookery Course* on an empty stomach.

I asked the ladies about kosher vodkas. 'All vodkas are kosher,' they said in chorus and told me about the 'war' between the remaining two Polish rabbis for the right to award the coveted Kosher Certificate to vodkas.

Agros's offices were brimming with all sorts of vodka memorabilia: vodka pens, vodka notebooks, vodka T-shirts. On one of the walls, there was a poster with a quote from Pablo Picasso: 'The three most astonishing things in the past half-century were: the blues, cubism and Polish vodka.' Did Picasso really say this? The authenticity of the quotation was impossible to check, for the famous Spanish artist died in 1973.

I was dreading more vodka souvenirs: my suitcase was already bursting with them. And I was right: the ladies presented me with a set of a dozen small bottles of differently flavoured Wyborowa. Thank God, I was with Wanda, to whom I magnanimously presented the set the moment we left Agros's offices (she had just recovered after our descent from the twenty-eighth floor). She accepted the gift with tearful delight.

I happily spent a solitary evening at my hotel: Wanda – like Polish vodka – could be dangerous in excessive doses. I dined on an Iranian take-away kebab, which I had bought from a street stall in Marszalkowska, Warsaw's main street. The appearance of kebab shops was a sure sign of the final and irreversible triumph of capitalism in Poland.

Before going to sleep, I browsed through the brochures given to me at Agros. One of them, *Aqua Vitae*, was printed on imitation parchment. It was written in flamboyant and stilted English: 'Polish vodka, once called "gorzalka", then "okowite" (derived from Aqua Vitae) has got a long history equal to the history of the mankind. It is even said that Eva had sooner tempted Adam with a glass of Polish "gorzalka" than with an apple.'

So far so good. I read on: 'Our ancestor Noah waited until the last moment for Polish vodka to be delivered to his Ark, and only after having received it, he decided to shove off.'

At that point I decided 'to shove off', too. I dreamt of

Eva drinking Polish vodka with Noah and chasing it with an apple.

'I want to show you something,' Wanda said enigmatically next morning. From her handbag she produced two empty bottles of Wyborowa from the set that I had given her the day before. She had brought them with her deliberately, to impress me, or, maybe, to make me feel guilty for having snubbed her company for the night.

I was looking forward to catching up with my friend Adam Michnik. Who exactly was he? I would call him a revolutionary, had this word not been compromised by twentieth-century political rhetoric. A dissident intellectual, a human-rights activist and one of the founders of Solidarity, Adam was a political prisoner at 19, an MP at 43, and, finally, the editor of Poland's first independent newspaper, *Gazeta Wyborcza* ('The Election Gazette') at 46. What a life!

I first met him in Moscow in October 1989 at the International Press Institute (IPI) Round Table, shortly before I was forced to defect from the Soviet Union. His rebellious nature was reflected in his appearance: an open, youthful face, dishevelled hair, soft charismatic smile. He was permanently clutching a strong 'thermonuclear' Gitane cigarette. When walking, he stooped a bit, the result of six years in prison. They managed to bend him, but failed to break him.

Adam was an unwanted guest in the Soviet Union, and even the post-glasnost Moscow press referred to him as a 'troublemaker' and a 'CIA agent'. I remember how ardently he defended his cause against the rumblings of his, then tame, East European colleagues, much to the irritation of the Round Table Soviet hosts. Everything about him unnerved them, even the fact that he refused to wear a tie. They could not understand that six years behind bars had earned him the right to dismiss official etiquette.

As an editor, Adam continued to be a thorn in the side of the establishment, even if it was the post-communist Polish establishment, although the collapse of communism, as he once said to me, was the biggest joy of his life. On several occasions he annoyed his old friend Lech Walesa, who – in his capacity as president of Poland – wanted to sack him from the editorial post.

In his book *Letters from Prison*, Adam wrote: 'We need freedom. As we walk towards it, we carry in us the seeds of captivity . . .' This quote brilliantly sums up the present-day state of Eastern Europe.

'Prison was an ideal place to write: no vodka, no women, no phones – nothing to distract you,' he had told me during one of our previous meetings, at the IPI General Assembly in Venice and added: 'It is hard to be free.'

Having drunk vodka with Adam in the past, I thought it would be legitimate to ask him what brand out of the 1000 available now in Poland he preferred. I expected that, as someone who had initiated the Solidarity trade union, he would opt for Solidarna. But I was wrong.

'I drink Chopin Vodka,' he said, throwing a furtive look at Wanda, who was nodding in a chair in the corner of his office (he always had an eye for pretty women).

I was not surprised by Adam's choice. Even in the free post-communist drinking environment, he had to opt for the most controversial vodka which was in danger of being banned. A dissident is always a dissident.

It was a typical office of the busy editor of a big daily newspaper. Adam's desk was piled with papers, proofs, ashes and cigarette ends. Honorary diplomas from American and European universities were pinned to the wall, next to a photo of Adam with Kazakhstan's President Nazarbayev, whom he had recently interviewed.

'I don't drink S-solidarna,' he said with a slight stutter, another legacy of his prison stretch. 'Nor am I a member of Solidarity. Not any longer. When the first Solidarity collapsed in 1991, I left with a group of liberal democrats. The present-day Solidarity is a coalition of many parties. Inundated with right-wing rhetorics, revisionist tactics, populism, clericalism and ethnic nationalism, it is no longer my cup of tea, or my glass of vodka . . . I am now a businessman, not a politician. The political map of Poland is a complete mess. Communists stand for privatisation. Democrats want to tighten up the screws. And everyone supports NATO. Floods have exposed the extreme weakness of the government. If the elections were held tomorrow, communists would win by a landslide.'

'Are you still friendly with Walesa?' I asked him.

'Let's put it like this: we don't seek each other's company any more, although, on a purely human basis, we still maintain normal relationships.'

When we were leaving his office, Adam gallantly kissed the hand of the still sleepy Wanda, pressing it to his lips for just a fraction longer than mere politeness dictated.

'Good old Adam. He will never change,' I thought.

My last day in Warsaw. My last day in Poland. It is also the last day of my eleven-month-long East European travels.

I am having my morning cup of coffee in an open-air café, Nowy Swyat (New World), in the centre of Warsaw. Symbolically, the street, in which the café is located, is called Chmelna (Drunken Street).

At this early hour, when most of the Warsovians are busy making money, the café is empty, except for a handful of morning patrons. An elderly man at the next table is telling his friend over a coffee about his daughter's recent trip to Greece with her boyfriend. A couple of American tourists are giving an impromptu English lesson to one of the waiters. 'How . . . are . . . you? . . . My . . . name is . . . Jarek,' he slowly repeats after them. In the corner, three gangster-like Polish 'businessmen', with crew-cuts, tattoos, gold rings and mobile phones, are conversing in low voices. They are probably discussing their next protection-racket scheme. Naturally, they drink Smirnoff. The only word from their conversation which I can clearly discern is *'kurva'* (bitch). They diligently insert it into every sentence.

A tall long-legged blonde with two dachshunds on a leash enters a sex-shop across the street. 'Erotic Dance for You' says the sign above the entrance. Soon, she re-emerges into the street, this time without the dach-shunds. 'Erotic dance' was clearly not for her. Or can it be that she does the dance herself of an evening?

Two stocky lads in black uniforms with 'Ohorona' (Guard) written on their backs are hanging around the sex shop. They grin at the dog-less girl, and she smiles back.

On the table in front of me is a copy of Adam Michnik's recent article 'Gray is Beautiful. Thoughts on Democracy in Central Europe' from the American magazine *Dissent*. I browse through it slowly. 'Communism was like a freezer. Within it a diverse world of tensions and values, emotions and conflicts, was covered with a thick layer of ice. The defrosting process was a gradual one – so first we saw beautiful flowers, and only later, the rot . . .' And several paragraphs down: 'Democracy is not identical with freedom. Democracy is freedom written into the rule of law . . .'

Around me, Warsaw – a normal European city – is living through its normal working morning. More and more patrons are entering the New World café in Drunken Street. Somehow, they all look familiar to me.

Old faces in the New World . . .

A 'No smoking. Hollywood' plate was attached to the glove compartment of the cab which took me to the airport. Contrary to Wanda's warnings, the driver was nice and friendly, and the meter was on.

My luggage was in the boot, except for one – imaginary – piece which I was cradling in my lap. It was a compact battered leather suitcase: my grandad's old travelling-bag.

19 SLOVAKIAN 'RAMPAGE'

'In Slovakia, we drink everything. We drank under the Austrian emperor, under President Tomas Masaryk, under communists and under democrats . . . Recently I was helping my parents to sell their house. We drank for two days with potential buyers, but failed to reach an agreement.'

My new friend Fero and I were sitting in his tiny *pivnica* (wine-cellar) in the town of Vrbove and tasting his home-made *burchak*, a very young wine, no more than four or five days old.

The word '*burchak*' is onomatopoeic. Originating from the verb *burchat* (to grumble), it brilliantly conveys the character of this brownish, opaque and vomitingly sweet liquid, reminiscent of a brew rather than wine: it bubbled, breathed and hissed in the tank as if it was indeed grumbling at us. A large quantity of it was already grumbling in our stomachs, too.

Fero was a short, compact man with sharp brown eyes. A psychiatrist by profession, he was in his early fifties. For many years, he had worked at a tiny research institute of gerontology in the town of Zilina which studied mechanisms of human ageing with the aim of slowing them down, I presume. Shortly after the collapse of communism the institute ran out of funds and had to close down: the new Slovak capitalists were more preoccupied with making a quick buck than with problems of eternal life, which, obviously, was not achievable in free-market conditions.

Having been made redundant (together with all the other seven members of the institute's staff), Fero had to open his own home practice, hoping to make some money by conducting 'psychiatric expertise' of potential gun owners in need of a licence. His business soon ran into trouble. 'My licence-issuing practice went down, simply because everyone who wanted to have a gun in Slovakia had got it already,' he complained, clutching his glass of *burchak* tightly, as if he was worried that I would snatch it from his grasp.

Unable to make a living out of licensing, Fero switched over to treating alcoholics. He boasted of having cured one 'very senior Slovak politician' (he rolled his eyes up to the *pivnica*'s low ceiling) using a tested method, described in Chekhov's short story 'A Cure for Drinking Addiction'. The method was limited to beating a patient up after every binge.

'An alcoholic is anyone who drinks more than I do' was Fero's favourite saying.

There are many cases in the history of medicine when psychiatrists went mad themselves under the influence of their insane shut-ins. As often happens, Fero didn't notice he had become an alcoholic himself. This was partly due to the fact that many of his patients chose to pay their fees in kind, which in Slovakia (and all over Eastern Europe) meant booze. They brought him bottles of home-made *slivovica* (plum brandy), flasks of herb-based Becherovka liqueur and litres of Borovicka, a gin-like Slovak concoction made of juniper berries.

'Borovicka goes wonderfully well with beer,' Fero said, smacking his *burchak*-covered lips.

To support his addiction, Fero started growing grapes in his own backyard. 'Having done some digging in the garden, I come down to the cellar for a drink, then dig again . . . I drink five hundred litres of wine a year.'

To this impressive figure one had to add buckets of *slivovica* and Borovicka, which, in Fero's own words, he drank every day, and gallons of *burchak*, which, unfortunately, could only be drunk during harvesting season, when this baby wine for the impatient, as I had come to call it, was sold by entrepreneurial peasants from makeshift stalls lining Slovak country roads and dirt-tracks.

'Each Slovak must drink at least fifty litres of burchak during the season to make sure all his bodily juices are rejuvenated,' concluded Fero.

I am not a Slovak, and this is probably why, instead of rejuvenating my juices, *burchak* gave me a splitting headache and made my stomach feel (and sound) like a sack full of stirring and hissing snakes. I came to realise why the Austrians, Slovakia's next-door neighbours, called *burchak* 'Sturm' and why Slovaks themselves had nicknamed a fully fermented *burchak* 'Rampage': they probably meant the uproar it tended to create inside both their heads and their bellies.

It was hard to know where to put Slovakia on to my drinking map of Eastern Europe. Fero was right: they did drink everything there. My principle has always been: when in doubt, ask the locals (preferably, sober-minded ones – unlike Fero). According to the new *Slovakian Spectator* magazine, which modestly calls itself 'Slovakia's English-language newspaper', 'Alcohol is taken very, very [*sic*] seriously in Slovakia, and its [*sic*] not unusual to see someone start their [*sic*] day with a shot of liquor [*sic*].' To clear up (some of) the linguistic confusion, I should explain that in 'Slovakia's English' 'liquor' means 'liqueur', which in plain English means 'a highly flavoured spirit, intended to be drunk after a meal', according to *Collins Concise Dictionary*.

So liqueur it is! And since most Slovaks seldom look into the *Collins Dictionary* and so are unaware that liqueurs are 'intended to be drunk after a meal', they tend to drink it also before a meal, during a meal and instead of a meal, all of which allowed me to list Slovakia as part of East European Spirit Lands.

I tend to attract trouble. My previous visit to Slovakia was in November 1992, when it was still part of the Czechoslovakian federation. Two days after my arrival, Alexander Dubcek, Czechoslovakia's ex-president and a Slovak by nationality, died as a result of the wounds he had received in an extremely suspicious car accident several weeks before. His body was lying in state in the National Theatre in Bratislava. I stood outside, in the huge crowd of mourners.

This was not just the funeral of the famous politician, the proponent of 'socialism with a human face'. It was also the funeral of Dubcek's honest delusion that socialism and democracy could somehow co-exist in one country. He failed to realise that socialism on our planet had always ended up with only one face – the moustached and pock-marked face of Comrade Stalin, a stark contrast to the open and smiling face of Dubcek himself in the black-framed portrait above the theatre's entrance.

I remember Vaclav Havel saying at the funeral that Dubcek was 'a figure of simple shining decency' and 'the type of politician communism was not accustomed to'. Neither was capitalism. Could many Western politicians be called honest and decent without reservations? So, in a way, the funeral of Alexander Dubcek on that November morning in Bratislava was also the funeral of decency in politics.

And less than two months later Czechoslovakia ceased to exist. The decision to split was taken by the two premiers – the Czech Republic's Vaclav Klaus and

Slovakia's Vladimir Meciar – without consulting the populace. Opinion polls showed that the majority of Czechs and Slovaks did not think the division was necessary, but the promised national referendum on the issue was never conducted.

The 'marriage' of the two states lasted for seventy-four years – one year short of a diamond wedding. It had not always been a happy matrimony, but few marriages can boast an uninterrupted bliss. For seventy-four years, the spouses had adjusted to each other to become almost inseparable. That's why the division, which later became known as the 'velvet divorce' (to echo 'the velvet revolution' of 1989), had been so painful. It was triggered by political ambitions, not by the people's will. Well, to develop the analogy with a human marriage, it is not uncommon for the spouses' parents and relatives, rather than the spouses themselves, to be the main cause of a divorce. And who suffers most of all as a result? The children, or in this case the people.

Dubcek was an ardent opponent of Czechoslovakia's division, so his death was timely for the separatists. There were rumours of a conspiracy, masterminded by Vladimir Meciar, Slovakia's authoritarian prime minister, an ex-boxer turned politician, who benefited enormously from the split. It turned out that the uninjured driver of Dubcek's car on that fatal journey was one of Meciar's aides, at a time when the latter was Slovakia's interior minister. This gave rise to the following black joke: when was the last time Prime Minister Meciar wore blue overalls? Answer: when he was tampering with the brakes of Dubcek's car.

On 1 January 1993, at a time when many Cold War frontiers were disappearing from the map, the newest European border came into existence. The absurdity of this partition became obvious for anyone who crossed it by train, as I did more than once in the course of my East European travels.

At the Slovak station of Kuty, several dozen Slovak

border-guards, dressed in baggy uniforms of cheap khaki with the Slovak double cross (national emblem) on their sleeves, would board the train. With guns dangling from their belts, they moved through the carriages, assiduously checking the passengers' visas and imposing hefty on-the-spot fines on those who didn't have them in their passports. When the train slowly – almost reluctantly – crawled into the Czech frontier station of Breslav on the opposite bank of the Morava river, they would be joined by their grinning counterparts from the Czech border-police sporting smart black overalls with gleaming badges on their chests. Having completed their cursory examination of the travellers' passports, they would engage their Slovak colleagues (who, for some reason, would still be hanging around the train) in a friendly chat, and sometimes a drink, in the corner of a half-empty first-class carriage. There is no language barrier between them, for the Czech and Slovak tongues are similar. They treat each other like close mates, which they probably were before the split (they could even serve in one and the same frontier-guard unit). Curiously, even their different uniforms underline their similarity and make them look like twin brothers, separated by the will of their divorced irresponsible parents, who decided to split the children between themselves.

This time I entered Slovakia from Austria (Bratislava is just forty minutes' drive from Vienna). At the border I asked a Slovak frontier-guard whether I had to register with the police in Bratislava during my stay. 'No, you don't have to,' he assured me. Years of life under communists taught me not to put much trust in the words of a government official, and on my last day in Slovakia I decided to pop into the city police head-quarters (just to be on the safe side). The headquarters were located in a grey Stalin Gothic building, which the locals had nicknamed 'Februarka', in sad memory of the communist coup d'état in February 1948. As a sign of the new times, modern money-dispensers, accepting

Western credit cards, were built into its sombre walls, next to massive columns and sculptures of muscular workers with pneumatic drills in their sinewy hands which decorated its awe-inspiring façade (the secret police headquarters used to be located there, too).

'Of course you have to register,' I was told by a ruddy chain-smoking police captain with red lapels.

'But the officer on the border told me I didn't have to,' I objected meekly.

'You are old enough to know better,' he said dragging at his cigarette.

The impromptu visit saved me a lot of money, for the first thing they wanted to check when I was leaving the country next morning was . . . my police registration stamp. They were very disappointed that I had one in my passport.

As you can see, the newest European border, which Alexander Dubcek had tried so hard to avoid, made sense for border-guards alone. The only real frontier it marked was the one between the land where people drank mostly beer (the Czech Republic) and the country where they 'drank everything' (Slovakia).

With Fero, my voluntary drinking guide, we visited the Slopak factory in the town of Malacky where they make the famous Slovak liqueurs. To my considerable disappointment, the factory was at a standstill. Danitsa Gubova, the manager, explained that half of the workers were on packaging courses, and the other half had been commandeered by another factory. But I had the feeling that the real reason for the stoppage lay in the pressures of the emerging free market, of which Mrs Gubova kept complaining.

'We have to fight the Slavic mentality giving preference to everything Western,' she said. 'Our liqueurs and brandies are not worse than the ones from the West, and our Martingnac is better than all these so-called "Napoleons" made in Germany, but breaking into

Western markets is hard because of strong protectionism. Besides, the spirit, which we have to buy as a base component for our products, has gone up in price more than ten times in just a couple of years.'

We were given a quick tour of the stationary production line. There was something extra-terrestrial, even Martian, about it: the gleaming stainless-steel tanks, in which our distorted faces were reflected, were full of bubbling and smoking liquid looking suspiciously similar to *burchak* (Fero was sure it *was burchak*). Not a soul (except for us) was around. The heavy, sweet air smelt of severe hangovers and of mortuaries. Restaurants and pubs have a similar smell on the morning after a big all-night party.

'Here we normally make Milka, an alcohol emulsion with nut extract, chocolate and coffee,' explained Mrs Gubova, her vibrant voice ricocheting off the liqueur-stained walls. 'Milka is our pride: it was invented at this factory fifteen years ago. You can drink it neat, or add it to your coffee instead of cream.'

At this point, Fero made a soft smacking sound with his lips. He could not wait to proceed from theory to practice.

The tasting room of Slopak was decorated in inimitable Soviet fashion. On the wall, there hung a copy of the famous painting by Repin, a nineteenth-century Russian artist, *Zaporozhie Cossacks Writing a Letter to the Sultan of Turkey*. The Cossacks in the painting were red-faced and agitated, as if each of them had just had a glass of one of Slopak's famous liqueurs. A transparent figure of Lenin, made of Plexiglas, stood in the cupboard. It was a present from a sister Soviet factory to commemorate the billionth bottle of liqueur produced by Slopak. The exact meaning of this gift was a mystery to me, for Lenin himself was a convinced teetotaller.

'You must first hold the liqueur on the tip of your tongue, then move it to the root of your tongue and spit it out,' Mrs Gubova instructed us.

'No way!' said Fero. 'It is only in the West that tasters spit alcohol out. We Slovaks are much more economical: we swallow it.' And he did.

We tasted the famous Milka in all its creamy varieties: Mocha Cream, Chocolate Cream, Nut Cream, Mozart (!) Cream, etc. Each bottle had a label with a description of the drink, in Slovak and in 'Slovakia's English'. The latter read as follows: 'Its a delicate, fine structure, made from the best material. Excellent for ice and whipped cream glasses, swects [sic] and into coffee. Please stores by rooms temperature, mix and shake before use.'

Fero downed one glass of the 'fine structure' after another until cream and other 'best material' oozed from his small hairy ears. From the sombre expression on his face I could see that he was not pleased with the overall effect: Milka's alcohol content was a modest 20 per cent . . .

'Let's go somewhere else and try the real stuff,' he said, the moment we left Slopak. Before I could say 'Milka', he flagged down a taxi and pushed me inside.

We drove to Malokarpatsky Vinarsky Podnik, a wine factory near the town of Pezinok, where one of Fero's patients worked. On the way, Fero called him up on his mobile phone and asked him to arrange a tour of the factory, followed by a tasting, for a 'visiting British editor', or 'pan redaktor', as he put it in Slovak. Who is this editor? I wondered, before realising that he meant myself.

'Give a good drink to anyone who enters here,' read a slogan at the factory's entrance. 'We are in business,' said Fero rubbing his hands.

The factory, which used to specialise in wines, now produced a number of spirits, mostly brandies. 'The Slovaks drink more spirits than ever before,' Fero's friend explained.

We had a quick tour of the premises, where the smell alone could make one drunk. Fero insisted on tasting the factory's liquid products straight from the fermentation tanks. 'I want to ask for political asylum here,' he mumbled, emptying one glass after another. This reminded me of Evgeny Bulavin, who used to ask me whether I knew anyone – an agreeable foreign spy, for example – to whom he could sell his motherland, the great Soviet Union, for a crate of vodka. Coming from anyone but Evgeny, such a statement would have been regarded as a clumsy provocation. But in his case, it was but the scream of his permanently alcohol-thirsty soul. I was sure that, had he found such a spy, he would have willingly reduced the price of his motherland to just one bottle, or even one glass.

Fero's friend, who had worked at the factory for thirty-odd years, told us a remarkable story. In August 1968, during the Soviet invasion of Czechoslovakia, a group of drunken Soviet soldiers burst into the factory. Having spotted the tanks of maturing wine, they decided to have a drink and fired a mortar shell at one of them to uncork it. The tank contained more than a million litres, and all the soldiers drowned in the alcoholic tsunami they had unwittingly unleashed.

I looked up at one of the stainless-steel vats towering above our heads like a mountain peak. '12,276,190 litres' was written on it. Somehow, I did not feel much pity for the armed invaders who had drowned themselves in alcohol.

Inspired by the hapless Soviet soldiers, Fero was trying hard to drown himself in booze, only from the inside. Such was the impression I had during the tasting. We tried the three-year-old Karpatske brandy and the export-only cognac Slovak Gold, washing them down with a grape-based soft drink called Vinea, also made by the factory. It was not long before Fero started finishing off my drinks which I had just sipped (brandies, unlike vodkas, are not for gulping) without asking my permission. The scene reminded me of the description of a wine-tasting in alcohol-starved Norway which I once came across in a London broadsheet: 'Some of the tasters had poured all six of their wines into one large beerglass and downed the lot in one go. Others put the bread into their glasses and mopped it up like soup. There was even one guy who was drinking out of the spittoon bucket . . .'

I wondered whether that last guy could have been Fero and was tempted to ask him whether he had ever been to Norway.

When our hosts indicated that the tasting was over, Fero got angry and wanted to carry on. It was only when I said that his behaviour could undermine the improving British–Slovakian relationship (I was a 'British editor', after all) that he got frightened and stumbled towards the exit.

But this was not the end of our own 'Slovakian rampage'. Fero insisted that we went to a restaurant at the old Pezinok Castle, where he ordered several rounds of what he called 'Slovak combination'. It was an unlikely choice between beer with rum and beer with gin, mixtures I hadn't tried since my student days. After a couple of equally lethal alternatives, the world swam in front of my eyes and I can't recall much of the rest of the evening, except for a handful of details. I remember that the restaurant owner, who was also a friend (or a patient) of Fero's, was sporting a snow-white double-breasted cotton suit and snow-white shoes.

The restaurant was OK, and the food was fine (we had chips), except for the cheeky fleas jumping on to our table from the walls. Fero ferreted them out of his glass and smashed them against the table cloth with his thick, nicotine-stained thumb.

I was lucky that Fero didn't treat me to another popular 'Slovak combination', a cocktail called Hriatua, which is drunk on Christmas Eve in the town of Upper Hron. Its recipe is simple: vodka, honey and . . . goose lard (they drink it hot!). My stomach ulcer wouldn't have coped with it.

20 A LESSON IN SELF-APPLIED NARCOLOGY

Among the eternal questions which have haunted humankind since time immemorial ('To be or not to be?' 'Is there life on Mars?' 'What to do on a dull Sunday afternoon?' 'Why is water wet?' etc.), there is one which remains unanswerable: how does one avoid a hangover after a rough drinking night?

Hundreds of possible solutions have been offered through the centuries. The hung-over Japanese walk around wearing surgical masks soaked in saki. In Puerto Rico, they apply lemon or lime to their . . . armpits. In India, they mix a teaspoon of ground black pepper with a glass of water, boil it and drink. American wine guru Hugh Johnson recommends chicken soup. Russians prefer brine. Kazakhs and other former nomads of Central Asia opt for koumiss, fermented mare's milk, which, as my own experience shows, is probably the best hangover cure one can find (as long as there's access to an agreeable mare, which can be a problem in a big city).

My drinking tutor Evgeny Bulavin firmly believed in the hair of the dog. Kingsley Amis used to dismiss the whole concept by saying, 'He who truly believes he has a hangover, has no hangover'. The *Daily Telegraph* wine critic Richard Neill suggests the following morning-after cocktail: 'Take one tall glass, add two egg yolks, a spoonful of honey, the juice of a lime/lemon and top with orange juice.' Unfortunately, he doesn't specify whether the 'tall glass' should be consumed before or after the rest of the concoction.

None of these recipes, however, solves the problem. In the best of scenarios, they only slightly relieve the symptoms; in the worst, one can end up with a tall glass inside one's stomach. Therefore, the healthiest thing you can do is to try and strike an optimistic note, as was done by wine expert Peter Hampson, who once cheerfully exclaimed, 'What's wrong with having a hangover? It's the only thing that stops us all becoming alcoholics.'

Conclusion: there is only one effective cure for hangovers – to give up drinking altogether.

If Peter Hampson had been able to throw one quick look at my Slovak friend Fero on the morning after our 'Slovakian rampage', the smile would have disappeared from his face. The psychiatrist looked dreadful. His hands were trembling, his face was the colour of the *Financial Times* newspaper, his strawberry-shaped nose with protruding red and blue veins resembled a London Underground map, his eyes had all but disappeared – only two narrow slits were visible under the bushy dishevelled eyebrows stuck to his forehead like two black, untidy shrimps. He was the spitting image of Russia's boozy president, Boris Yeltsin, the only difference being that Fero was half his size.

'*Facies ebbrietica*,' he whispered (his voice had disappeared together with his eyes), when I told him about this striking resemblance.

'What?' I asked, fearing that he was becoming delirious.

'"*Facies ebbrietica*" in Latin means the puffy red face

of an alcoholic. This is exactly what Yeltsin is suffering from,' he explained.

'Look in the mirror,' I wanted to say, but thought better of it.

Having treated alcoholics for many years, Fero knew what he was talking about, and the fact that he had contracted the disease himself did not matter. I had come across similar cases before, the most memorable of them being Eduard Drozdov, the chief narcologist of Moscow in the late eighties.

Before you reach for the dictionary, let me explain that narcology is a branch of medicine dealing with alcoholism, drugs, smoking and other addictions. In Russia this word is primarily used to describe the most unrewarding medical task, the treatment of heavy drinkers. In the West, for some reason, they prefer other terms.

Anyway, in 1986, or '87, when I was working as a special correspondent for *Krokodil* magazine in Moscow, I received a reader's letter complaining that a vodka shop was functioning on the territory of Moscow's biggest narcological clinic, where several thousand alcoholics were undergoing treatment. My first instinct was to dismiss this bizarre complaint as a grotesque lie, but knowing that everything was possible in the absurd reality of the Soviet Union, I decided to check the 'signal'.

To my astonishment, I discovered that the letter told the truth: a small vodka shop was indeed doing a brisk trade right under the windows of the alcoholics' hospital. A bucket tied to a rope was going up and down from the hospital window: down, with several rumpled roubles in it; up, without roubles, but with a bottle of vodka. No wonder the efficacy of the narcology treatment at the hospital left much to be desired.

The case was so outrageous that I decided to see the hospital's chief physician. That was how I met Eduard Drozdov, Moscow's chief narcologist, professor of medicine, city council deputy, Hero of Socialist Labour and ... a drunkard, although that last incarnation of his did not reveal itself until later.

Professor Drozdov expressed his horror at the existence of the vodka shop (of which he claimed complete ignorance) on the territory of his clinic and promised to attend to this 'scandalous breach of regulations' as soon as he had a spare moment. The problem was that he didn't have many. His working diary was full for days ahead. To demonstrate how busy he was, he kindly invited me to spend some time in his office while he was receiving visitors and patients.

For me, it was an unforgettable experience. From a cosy armchair in the corner of Drozdov's spacious study, I witnessed a succession of grief-stricken wives, mothers and sisters of alcoholics. The women were all crying, telling heart-breaking stories and begging Drozdov to save their drink-sodden husbands, sons and brothers. He tried to calm them down, and gave each of them a packet of some 'miracle drug' which, as he would say, might help their beloved. Before leaving his office, each woman would leave a carefully wrapped parcel on his desk. Drozdov would lock it up, without un-wrapping it, in his capacious office safe. Watching the women was the best anti-alcoholism propaganda one could imagine, and by the end of the day I had solemnly promised myself to give up drinking from the following morning.

But Drozdov himself was much less affected. At exactly 6 p.m., when the door closed behind the last weeping woman, a young, long-legged nurse pranced into the office. She was on suspiciously familiar terms with Drozdov. 'Well, Edik, what have we got in the takings tonight?' she sang playfully. Without asking for the narcologist's permission, she opened his safe, took out several parcels left by the women, and hastily unwrapped them. They contained bottles of booze.

'What shall we have tonight? Napoleon cognac?

Possolskaya vodka? Whisky from Scotland?' she asked Drozdov.

'Hush, Lyuba, there's a journalist here,' he interrupted, pointing at me.

'So what?' giggled the unstoppable Lyuba. 'With your reputation and your party record, you have nothing to worry about.'

She was right: the chance that the vigilant Glavlit censors would allow a story about Moscow's chief narcologist and a high-ranking member of the Soviet establishment taking bribes in the form of booze into print was less than zero – it was minus ten!

'Hey, journalist, will you have a drink with us?' Lyuba asked, winking at me mischievously.

Three hours later we were still sitting in the side-room of Drozdov's office finishing off the third (or was it the fourth?) bottle. The chief narcologist was dead drunk.

'This is narcology in action for you, Vitali,' he said. 'We are not simply drinking here. We are ex-pe-ri-men-ting! This is your first lesson in self-applied narcology. Like all pioneering physicians, we are testing the effects of the drug – courageously – on ourselves!'

He produced a white pill out of his pocket. 'Take it! It will kill the smell of booze, and your wife won't suspect a thing!'

'What sort of pills were you giving to the visitors?' I asked him.

'Ha! You won't believe it, but they were simple mints. Alcoholism is incurable, but my theory is that you can affect a patient psychologically, if he believes that he is taking a powerful anti-drinking drug.'

I could hardly take in any more alcohol – or any more Drozdov, for that matter.

'Look, Vitali, can you do me a favour and forget about the vodka shop?' he asked me suddenly. 'Leave it alone. Let it operate. I don't want to spoil my relationship with the local council.'

'I can't promise anything,' I said, and I stood up to leave.

'They won't allow you to publish the story anyway!' Drozdov cried at my hastily retreating back.

Needless to say, my wife detected the smell of booze even before I unlocked the door of my flat. In this respect, Drozdov's pioneering experiment proved a failure.

In all other respects, however, it was a staggering success. Next morning, an authoritative phone call from the Communist Party Central Committee was received by my editor. The caller strictly forbade the magazine to publish or even to consider for publication anything connected with the narcological clinic or with the highly respected Professor Drozdov.

In the following years, I often saw the chief narcologist on television and heard him on the radio. He spoke about the dangers of alcoholism and called for complete and total sobriety. The sound of his voice invariably made me sick, as if I had indeed taken a vomit-inducing anti-drinking drug.

This incredible, yet hundred-per-cent truthful, story, another proof of one of the main principles of corrupt Soviet-style socialism, 'I feed on what I fight', appears here, in this book, for the first time (I hope the tentacles of Drozdov's pull haven't reached Britain yet). It gives me enormous pleasure to make it public after all these years.

Even the powerful science of self-applied narcology and its distinguished representative Professor Drozdov were helpless against hangovers, I am sure. But, back in Slovakia, Fero had his own secret recipe. His favourite hangover cure was a quick dive into a pool of thermal sulphurous water at the famous Slovakian spa town of Piestany, where one of his patients worked as a doctor. One could be forgiven for thinking that Fero's patients constituted a large proportion of Slovakia's 5.5 million population, which, in turn, made one wonder why his psychiatric practice was not exactly thriving.

Off we went to Piestany, which luckily was not far from Bratislava, where I was staying: in Slovakia – a relatively small country – almost everything was within easy reach.

While Fero was undergoing his water treatment, I took an unhurried walk around the town, which is divided in two by the quiet and scenic River Vah. What struck me in Piestany was the over-abundance of alcoholic drinks in the town's shops. Spirits were sold everywhere: at newsagents', at florists', even at hair-dressing salons. Could it be that it was the combination of thermal waters, therapeutic mud and booze that had made Piestany into Slovakia's premier health resort?

In a shady park on the bank of the Vah, elderly couples in track-suits were strolling hand in hand under ubiquitous banners with a somewhat dubious logo: 'Piestany is the town of rheumatics of the whole world'. The atmosphere was reminiscent of the decaying north Welsh resort of Llandudno, where spotting anyone under 60 years old is almost as hard as pronouncing the town's name without stumbling.

'Balneological Museum' was written on a low-built old house under a chestnut tree. I stepped inside.

'Clean your shoes', ran an angry English sign on the front door. I instinctively looked down at my trainers before realising that what they had probably wanted to say was 'Wipe your feet'. The elusive 'Slovakia's English' kept playing tricks on me.

The circular museum lobby was dominated by three colourful panels hanging next to each other. It didn't take me long to grasp that they were thematically connected. The first one showed a group of legless and armless cripples with crutches being welcomed to the spa by a smiling toga-clad lady. In the second, the same invalids were blissfully relaxing in the healing mud, with their stumps miraculously regenerating. In the last picture, one former cripple was cheerfully leaving the temple-like spa building with all his limbs firmly in place, while another ex-invalid was portrayed breaking his no-longer-needed crutch into two with his newly grown muscular hands. What happened to all the other paraplegics, who had featured prominently in the previous panels, remained a mystery. They must have all drowned in the therapeutic Piestany mud.

Going from one room to another, I was on the lookout for a mammoth's bone, a regulation exhibit of any provincial museum, notwithstanding its speciality. And there it was, next to an ossified human skeleton – probably the result of too intensive a treatment. And next to the anonymous skeleton, there was a no less anonymous crutch, which had probably belonged to the skeleton when he (or she) was not yet a skeleton but a joyful flesh-and-blood invalid, who had come to Piestany in search of a cure and ended up as a skeleton. Or so I thought.

I was the only visitor at the museum. As I walked around, I was closely followed by an angry-faced woman with a broom and a mop who swept and mopped the floor after my every step, as if she suspected me of being contaminated with leprosy, AIDS and CJD all at the same time.

When I finally caught up with Fero, he was un-recognisable: normal colour had returned to his face, and his eyes had reappeared and were frantically rotating in their sockets, looking for something to drink.

Having left the rejuvenated Fero to enjoy himself in Piestany, I took a train back to Bratislava, where I had an important appointment with Dr Jean Pierre Fekete, who, unlike almost all my previous Slovak contacts, was – surprise, surprise – not a patient of Fero's. Dr Fekete was the director of Bratislava's only sobering station, which he himself preferred to call a 'narcological centre'. Now you will understand why Fero had staunchly refused to accompany me to that particular meeting.

The sobering station was appropriately located in Moskovska (Moscow) Street in Bratislava's Soviet-style suburb of Petrzalka, once described by Jan Morris as 'a communal forest of high-rise tenements, a tundra of concrete, treeless, chimney-less, spireless, all new, all right angles, one block in merciless enfilade behind another'. The place itself could serve as one big sobering station for those Western champagne socialists who get easily inebriated on nice-sounding socialist rhetoric.

One side of Petrzalka faced a narrow patch of forest, behind which lay the Austrian border. In communist times, the forest was a vigilantly guarded no-go area and played a role of a natural barrier between the East and the West. A local resident told me that bursts of gunfire were frequently heard from there during the night. Such was the response of the communist regime to those Slovaks who ventured to test their constitutionally guaranteed freedom of movement.

I had feared that Dr Fekete would turn out to be Bratislava's answer to Professor Drozdov. To my relief, he was totally different. A quiet, soft-spoken man, he was half French by origin, which explained his double-barrelled and exotic (by Slovak standards) first name 'Jean-Pierre'.

The atmosphere of his office could be described in just one word – 'poverty': scratched furniture, battered walls, bare light-bulbs, no sign of a computer. His laboratory equipment was limited to a dirty sink with a solitary leaking water-tap. The reason for this indigence was simple: the centre was run by the state.

'We are a state-owned public health facility acting as both a narcological clinic and a sobering station,' he said in a subdued voice. 'We earn our living by scoring points from insurance companies.'

He went on to complain that they only had fourteen beds, which was nowhere near enough for Bratislava. The standard fee for sobering up one drunkard was 600 crowns (about £11), and the whole procedure took approximately eight hours. The station suffered losses of about 60,000 crowns a month, because most of its clients (or 'patients' as Dr Fekete discreetly called them) were unemployed and couldn't afford to pay.

'Alcohol is the number-one toxin in Slovakia, and drinking seems to be on the rise compared to the times of communism,' he continued. 'The reason? Psychological impact of political and economic changes, which makes people increasingly turn to alcohol for comfort. What worries me is the growing number of highly intoxicated patients in the third stage of alcoholism and beyond.'

'What are the symptoms of this particular stage?' I asked.

'Between the third and the fourth stages of alcoholism, the patient drinks anything that contains alcohol and becomes a danger to himself and to society.'

I thought that Fero must be slowly but surely approaching the fourth stage.

At the end of our conversation, I asked Dr Fekete about the difference between running a sobering station under socialism and under capitalism.

'Under the communists, the police tried to bring in as many drunks as possible, because their salary depended on that. Often they would grab a perfectly sober person from the street, beat him up and bring him here. As a result, statistics were severely distorted.'

At this point, I had a sudden flash of recollection.

In 1982, *Krokodil* received a reader's letter from the Urals city of Kirov claiming that the local police, operating by profit-and-loss accounting, were in the habit of arresting sober people in the streets and taking them to sobering stations. I went to investigate.

Kirov was drinking itself into oblivion. There was nothing on sale, despite the ration cards on which the locals somehow survived. To soften the harsh reality, the city's wine factories were supplying the shops with thousands of decilitres of cheap, strong rotgut.

I remember going elk-hunting with the permanently drunk city mayor, who kept hitting bottles instead of elks, thank God . . .

As to the facts in the reader's letter, they proved correct and were confirmed by the head of Kirov's main sobering station, a podgy police colonel with unhealthy flushes on his cheeks. Having revealed the truth, he probably got frightened of possible repercussions for himself after my would-be article. That evening, he tuned up at the door of my hotel room with two bottles of pure alcohol (96 per cent proof) hidden in the sleeves of his police uniform, with the aim of 'establishing better contacts with the Moscow press' (as he put it). I didn't want to appear inhospitable, so I invited him in, and we started 'establishing contacts', i.e., drinking.

After the second shot of the fiery spirit, the colonel suddenly gave out a loud grunt and collapsed on to the floor (he was obviously an alcoholic). My situation was tricky: there, on the floor of my hotel room, lay the head of the city's main sobering station in his colonel's uniform – drunk out of his mind. I tried to move his motionless body, but failed to shift him an inch: he was massive, and being drunk made him seem (and feel) even heavier than he was.

Finally, after some hesitation, I dialled the sobering station's emergency number and explained the situation to the operator, who was not in the least surprised. 'We are sending a car,' said he.

Three burly policemen arrived shortly. With an effort, they lifted the colonel from the floor, carried him out into the street and tossed him into the back of the waiting sobering-station van, as if he were a lifeless log (which he was). They were clearly accustomed to the drunken idiosyncrasies of their boss.

I left Dr Fekete's office with a good feeling. It was pleasing to realise that not all heads of sobering stations and not all chief physicians of alcoholics' clinics were secret (and sometimes open) dipsomaniacs willing to subject me to stupid drinking tests and to cruel lessons in self-applied narcology.

21 I SAW THEM DRINK AND FIGHT

'We Slovaks are cautious people. On 17 November 1989, when the revolution happened, we all went to Bratislava's central square, not far from here, and started jingling our keys in our pockets in anti-communist protest. So here we had a key revolution, not a "velvet revolution" like in Prague ...'

Fero and I were having a belated midday breakfast at Bratislava's only McDonald's restaurant. The place was full of happy, glossy-eyed kids, blissfully and forgetfully, as if in a semi-trance, gobbling their Big Macs. (Why do children all over the world adore junk food? Is it because of some mysterious 'junk-food gene', retained in human bodies until the age of 15–16, when it is replaced by the sex drive?) A tired cleaner-girl, with hopelessness written all over her face and with an 'M' badge on her chest, was reluctantly sweeping the floor. Three broad-shouldered security guards in Group 4 T-shirts were shifting from one foot to the other near the door. Fero explained that they had started guarding the restaurant after a series of 'anarchist' attacks in the Czech city of Brno, where the local McDonald's outlets had been splashed with paint. The 'cautious' Slovaks, however, were unlikely to do any damage to the McDonald's. The only thing local anarchists and environmentalists were probably capable of doing was some discreet jingling of coins in their pockets while they ate their Big Macs.

I ordered myself a sandwich which the menu called 'Fish Mac iz ryboi'. Translated word-for-word into English, this meant 'Fish Mac with Fish'. Fero's breakfast consisted of two (liquid) courses of his change-able 'Slovak combination': he was drinking Borovicka liqueur from a flask and washing it down with beer.

'Look, Fero, you are a psychiatrist,' I said to my friend. 'You are also a physiognomist. Remember how you were able to diagnose Yeltsin's alcoholism from his puffy face? What can you say about your controversial prime minister, Vladimir Meciar? What does his face tell you? Is he a drinker, too?'

On hearing the name 'Meciar', Fero shrank and nearly choked on his beer. 'No comment,' he mumbled.

It was not only Fero who was afraid to make any comments about Meciar. Most of my Slovak contacts would recoil when asked to express their opinion of the country's ebullient prime minister. In the old Soviet fashion, they would roll their eyes up and press a finger to their lips – the body language which we often used in Moscow when we wanted to convey to our interlocutors that 'walls had ears' and that we were unable to talk openly, because Big Brother might be eavesdropping.

But I was extremely interested in Meciar, who had been effectively ruling the country since his party – the so-called Movement for a Democratic Slovakia – took office in January 1993. He came to power on the wave of Slovak nationalism sparked by the 'velvet divorce' from the Czech Republic, of which Meciar himself was one of the main instigators. His dictatorial rule was marked by the ever-growing role of the Slovak Intelligence Service (SIS) and its chief, Ivan Lexa, a close friend of Meciar's, in all spheres of life; by stifling the liberal press; by political deceit, fraud and intrigues. Meciar presided over the introduction of the Anti-subversion Law (later vetoed by President Michal Kovac), under which jail terms could be imposed on Slovaks found guilty of 'disseminating false information abroad damaging to the interests of the republic', or organising public rallies judged (by Meciar) to be 'subversive'. This law effectively meant a return to the times of censorship and political repression.

In 1993, Meciar ordered a cut in family benefits for the Slovak gypsies. He justified this move by the declaration (which would have made Hitler green with envy) to the effect that the cuts were intended 'to achieve a reduction in the extensive reproduction of the socially unadaptable and mentally backward population', meaning gypsies of course.

It was hard to find any part of Slovakia's life which had remained untouched by Meciar's authoritarian hand. Even the neglected streets and tattered, unpainted façades of Bratislava were explained by the simple fact that the municipal elections in the capital had been won by a coalition which was in opposition to Meciar. In retaliation, the prime minister ordered that municipal funds be cut, that Bratislava be deprived of its 'special status' as the nation's capital and that some government offices be moved to the town of Banska-Bystrica.

But Meciar's biggest notoriety was achieved in the feud with President Kovac, the prime minister's sworn political enemy, who tried to oppose some of Meciar's most reactionary decisions. This Meciar-inspired vendetta eventually led to one of the biggest and zaniest political scandals of the nineties – not just in Slovakia, but in the whole of Europe.

The chronicle of this scandal reads like a poorly plotted Mafia thriller. On 31 August 1995, President Kovac's son, also named Michal, was kidnapped and taken to the Austrian border town of Heinburg, where he was dumped dead drunk on the steps of the local police station (he later claimed that two bottles of whisky had been forced down his throat by the SIS agents who were behind the kidnapping). Meanwhile, Ivan Lexa issued an international warrant for Kovac Junior's arrest in connection with some mysterious corruption case. A falsified account for 200 million shillings in Kovac's name was promptly traced in Austria.

The president's son was held in Vienna until he was released on bail on 2 October and returned to Slovakia, where he was placed under house arrest. His passport was taken away. A Slovak police investigator assigned to his case failed to obtain any incriminating evidence against Kovac, but discovered a possible link to the SIS. Under pressure from Lexa, he was dismissed and another investigator, 26-year-old-Robert Remias, was appointed in his stead. It didn't take Remias long to arrive at the same conclusion: the kidnapping had been masterminded by the SIS. He established a rapport with Oscar Fegyveres, a former SIS officer, who had proofs of the SIS involvement in the kidnapping and was willing to disclose them. On 29 April 1996, Remias died after his car burst into flames on the outskirts of Bratislava. Within hours of the incident, Meciar's office announced that it had been an accident. But police investigators working on the official probe conceded that a piece of metal resembling a bullet had been found in Remias's body. Fearing for his life, Fegyveres fled abroad.

During my visit to Slovakia, the tape of an alleged bugged telephone conversation between Lexa and Slovakia's interior minister, another pawn of Meciar's, was made public. In this conversation, the two men, using extremely foul language, discussed how to mislead the investigation into Remias's death. Printed transcripts of the tape were placed on public notice-boards all over Slovakia. Naturally, the official government sources questioned the authenticity of the tape, claiming that it was a fake. In a brazen gesture of defiance, Meciar, who had probably decided that an offensive would be the best form of defence, publicly asserted that it was President Kovac who had organised the kidnapping of his own son in an attempt to compromise the SIS and Meciar himself.

My attempts to secure an interview with Meciar came to nothing. An influential contact assured me that 'even for the American ambassador', it was impossible to see the reclusive prime minister, whose office was, allegedly, run by an undercover agent of Lexa's. What a mess!

I tried to send a fax with my credentials to Meciar's office, but couldn't get through. After the fourth attempt, someone picked up the phone just to say that the prime minister's fax was out of order.

There was another person in Bratislava, who, I was told, knew as much about the kidnapping as Meciar himself, and possibly more. His name was Peter Toth and he was a young investigative journalist with *SME*, the daily newspaper of the Slovak opposition.

We agreed to meet in a small coffee shop near *SME*'s offices in the centre of Bratislava. I didn't know that seeing Peter would be like an excursion into my own past as an investigative journalist in the KGB-controlled Soviet Union.

Several tall men – all in dark glasses and with mobile phones – were hanging around the café's entrance. A couple of their twins were comfortably seated inside the semi-dark café, with their sunglasses still on. I couldn't help feeling that I was playing a role in a badly scripted spy movie.

Peter Toth was a handsome 25-year-old, with an open, intelligent face and velvety dark-brown eyes. He spoke good English.

Throwing furtive looks at the men in dark glasses, he said that he was used to these 'escorts', who had followed him everywhere ever since he started his coverage of the kidnapping case.

'These guys are OK. They simply tail me everywhere,

and it is enough to drive through a red light to shake them off,' he said with a smile. 'I have had much more unpleasant encounters. My phone is bugged. I was attacked and beaten up in the street. My wife had an anonymous phone call threatening her and our three-year-old son with something awful, if I didn't give up writing about this case. They tried to provoke me into committing a crime by using stooges who said to me that to get some exclusive information about the case I had to break into a private flat. Another provocateur offered me a gun. I refused . . . They also tried to sue me for defamation, whereas the only thing I am determined to do is uncover the truth.'

It sounded like an almost exact description of the trials I had to go through when investigating the Soviet mafia in Moscow in the late eighties. The methods of intimidating 'nosy parkers', used by secret services, are more or less the same all over the world and do not change with time.

'Why are they so worried about your writing?' I asked him.

'I was a close friend of Remias. Two hours before he died, he came to my flat and said that he was prepared to testify against Meciar. And my flat is bugged of course. So I became personally involved in the case, so to speak. His death showed me that this government was capable of anything, and I think it would be wrong to let them get away with it.'

Peter was the only person in Slovakia who did not look the other way and didn't try to hush me up, when I asked him, 'What do you think of Meciar?'

'Meciar takes politics very personally. He is a talented public speaker with the ability to touch the worst parts of the Slovak soul – here lies the secret of his appeal among certain groups of the population. He keeps saying that his aim is to turn Slovakia into a "Switzerland of Mitteleuropa". This could have been achieved, by the way, had it not been for Meciar himself, who is like Lenin, Hitler and Milosevic – all in one person. He is totally unable to take criticism and doesn't like freedom of expression. He is also a pathological liar, although I think he has reached the point when he has started believing his own lies.'

'What motivating force is behind his hatred of President Kovac?'

'Kovac used to be a member of Meciar's party. They are both former communists, but Kovac is able to evolve, whereas Meciar isn't. Their feud started when Kovac vetoed Meciar's nomination of his pal Lexa as the head of the SIS. After the veto, Meciar tried to appoint Lexa the minister of privatisation, but Kovac vetoed him again. Then Meciar changed the law, and presidential approval was no longer necessary – as usual, he had his way in the end. But Meciar never forgives. That's why he decided to stage Kovac's son's kidnapping. He wanted it to look as if Kovac Junior was kidnapped by his own mafia accomplices, but messed up the whole thing from the start. He couldn't even stage a kidnapping properly.'

'Does Meciar drink?'

'No, he is a teetotaller.'

Peter left the café without looking back at the men in dark glasses. Ten seconds after he disappeared, they put down the newspapers they had been pretending to read, and dashed after him, talking on their mobile telephones as they ran.

About a year later I learnt in London that Peter's car had been set on fire by unknown wrongdoers. This time – again – he escaped unhurt.*

---

* On 2 March 1998, after Michal Kovac's presidential term ended and parliament failed to choose a successor, Meciar grabbed presidential power and became Slovakia's effective dictator. Significantly, the first decision of the self-appointed President Meciar was to halt the prosecution of officials linked to the kidnapping of ex-President Kovac's son.

In the restaurant car of the train from Bratislava to Budapest, I got talking with a gay Canadian young man, who was travelling around Europe. Dressed in black leather pants and a black T-shirt, he was drinking beer and chain-smoking. A big white scar lay across his round, clean-shaven skull.

I asked him what he thought of Slovakia.

'I've only been to Bratislava,' he said waving his Gauloise-clutching hand. 'There I rented a room from a young woman who was a whore. For that, she was constantly told off by her religious mother, with whom she fought every day. Golly, how they fought! They would get drunk and start throwing crucifixes and pictures of Madonna at each other . . . I hate fights. I hate religion. I hate my mother, who is a fat Roman Catholic in Vancouver . . . As to Slovakia, I don't know . . . As I've just said, I've only been to Bratislava, where I didn't venture outside for once – just sat there and watched them drink and fight.'

He was literally fuming with angst (or was it just cigarette smoke?), this young Canadian traveller, who, by the way, was 25: the same age as Peter Toth.

And I suddenly thought that his impressions of Slovakia were amazingly correct and to the point, despite the fact that he had spent all his time stuck in his jolly rented flat amid a rowdy family quarrel.

'Just sat there and watched them drink and fight . . .'

22 THE LAST EIGHTEEN DROPS OF SPIRITS

Few things in life were capable of making my drinking supervisor Evgeny Bulavin as distraught as the sight of an empty vodka bottle. Having placed the 'dead bottle' horizontally on the table, like a perished valiant soldier laid to rest by his comrade-in-arms, he would watch its neck closely, trying to hypnotise it into filling up with vodka again. His theory was that, no matter how empty the bottle might seem, there were always eighteen drops of vodka left in it. After several minutes of silent grieving, he would lift the bottle from the table, turn it upside-down and shake it patiently over a glass. Miraculously, eighteen indolent vodka drops would indeed emerge from its neck one after another. Until now, I have not been sure why the number of the remaining drops was always the same – not sixteen, not nineteen, but invariably eighteen! You can check it yourselves, if in doubt. Some abstruse and yet undiscovered physical law must be hiding inside the empty bottle of vodka.

There are several things I want to pour out in my 'last eighteen drops of spirits'. The problem with the second part of this book, just as with the previous 'beer' one, was how to fit East Germany into it. The reason, as I have said once before, is that, probably due to their extremely confusing and ambivalent geo-political reality, the 'Ossies' prefer unlikely combinations of several drinks to any pure drink in particular. Or is it something to do with the Germans' innate love of tacky variety shows, like the one I saw at the famous Wintergarten Cabaret in West Berlin?

Whatever the reason, it does not mean that the traditional German *Schnaps* (or *Schnapps*, if you order a double – only joking) is totally out of the picture. In one of the trendiest new bars of East Berlin called VEB-Ost Zone, I tasted a popular 'post-communist' German *Schnaps*, Erichs Rache (Erich's Revenge), poured by the barman from a bottle with a portrait of the infamous East German communist leader Erich Honecker on the label. In full accordance with its name, the *Schnaps* was disgusting (it had to be). Yet the patrons of VEB-Ost Zone were masochistically drinking it in large quantities in an attempt to drown their nostalgia for communist times, or *Ostalgie*, as it had come to be known in the German press. (I joined the patrons in a toast to the health of Honecker and spilt my vodka remembering that he had been dead for several years.)

The interior of this peculiar watering hole in Oranienburger Strasse, a stone's throw from where the Wall used to be, deserves a proper description. Framed portraits of the bespectacled Erich Honecker and other leaders of the former German Democratic Republic adorned the walls. The patrons sat on wobbly bar stools, or in booths made from the back seats of old East German Trabant jalopies, affectionately nicknamed 'Trabbies'. They smoked Karo or Cabinet cigarettes, popular 'communist' brands which tasted (and smelt) of burnt rags. Sometimes, they mixed their *Schnaps* with Rotkäppchen ('Little Red Riding Hood'), a cheap GDR sparkling plonk, or with water, to form *Braunie*, another sickening East German concoction. This bar was like a theme park recreating the half-forgotten communist environment, for which lots of former 'Ossies' still seemed to be nostalgic (or 'ostalgic').*

The only sign of the changing times in VEB-Ost Zone was that it now had its own website on the Internet. Call me retrograde, but to a semi-computer literate person like myself, the purpose of this website remained obscure: why should anyone bother to access it? To have a virtual-reality drink? But isn't that like sending a pizza by fax?

There is no denying the fact that spirits continue to be enjoyed all over Eastern Europe, but only Poland and Russia remain pure and unshaken strongholds of pure and unshaken strong drinks. In 1997, a plastic pipe running beneath the border of Estonia and Latvia into Poland was discovered by border-guards. It was used for smuggling bootleg vodka.

Whereas in post-communist Poland they started building vodka distilleries on the grounds of former Soviet military bases, in no-less-post-communist Russia they went even further by building a vodka factory on the site of a former nuclear reactor in the city of Nizhni Novgorod. The vodka, which is distilled in the reactor's

---

* A similar theme park recreating a communist East German town, complete with crumbling apartment blocks, empty shops and Stasi agents on every corner, had been seriously considered by Berlin authorities, who had been planning to build it in the outskirts of the city to attract Western package tourists. The idea was that visitors would be accommodated in spartan 'socialist' flats and would do their own shopping in the barren stores for the duration of their tour, no matter what. Those who got fed up and decided to escape earlier, would be denounced by the 'Stasi informers' (played by specially hired actors), interrogated and even 'imprisoned' – until their vouchers expired, of course. The designers of the would-be park must have gone a bit too far in their imagination: the whole project was eventually dumped as too costly, unrealistic and lacking in taste. What a pity!

converted water filters (!), is in great demand in the city: sales figures show 1 million bottles of it sold every month (the population of Nizhni Novgorod is 1.5 million). The locals lovingly christened it 'Nemtsovka' after the city's popular mayor, Boris Nemtsov, who was later promoted by Yeltsin to become Russia's first deputy prime minister (I think I can guess why). They might just as well have called it 'Termoyadernaya' ('Thermonuclear') vodka, or even 'Chernobyl' vodka, which, I am sure, would have boosted the sales even further.

In all extremities, the spiritual qualities of vodka as the best available provider of brief escapes and temporary 'obliterations of reality' as long as there are people who need them (and in Eastern Europe they certainly do) remain both unchanged and unchallenged. The fact that I personally have given up drinking it does not in the least alter my unfailing appreciation of aqua vitae's unique and wondrous qualities.

I would like to finish our excursion to the Spirit Lands of Eastern Europe with a paragraph from *Story of a Life*, by my literary mentor (not to be confused with my drinking tutor), Konstantin Paustovsky, an incorrigible romantic and a brilliant stylist – never a heavy drinker himself, by the way.

As I drank the vodka I kept marvelling at its extraordinary property: my head remained quite light, but all the thoughts wandering about in it seemed to me as fresh as a young magnolia blossom . . . and as bright, and even perhaps as sticky to the touch, as a newly painted felucca. It was a wonderful feeling.

III: WINE LANDS

Hungary, Bulgaria and Romania, with a hint of East Germany

23 WINE LANDS BEGIN IN SOUTH RUISLIP

If my knowledge of vodka culture could be described as in-depth (both in theory and in practice), and my understanding of beer-drinking was more or less adequate, wine culture remained as remote, puzzling and unexplored as Lake Titicaca.

Not that I was totally unaware of wine's (or Lake Titicaca's, for that matter) existence. From my school times, I remembered some lines from Pushkin's *Eugene Onegin*: 'At first, these fated conversations/ between the wines, Cliquot, Lafite,/ were simply friendly altercations . . .' (Or was it 'revelations'? Something of the kind . . .)

Among other diluted images evoked by the word 'wine' was that of the head of my dead-drunk carousing supervisor Evgeny Bulavin resting on a restaurant table and calling out to the waitress: 'Another bottle of *sukhen'koye* ["little dry wine"], please!' Instead of bringing another bottle, she hit him on the head with a tray – and rightly so!

There was also a thing called Vino Bile Mitsne (in Ukrainian), which meant 'Strong White Wine', although 'strong' was the only true word on its label, for, in actual fact, it was just a cheap brownish plonk, popularly known as 'Biomedicine'. It was sold in huge missile-shaped bottles nicknamed 'fire-extinguishers', and was famous for its amazing ability to give you a severe hangover even before you started drinking it. Bio-medicine was popular among students, and among some of our university teachers, too. I remember that the first flesh-and-blood English person I ever saw – a female exchange-scheme teacher from Cornwall who was supposed to teach us English – got so addicted to Biomedicine that, in her own words, she had come to prefer it to all the Bordeaux and Burgundies of the world. Mysteriously, Biomedicine tended to improve her speech defect – a heavy stutter aggravated by a slur.

Then there was black, smelly Solntsedar, which translated as 'a gift of the sun', but in effect was a 'gift' of the Soviet chemical industry, which manufactured it from oil, coal and, possibly, nuclear waste. This 'wine' could be used successfully as an insecticide, as many of my bedbug-ridden friends testified. Its popular name was *bormotukha* – literally, 'the stuff which makes you mumble'.

The first ever wine, or rather 'wine', that I tried at the tender age of 16 was of the *bormotukha* family. It was called Lydia. I drank it with my classmate Sergei Sibartsev, an overgrown bully and a dunce, during a compulsory First of May demonstration. Having escaped from our school's festive procession, we sheltered in an empty boilerhouse, where we tried to open the bottle with our bare hands. To our dismay, it was firmly sealed with an unremovable plastic cork. After several futile attempts, we simply broke the neck by hitting the bottle against a brick and hastily – taking turns and cutting our tongues on the sharp edges – swigged the foul-smelling oily contents. Our tongues were sore for days afterwards. A modern wine critic could safely describe Lydia as 'having a cutting finish'.

Wine as such was never treated seriously in the Soviet

Union. Like beer, it was only good for curing hangovers and for 'polishing up' more serious reality-obliterating drinks (vodka, moonshine, eau-de-cologne, shampoo, etc). Also, it was always in short supply, especially during Gorbachev's anti-drinking campaign, when many vineyards in the south of Russia were axed and several prominent wine-makers committed suicide.

A well-known Moscow writer told me that he was once presented with a moss-covered bottle of an extremely old and indecently expensive vintage Bordeaux during a visit to France. Back in Moscow, he put the bottle in the fridge (!) and forgot about it. One day, he was entertaining some friends and decided to put the bottle on the table, but couldn't find it. After a while, his wife recalled that she had given the wine to the plumber, who had drunk the whole bottle after fixing the leaking toilet a couple of days before. The following morning, the writer confronted the plumber and asked him whether he had liked the wine. 'Crap!' the plumber replied. 'Sour and weak crap!' 'How did you drink it?' asked the writer. 'I downed one glass, then another, all in ten seconds – how else?'

When I worked as an interpreter for the Mitchell Beazley stand at the Moscow International Book Fair in 1979, I was presented with a copy of Hugh Johnson's *Pocket Wine Book*. With thousands of wine descriptions of the type 'Frascati Lat DOC w dr/sw (sp) DYA', for someone like myself, who had been aware of just two varieties of wine, Biomedicine and *bormotukha*, it was as informative and as exciting as a collection of Mao Tse-tung's quotations in Mandarin Chinese.

True, bits and pieces of wine culture were preserved in southern parts of the Soviet Union, in places like Georgia, Armenia, Moldavia (now Moldova) and in the south of Ukraine. My introduction to real wine culture occurred during a journalistic investigation in Moldavia, where I got a unique chance to visit the old wine cellars in Novie Maleshty. The 42-kilometre-long cellars were like an underground city, complete with streets, lanes and crossroads. 'Champagne Avenue', 'Port Wine Street', 'Cabernet Road', the dimly-lit plates stated. The streets were so wide that lorries drove freely along them. On both sides stood huge barrels, in which good Moldavian wines were maturing.

I was escorted by a local wine-maker, who had a professional wine-glass corn on the bridge of his nose, the result of years of intensive wine-tasting. He had a puffy purple face, which was the main symptom of 'winism' – a professional wine-makers' disease, as he explained. Looking back now, I am inclined to think that he was simply an alcoholic. But then I was very impressed.

At one point of the tour, my escort took me up to a solid wall, groped along its absolutely flat surface, then made a pressing movement. The wall slid open like a theatre curtain, revealing a spacious, brightly lit underground hall with chandeliers, parquet floor, a tiled fireplace and, in the centre of the room, an ornate fountain with goldfish. Elaborate wooden sculptures in an avant-garde style were scattered here and there, each one illuminated from underneath by a spotlight. There were several other rooms in that fairy-tale palace. In one of them stood a long table with exquisite Arabic chairs.

I went numb. 'What is this? A museum?' I asked my red-nosed guide when I regained the power of speech.

'No, this is the place where the party leaders of our republic receive their guests, taste Moldavian wines and throw banquets,' he explained.

It was then that I realised for the first time that drinks in the Soviet Union were stratified and segregated along the same lines as society as a whole. Having left the people to strive for oblivion with the help of vodka and cheap plonk, the Soviet rulers reserved the sophistication and subtlety of wine-drinking for themselves, simply because their reality was incomparably better and did not require any 'obliteration'. Stalin himself, being a Georgian, used to opt for good-quality Georgian wines (his favourites were white Khvanchkara and red Kindzmareuli), and left his minions and factotums to drink vodka, which he used literally to force down their throats. He especially enjoyed humiliating Molotov, his tame and cowardly foreign minister, who could not hold drink well, by making him gulp glass after glass in front of his obsequiously giggling Politburo 'comrades'.

There, in the cellars of Novie Maleshty, I came to understand that, apart from sugar and alcohol, drinks had significant social, and even political, contents.

When I found myself in Australia, one of the world's leading wine-making countries, I couldn't help noticing how differently wine was perceived there. The newspaper for which I worked employed a bunch of cheerful and ruddy-faced wine critics. How someone could write about nothing but wine and still call himself a journalist was beyond my comprehension. Fresh from the Soviet Union with its never-ending hardship and tragedy, I solemnly promised never to write about either food or drink. The promise soon shrank under the pressure of the all-permeating hedonism of the Australian society, and less than a year later I became a regular contributor to the newspaper's sixteen-page Epicure section. And here I am – more than half-way through a book on drinks and drinking.

My new 'mates', Australian hacks, would happily consume a couple of bottles of wine each during an ordinary lunch (as long as it was on expenses, of course; otherwise they went for beer). It was with their help that I discovered that wine was an extremely image-oriented product. At one of those journalistic lunches a bottle of South African red wine appeared on the table. It was in 1991, and apartheid was still alive and well. 'I won't touch this racist wine with a bargepole,' one of the hacks noted angrily. 'Why not? After all, this wine is not white, it is rather black,' I objected sincerely, pointing at the bottle. The fact that wine could be 'racist' was quite a revelation to me (and still is).

Shortly after apartheid came to an end, the same South African wine became a best-seller in Oz.

Once, my newspaper sent me to South Australia. Without consulting me, the local tourist board arranged a tour of five Barossa Valley wineries – all in one day. On the night before the tour, I had an attack of stomach ulcer. The fit was so nasty that while visiting the wineries on the following day I had to forgo the tastings. When at the last winery I asked for a can of Coke to quench my thirst, the owner nearly fell off the mini-tractor on which he was driving me around his vineyards.

To be honest, even without my ulcer, I wouldn't have enjoyed tasting the wines anyway. My taste-buds were ruined almost beyond repair by vodka, pure alcohol and *bormotukha*-style Soviet 'wines'. In my mind, I kept comparing drinking vodka to flying a Qantas jet, which brought you to your destination (of temporary oblivion and near-bliss) smoothly and on time, whereas drinking wine was like embarking on a long, bumpy and congested Aeroflot flight, during which you never knew when you would arrive and whether you would arrive at all.

Living in Britain, a country which *The Oxford Companion to Wine* calls 'one of the most fastidious, yet open-minded, wine-consuming nations', I got the impression that I was constantly surrounded by wine connoisseurs of the highest calibre. At parties and lunches, my British friends and contacts took genuine pleasure in sniffing wine, swirling it in their glasses, 'allowing it to breathe' and making loud slurping sounds with their lips before swallowing it. As I came to realise, many of them, rather than being connoisseurs, were 'wine snobs', trying to camouflage their dipsomania by pretending they cared about what they drank. One of them was a compulsive eater, who used to measure sausages by metres ('I ate half a metre of sausages for breakfast'). He drank wine in large quantities in between courses 'to clear his palate', as he would put it. He queried waiters about the vintage with the same ardour KGB interrogators used when questioning suspected dissidents. He sniffed the cork and dutifully swirled the wine in his glass, only to gulp it down greedily before biting into a sausage.

Examples of wine snobbery were numerous. A businessman who paid £4,950 for a bottle of 1985 Romanée-Conti. A case of Château Petrus sold for £22,848 at Sotheby's. I learnt of the existence of the National Correspondence of Corkscrew Addicts organisation (NCCA), whose members wrote letters to each other on a single subject: which corkscrews were the best for opening wine bottles. And once in Fortnum & Mason I saw on sale a CD entitled *The Sound of Wine*, on which the fermenting noises of fourteen different wines were recorded. What a productive pastime: to sit in an armchair listening to the melodious noises of wine fermentation! It was hard not to agree with the American authors of a useful and witty book, *Wine for Dummies*, the first book on wines that I acquired for myself: 'In some parts of the world, people have a very interesting attitude toward wine. They just drink it.'

Britain certainly belongs to a different part of the world, where people prefer talking and writing about wine, even listening to it, and thinking of themselves as ultimate wine experts. Actual drinking does not matter. But it is next to impossible to find a person prepared to confess his (or her) ignorance in matters of wines and wine-making (they would be more willing to confess to not remembering the prime minister's name). I was probably the only one . . .

I realised that prior to heading for the Wine Lands of Eastern Europe, I had to get some nitty-gritty on wine culture and wine in general. In search of enlightenment, I started looking through the Food and Drink pages of London broadsheets, but ended up even more confused by such descriptive eulogies to wines as 'Best served chilled on a balmy midsummer morning with a fresh peach or apricot' (it was probably the wine critic himself who went 'barmy' on a 'midsummer morning'); 'has remarkably fine weave of pure silk, flavours form a pastel fresco of tones and tint'; and 'A faint whiff of gunsmoke gives this stylish, pretty sylph of a wine some of the complexity that unoaked Chardonnay yearns so longingly for'. Reading this last, I yearned longingly to get hold of a device that produced real gunsmoke and to aim it at the sylph-obsessed wine writer.

Having despaired of learning from broadsheets, I turned my attention to specialist magazines, of which there were two, *Decanter* and *Wine*, at my local W.H. Smith.

The glossy *Decanter* opened with a column entitled 'Michael Broadbent's Tasting Notes Number 228': 'Having long since become somewhat bored with the ubiquitous Sauvignon Blanc and Chardonnay, and to a lesser extent with unblended Cabernet Sauvignons, I now observe that in some quarters the reaction is in full swing.' I immediately got bored to quite a large (and totally unblended) extent. I had a similar sensation at the first university lecture in logic which I had bothered to attend (it was the last one in the course, by the way): I could understand each separate word of the lecturer, but when these words were brought together into a sentence, they became meaningless and mildly intimidating.

Wine also opened with a column: 'Recently, I met a Belgian who wanted to buy some Le Pin 1982. The trouble is he couldn't afford it – just like almost everyone else, except the Far Eastern collectors who are currently snapping it up wherever they find it.' At least it was clear and down-to-earth. After some hesitation, I rang up Susan Low, the editor of *Wine*, and made an appointment. I was slightly puzzled by the fact that the offices of the magazine were in South Ruislip.

Getting to South Ruislip was almost as complicated as getting to Liechtenstein. The journey on the Central Line of the London Underground seemed endless. Soon I was the only passenger left in the carriage: no one else in the world had any business in South Ruislip on that particular Tuesday afternoon.

The suburb where I finally arrived did not look like London – or England, for that matter. Its windswept and deserted streets were lined with hangars, store-houses and ugly American-style shopping malls. I had a ticklish and unsettling feeling of being abroad without a proper visa.

'Toilets will be closed from 10 February 1992. London Borough of Hillingdon', ran a sign near the Tube station. It was July 1996, and toilets were still closed. They were probably closed for ever. But it was reassuring to know that I was still in London.

I was able to locate the *Wine* offices by the dozen or so empty wine bottles displayed in its windows.

Susan Low was a young and attractive lady. She was also extremely busy and could only spare me a couple of minutes. Besides, she couldn't offer many tips as to the wines of Eastern Europe. 'The problem with that part of the world is that the quality of wines is extremely uneven,' she said. 'You can have an excellent wine in one place and an absolutely awful one next door – simply because they forgot to wash the bottles properly.'

'Just like everything else in Eastern Europe,' I wanted to say, but Mrs Low looked so busy that I decided not to waste her precious vintage time on having to listen to the frivolous comments of a wine-ignoramus, like myself. And then she said something that I was extremely pleased to hear: 'In Britain, wine has been made too complicated, so, maybe, in Eastern Europe you will be able to discover it for yourself in all its beautiful simplicity.'

Walking back to the Tube station – past warehouses and rubbish dumps – I suddenly realised that my travels to the Wine Lands of Eastern Europe had started there, in South Ruislip, a part of London which didn't look like London, but had a distinctive East European touch.

24 IGOR'S NITTY-GRITTY

My long and dangerous journey from Muswell Hill to South Ruislip had not achieved much, apart from kick-starting my exploration of East European Wine Lands. I definitely needed some more nitty-gritty about wine and wine culture, and no one was better qualified to provide it than my good friend Igor Pomerantsev, a poet, a novelist, a radio journalist and the first and only Russian wine-writer in existence.

An émigré of more than twenty years' standing, he used to be the head of the London bureau of the Munich-based Radio Liberty/Radio Free Europe. In 1995, the US Congress, which had supported this excellent radio station since its foundation, drastically cut its funds on the grounds that, due to the end of the Cold War, its services were no longer in great demand. The station had to abandon its costly Munich headquarters; it relocated to Prague on the kind invitation of President Vaclav Havel, who had been an avid listener to Radio Free Europe during his dissident years.

I decided to catch up with Igor in Prague on the way to Hungary. We agreed to meet at Radio Liberty's new offices in the former parliament building in Vaclavske Namesti.

'This is not the entrance to the State Opera,' said the strict sign at the radio station's front door. And it wasn't. I was going to the offices of Radio Liberty with some inner trepidation. And not just because I used to be the station's Australian correspondent. The memories of my brief visit to its Munich headquarters in 1992 were still fresh. Then, the station had occupied considerable territory in the prestigious English Garden area. The complex was surrounded by a massive concrete fence with barbed wire and security cameras on top: a thorn in the side of the communist rulers, Radio Liberty was considered a likely target for KGB terrorist attacks. My pass had to be ordered a week in advance, and the guards only agreed to let me in after a thorough examination and extensive questioning.

Times had certainly changed since then. Radio Liberty's new headquarters in Prague looked like an ordinary East European office. Instead of armed guards, an elderly babushka-like charwoman was knitting in the lobby under a key-rack. She didn't bother to look up as I went inside through a rotating turnstile.

Igor invited me to attend an editorial meeting, which was relaxed and convivial: journalists were discussing the broadcasting schedule for the day and exchanging the latest Yeltsin jokes. In an extraordinary twist, Radio Liberty's broadcasts, which used to be severely jammed and could be received only at crazy hours of the night in the old Soviet Union, were now retransmitted by several dozen Russian radio stations.

In the evening, Igor took me for dinner to a restaurant in the Palffy House, an eighteenth-century baroque palace in Mala Strana. It was one of his favourite drinking haunts in Prague. To begin with, he ordered a bottle of white Bohemian wine.

'In the Czech Republic, which has an Austrian wine culture, you can only drink white wine,' he remarked, sniffing the cork which the white-aproned waiter (Pan Vrkhny, alias Mr Upper) put on the table in front of him.

'Bohemian white table wines are sort of OK, not sweet like German ones. The Czech climate – rainy and cloudy – is good for them,' he noted, before emptying his glass in one gulp. Having intercepted my stunned glance, he explained: 'Table wines should be gulped. Besides, I felt very thirsty, and table wine is like water. Good table wine should be democratic, simple and elegant, without an aquiline nose, so to speak. I drank such wines in northern Italy and in Turkey. Turkish table wines are amazingly fresh.'

I followed Igor's example and gulped down my glass.

'But don't you ever drink Czech red wines, which are bland and talentless, although not immoral,' he continued.

'Immoral wines?' I asked in disbelief.

'Yes.'

'What wines can you classify as immoral?'

'Cheap supermarket ones which destroy the very tissue of wine. They are semi-dead – like pulp fiction, or like badly translated poetry. The wholesale wine trade kills the quality. Also, German sweet whites, which represent the biggest fiasco in the history of wine-making. They stand for unadulterated kitsch. I had to leave Germany, where I had lived for several years, because I could not stand their wines. They were so monstrous that I could hardly believe my tongue. Yes, they are popular, because the masses love kitsch, not just in wines but in poetry, music and other forms of art.' He pointed at the excessively ornate walls of the room where we were sitting.

'How come you, a carrier of Russian culture, became a wine expert and a wine-drinker?' I asked Igor.

'Russian culture? What is it? It is the culture of Dostoevskian epilepsy, in which everything is achieved through pain and suffering. Masochistic to its very core,

it is about achieving happiness through constant misery
. . . I grew up in western Ukraine, to where I was brought
from Siberia as a child. My mother was a Russian, my
father a Jew from Odessa – an interesting cocktail. My
grandad was a "*tseloval'nik*" ["a kisser"]; he had his
own wine shop. Wine and vodka shop owners were
called "kissers", because they were supposed to kiss the
tsar's seal on the licence allowing them to trade in
alcohol. Western Ukraine, where I grew up, used to be
part of the Austro-Hungarian empire. It was a semi-
forgotten Atlantis on Soviet territory. Mediterranean in
spirit, it was resplendent with colour, apples, pears,
wines. We didn't drink vodka there, we went to wine
cellars. We preferred Kafka to vodka.'

'How do you differentiate between wine culture and
vodka culture?'

'Wine is the sun, the earth and the grape. Vodka is a
volatile sperm of a nation. It is a shock, an aggression,
an epileptic attack, a blow below the belt. Drinking in
Russia often ends up in scuffles and ugly fights –
something that rarely happens in wine countries like
Italy or France. Vodka culture is the culture of spasm
and hysteria. It is happiness through nausea and disgust.
No one in his right mind can claim that vodka is tasty.
This is why it is gulped, not sipped. It is only the uncultured West Europeans who sip vodka, which shows
their lack of understanding of vodka culture. Wine, on
the other hand, is gradualness, enjoyment, delight. It is
happiness through happiness. It does not lead to
oblivion, but provides communication along horizontal,
rather than vertical, lines. Good wine is like blotting
paper: it absorbs you into its own life, it flows smoothly
and unhurriedly from one soul into another like sand in
a sand-glass. It has its own history and its own memory
– the memory of the soil, the memory of the vine, the
memory of the grape. It has its own distinctive culture,
as ancient as that of poetry or dance. "Wine ennobles
human faces", as a poet once put it.'

'How about beer?'

'Beer culture is anal – that's all I can say.'

We ordered another bottle of wine.

'Look at my wine glass,' said Igor. 'Isn't it beautifully shaped? It is not by chance that a wine glass is designed to resemble an overturned church dome. In Christianity, the dome symbolised conciliarism. For me, drinking wine is like praying, or like reading poetry. This is why I see no harm in drinking, say, half a bottle of a classic Bordeaux on my own. It is a serious occupation. I fully concentrate on the wine, which, for me, is not an accompaniment to music but music itself. It is like discovering the world, like a long-awaited tryst of two lovers – a drinker and a wine.'

'Do you think that after years of drinking rubbish I still stand a chance of learning to appreciate wine?' I asked Igor.

'I don't know,' he replied after a protracted sip from his glass.

I thought that he was reluctant to upset me – like a doctor who looks for a suitable euphemism to soften the diagnosis of a terminal illness. We were now drinking red wine (not the 'immoral' Bohemian one, God forbid), which was supposed to be sipped.

'It may be too late for you, Vitali,' Igor said gravely. 'Your taste-buds might have been irreparably ruined. One has to be born with them, and to nurture them all his life. They require constant exercising, like muscles. You have to train your tongue, your palate, your alveoli. There is only one way to understand wine, and that is to drink it. To drink as much as you can – the more the better. For this understanding, one often has to pay with a ruined liver, with a malfunctioning heart and brain. I have spent my whole life trying to achieve it. Now I drink no less than half a litre of wine a day. Sometimes more. For me, it is like a daily portion of happiness. When I was researching my novel *The Basque Dog* – the first Russian novel about wines – I had to go to Spain and stayed there for three months, drinking. It was a high-risk zone. I ended up with bad liver-poisoning and had to go on a strict diet for weeks afterwards. But, despite this, I still insist that the secret of understanding wine lies in drinking lots and lots of it.'

'Do you think that wine-making is an art? Or is it just an industry, a technological trade?'

'It is an art which includes technology. The technology of wine-making is as old as wine itself. Ancient Greeks used to add sea-water and marble powder to their wines as preservatives before transporting them. Louis Pasteur worked hard at finding better ways to keep the qualities of wine intact for as long as possible. Or take the invention of the barrel. It was a real technological revolution. History has shown more than once that those wine-makers who neglect technology end up as losers.'

'What's your opinion of all these wine critics, wine gurus and wine experts claiming to possess the ultimate authority in the matters of wine and wine-making? How genuine are they?'

'I respect Hugh Johnson, the American wine writer. There are hundreds of real connoisseurs in Britain, but many more latent alcoholics who camouflage their illness by rituals – all these glass-twirlings, sniffings, drink-red-wine-with-meat, drink-white-wine-with-fish and other nonsense. They are totally meaningless. The club of real wine connoisseurs is an open house. Anyone who knows the password can enter it. And this password is in one's tongue.'

It was past midnight when we left the Palffy House and – a bit unsteadily – started trudging down the hill towards the Charles Bridge. The bubbles of city lights, mixed with the stars, were blinking and bursting merrily down below, like the exquisite champagne of the night spilt from the overturned glasses of church domes on to the black table-cloth of the Prague sky. On our way down, we were able to taste that truly divine drink.

We parted at a taxi rank. I had to go to the railway station to catch the last train to Budapest. Igor took a cab home to the Prague suburb of Vinohrady – which is Czech for 'grapes'.

25 'BRUDERSCHAFT' SNEEZING IN BUDAPEST

Budapest has a great deal of trade with ships up the river, which bring them many things from foreign countries. I cannot tell you how much they value a piece of English cloth, or even a paper of English needles!

Near Home or Europe Described,
Longmans, Green, & Co., London, 1910

'Ah-tishoo!' I was woken by my own sneeze and realised, with horror, that I had flu. I looked out of the window. It was early morning. My train, the Pannonia Express, was stationary. There was a sign with a frightening word, 'Szekesfehervar', in front of me. A station name like that could exist only in one country: Hungary.

With an effort, I remembered that the night before I had been drinking with Igor in the Palffy House; that I had then dashed around Prague Central Station in search of a pharmacy (I could feel a cold approaching) and failed to find one; that the unending passport controls had kept me from sleeping during the night as the train was crawling across the brand-new East European borders, from the Czech Republic into Slovakia and then into Hungary.

I recalled that at 3 a.m. a Slovak border-guard, a slim young woman in baggy uniform and with a gun

dangling from her belt, asked me in Russian to translate
to a visa-less Australian in the next carriage that he had
to pay the fine. I enquired whether I would be eligible for
the Meciar Cross, Slovakia's highest award (invented by
me), for that and advised her to shoot the recalcitrant
Aussie straight from her lovely hip (I didn't remember
whether I had said the last five words out loud).

Later, the Australian, who had eventually agreed to
cough up, came to my compartment to complain (and
woke me up again). He was red-eyed and dishevelled,
and had the peculiar disgruntled look of a man who had
just been mugged. I tried to comfort him by saying that
he was lucky not to have been shot, according to my
advice.

'Ah-tishoo!' My nose was blocked. An uninterrupted
buzzing noise from the headphones, which I wasn't
wearing, resounded in my clogged ears. A didgeridoo
was playing inside my brick-heavy head. I felt dizzy,
queasy and uneasy. Evgeny Bulavin used to like having
colds, because, he asserted, they made him feel as if he
was drunk. I might have enjoyed my cold, too, had it not
been for several days of intensive wine-tasting which lay
ahead of me. In this condition, I couldn't tell a Bordeaux
from a *bormotukha* (to be honest, I was not sure
whether I could have done that even if completely
healthy).

I asked an attendant for some Panadol pills. He was
Hungarian and didn't understand: the word for Panadol
was probably not dissimilar to 'Szekesfehervar' in
Hungarian – the mind-boggling Finno-Ugric language,
in which *'ugly'* means 'galoshes'.

At Keleti, the main station of Budapest, I was greeted by
a lanky young man in a baseball cap, a driver from the
Tourism Bureau.

'A-ah-tishoo!' he sneezed, shaking my hand.

'Ah-tishoo!' I replied.

'My name is Attila,' he said.

'What?' I asked, thinking that he had sneezed again.

'Attila,' he repeated. 'Like Attila the Hun – ah-tishoo! Sorry, I have a cold.'

'It makes two of us. At least we won't infect each other. Let's sneeze *"Bruderschaft"*,' I suggested.

We decided to go to one of Europe's most famous cafés, Budapest's Café New York, for a welcome-to-Hungary drink. Having squeezed ourselves into Attila's battered Suzuki, we drove off, all three of us (including the Suzuki) constantly sneezing.

Like his distant ancestor and namesake, the legendary Hunnish king, nicknamed 'the Scourge of God' by his contemporaries, Attila was a bit of a daredevil. If Attila the Hun was notorious for his belligerence, grim disposition and reckless horse-riding, Attila the Hungarian was the wildest car-driver I had ever come across.

'I am taking you along the same road that our president normally travels,' he told me proudly in his amazingly good American English (he had spent a year in the USA), swerving his jalopy to the right and nearly hitting a traffic policeman. I was sincerely hoping that the incumbent Hungarian president, Arpad Goncz, was not travelling along his favourite road at the same time as we were: all wine-tastings were likely to be cancelled if Hungary was suddenly thrown into several days of national mourning.

Attila's driving was such that, for the first time in years, I rejoiced in having grey hair: had it not been grey already, it would have certainly gone snow-white after a ride in his Suzuki. He took short-cuts across parks, street pavements and shopping malls. He zig-zagged through the narrow lanes of Buda, the old town. He would stop in the middle of a busy thoroughfare for a chat with his 'university mate'. Besides, he kept talking non-stop on his mobile phone, letting go of the wheel and gesticulating wildly with both hands.

'To drive in Budapest, you need fast reactions and

smartness,' he told me, chasing an old lady with shopping bags along the pavement. The lady was waddling away from his barmy Suzuki with the speed of a hurricane.

'Honk! Why don't you *honk* at her?' I screamed.

'I never beep at pedestrians. The police do not allow beeping in the city,' he replied calmly.

'But they obviously don't mind running over old ladies,' I thought.

When we stopped near a pharmacy to buy us some Panadol (I noted with fiendish satisfaction that the Hungarian word for pharmacy was '*gyogyszertar*'), Attila triple-parked his car in such a way that it blocked three lanes of moving traffic, which came to a halt and became honking traffic for all the ten minutes we spent at the pharmacy. Attila listened to the honking with unhidden delight, as if it was the famous 'Faust' Symphony by the great Hungarian composer Ferenc List.

'In Budapest, you can park anywhere. I normally park on the pavement,' he explained.

Indeed, all the places on the pavement near the pharmacy had already been taken by mechanical stallions driven by other wild descendants of the lugubrious king of the Huns.

When we were crossing the impressive Erzebet Bridge, I looked down and was upset to see that the water in 'the blue Danube' was actually not blue but brown. 'They add paint to the water to make it blue during festivals and national celebrations,' Attila reassured me, narrowly avoiding a head-on collision with a tram.

The dreary Soviet-style façades and formerly grand *fin-de-siècle* boulevards of Pest, Budapest's newer area, which, surprisingly, was much more run-down than its older part, Buda, were – like the Danube – in need of repainting. They were somewhat animated by the newly erected advertising cylinders, covered with ads for Marlboro and Pepsi.

'Hungary is the only country in the world where the sales of Pepsi are almost as high as those of Coca-Cola, and their competition is fierce,' said Attila.

According to him, Pepsi targeted Budapest trams and covered them with its logo. In retaliation, Coca-Cola had set its sights on the historic graffiti-ridden Chain Bridge, having offered to scrub it clean and replace graffiti with Coca-Cola ads and decorations.

'Can it be that an explanation for the brown waters of the "blue Danube" lies in this unscrupulous rivalry?' I thought, remembering that blue was the 'official' Pepsi colour. I wouldn't have been particularly surprised to learn that it was indeed Coca-Cola which – in an advertising frenzy – had repainted the great European river brown. If so, the Pepsi manufacturers could console themselves with the fact that when Coke first went on sale in China under the name Ke-kou-ke-la, it turned out that in some Chinese dialects this means 'female horse stuffed with wax'.

I was a bit wary of Budapest restaurants and cafés. My fears had been triggered by multiple stories in London newspapers about the large-scale fleecing of foreign visitors by charging them thousands of dollars for no more than modest meals and drinks. Four Danish tourists were, reportedly, presented with a bill for a million forints (£3,400) – enough to buy a nice new car in Hungary (which was probably their waiter's dream) – for a humble non-alcoholic dinner at a Budapest restaurant. 'These are our night prices. We charge what the market will bear,' the restaurant manager explained. Even if the market could bear it, the determined, cold-blooded Danes could not. Their complaint led to an investigation, the subsequent closure of several dozen 'guilty' restaurants and an official warning by the US embassy in Budapest, urging Americans 'to beware cafes and night-clubs where bills can require a second mortgage'. (As to non-Americans, the embassy did not seem to mind them being robbed.) A useful tip from the Union of Hungarian Restaurateurs was that 'a good meal in a Budapest restaurant should not cost more than £5 (about 1,600 forints)'. What exactly they meant by 'a good meal' remained a mystery. What if the meal was 'very good', or (improbably) 'excellent'? Clearly, Hungarians were taking the words 'free market' at their face value. Or maybe, in accordance with the old Hungarian saying 'We are poor but we live well', they were all desperate to get themselves new cars?

The other sign of the emerging Hungarian qualms-free market was the introduction of package dental tours of Budapest, which had received a lot of publicity in Britain. Prices started at £175 for three nights including flight, hotel, a consultation with a dentist and examination. If the dentist thought treatment was necessary (it was highly unlikely that he would determine otherwise), a tourist had to cough up a further £280 for dentures and a mere £22 to have a tooth extracted. In between filling and drilling sessions, guided tours of Budapest were offered to the travellers (or rather to the patients) – for an additional price of course. In short, anyone subscribing to these package holidays, which were sinisterly advertised as 'dental breaks', faced the cheerful prospect of returning to his home country not only broke but also toothless.

It was 11 a.m., and the Café New York in Andrassy Street was half empty: the breakfast patrons had already left and the early lunchers had not turned up yet. The *belle époque* interior of the place was grand: mirrors, columns, chandeliers, furniture of polished mahogany. It reminded me of the famous casino at Monte Carlo. I hoped that the resemblance stopped there and that having a drink at the Café New York wouldn't be much of a gamble: unlike some wealthy Americans, I couldn't afford a second mortgage. To be honest, I couldn't afford the first one either.

We sat down at a heavy dark-wood table and swallowed a couple of Panadols each before reaching for the menus.

'Czechs have beer in their veins, Austrians coffee, and Hungarians – wine!' Attila chanted nasally (his nose was as firmly blocked as mine).

He was probably right, for even the weather forecast in one of Budapest's English-language weeklies, which I had read on the train, contained the following advice: 'Sunday will be partly cloudy again with occasional showers. We'd recommend warming some wine.'

But the idea of what Attila's driving might be like when he was drunk was so terrifying that it defied contemplation.

'I would rather you be an Austrian just for now,' I muttered.

A tuxedo-clad waiter-boy, who was 15 (we had asked him) but looked 11, brought us coffee and bread, but no butter.

'We don't serve butter before dinner,' he explained.

The coffee was excellent and fully corresponded to the Hungarian proverb 'Coffee should be black like the devil, hot like hell, and sweet like a kiss.' A group of chain-smoking young girls sat in the corner, living proof of the fact that Hungary is the eighth heaviest smoking nation in the world, and every statistical Hungarian smokes 3177 cigarettes a year, slightly fewer than an average resident of the United Arab Emirates (3218), but more than a happy citizen of the world's wealthiest state, Brunei (3158). In front of our eyes, the girls were quickly approaching their annual smoking quotas.

At the turn of the century, the New York was the liveliest of Budapest's four hundred cafés and one of the best in the whole of the Austro-Hungarian Empire. On its opening day, a group of satisfied customers threw its key into the Danube so that it would stay open day and night. In 1910–30 it became the favourite haunt of Budapest literati. Struggling Budapest writers scribbled away on the free paper provided by the café. A special (and fairly frugal) 'writer's platter', consisting of cold meat, cheese and bread, was the most popular item on the menu. Here, the aspiring authors could also catch up on the latest news, for the café proudly stocked 'all the dailies and arts journals of the world'. Writers were followed by journalists (after all, as one of my Moscow friends used to say, a writer is a journalist who can't get his copy into print), and some of Budapest's best-known newspapers and magazines were edited in the café's first-floor gallery.

Among the café's old-timers was Ferenc Molnar, the renowned Hungarian playwright of Jewish origin. In the New York, he had his favourite chair, in which he would sit for hours, drinking coffee and writing. After the 1938 Anschluss, when neighbouring Austria was annexed by Germany and got fully incorporated into Hitler's Reich, a friend asked Molnar, who was sitting in his beloved café New York chair: 'Ferenc, aren't you afraid? Why don't you save yourself by emigrating to America?' 'It is easy to emigrate to America,' replied Molnar, 'but it is difficult to get up from this chair.'

After the Second World War, the New York became a shoe-shop before re-opening as a café in 1954, two years prior to the Soviet military invasion, as a result of which real writers disappeared from the café (and from Hungary in general) for many years to come. The New York survived the thirty-two years of Janos Kadar's rule, popularly known as 'goulash communism', when certain economic freedoms, unheard of in other Soviet-bloc states, were preserved by the cunning communist leader. Nowadays, some of the writers have returned to the New York. And although the 'literary waiters' of the '20s and '30s, who used to call all their clients by their first names and read all their works, had vanished for good, the café still boasted a 'literary toilet attendant', a well-read elderly lady, who did not charge her favourite writers for the use of her vital facility. She did charge me, but that was probably because she didn't know English and hence hadn't had a chance to read any of my books.

In the ante-room of the café's grand literary toilet, I picked up a promotional leaflet saying, 'Welcome to Budapest. Congratulations! You are in the right place at the wrong time – but that's our job!' This reminded me not just of the peculiar Hungarian sense of humour but also of another place that I wanted to see in Budapest, a place which was closely connected with the caustic and self-deprecating Hungarian wit.

A couple of months before my trip to Hungary, several London newspapers had run a story about a certain Ferenc Kovacs, who had opened the world's first and only joke shop in Budapest. The shop was aimed at relieving the famous Hungarian depression and pessimism. According to the papers, the entrepreneurial Kovacs charged 3 forints (1.5p) for making a customer smile, 7 forints for provoking a grin, 9 for a chuckle, and 12 (plus VAT) for making one laugh one's pants off.

There was even an example of a 9-forint joke: 'A policeman is shaving in the bathroom, when his wife comes in. "You have cut yourself, darling," she says. "I know," replies the policeman. "I did it deliberately when you came in, just so I know where to start again when you leave."'

The joke shop (reportedly) sold musical condoms with the choice of two tunes – an old communist song called 'Arise, You Red Proletarian' and 'You Sweet Little Dumbbell' – which played as the condom was unrolled.

'What does a joke shop, with all these singing condoms, have in common with exploring Hungarian wines?' you might ask. The connection is both simple and logical. Hungarian Panadol didn't seem to work, and since the next day I had to be ready for the wine-tasting in the Tokaji region, I had to get rid of my cold by hook or by crook. And nothing cures a cold as efficiently as a good laugh.

Unfortunately, the papers did not give the address of the joke shop, and the street-wise Attila expressed total ignorance not just of its whereabouts but of its very existence, too. He rang several of his friends at the Tourism Bureau on his mobile, but none of them had ever heard of either Ferenc Kovacs or his joke shop, which only increased my desire to find it.

In Attila's faithful Suzuki we combed the whole of central Budapest. Several times we whooshed past the newly reopened Great Synagogue, Europe's largest, in Dohany Street. Every two minutes, Attila would jump out of the car and start questioning passers-by about the joke shop and Kovacs Ferenc.* The pedestrians only shook their shoulders, and one of them remarked in truly Hungarian fashion, 'You can pay me, and I'll tell you a joke!'

Having quadruple-parked the car in the middle of a pedestrian crossing, we began door-knocking, but the result was the same: the residents of Budapest had never heard of Ferenc Kovacs – sorry: Kovacs Ferenc – and/or his joke shop.

After a couple of hours, it dawned on me that the joke shop had never existed, and the whole idea, fed to gullible and news-hungry British journalists who had spread it all over the UK without checking, was but a product of the elusive Kovacs Ferenc's imagination and his typically Hungarian sense of humour. At this point, I burst out laughing. Soon I was joined by Attila. We laughed our pants off until we both stopped abruptly, having realised that we had just earned Kovacs Ferenc 24 forints plus VAT.

Late in the afternoon, Attila dropped me at Honved Hotel in Pest. He was to come back tomorrow morning

---

* In Hungarian, not only are prepositions added on to the end of the words, but last – family – names precede first ones, which would make me into 'Vitaliev Vitali' and, say, Boutros Boutros Gali into 'Gali Boutros Boutros'.

to give me a lift back to Keleti station, from where I was to take a train to Tokaji.

My room was filthy, and the bathroom sink was blocked. 'Our Hotel is taking care on [*sic*] environment' said a sign on one of the dirty, fly-stained walls with peeling wallpaper. 'Not *on* its own environment though,' I thought ruefully.

The hotel restaurant was closed, which was probably for the best.

'There is a good restaurant nearby,' said the receptionist. 'It is called the Goldfish.'

The area around the hotel was unkempt and run-down. The familiar Ikarus buses (we had plenty of them in the Soviet Union) rattled past me nonchalantly as I trudged along the rugged pavement trying to spot any place that distantly resembled a restaurant called the Goldfish. It was hopeless. For a good ten minutes I stood in front of a sign saying 'Kerjuka Kaput Belsukni', trying to guess what on earth it could mean.*

The only readable sign in the vicinity was above a chocolate shop. 'Bon Bon Hemingway', it said in English. I thought that Hemingway himself would not have been pleased to see a shop selling chocolates, not booze, named after him.

I finally located the Goldfish, having spotted a picture of a fish in its window (how very clever!). You will never guess what its name looked like in Hungarian: 'Aranigal Vendeglo'.

Sitting in the cosy, small restaurant surrounded by locals, whose language remained a total enigma for me, I was slurping a hot and spicy fish soup (good for my sore throat). Everything was fine until I asked the waiter

---

* In reproducing Hungarian words, I deliberately omit accents above the vowels: nearly all Hungarian vowels are accented, and all the accents are different. So – just as in other parts of this book – I decided to take pity on its British typesetters, and on the readers, too.

for a bottle of mineral water. To be on the safe linguistic side, I said it in four languages: 'mineral water' in English, 'mineralnaya voda' in Russian, 'l'eau minérale' in French, and even – God knows why – 'aqua minerale' in Italian. The waiter nodded and promptly brought me . . . a Hungarian newspaper, which I couldn't read, let alone drink.

I slept badly during the night. Cockroaches rustled matter-of-factly behind the peeling wallpaper. The blocked bathroom sink stank. At about 3 a.m. I was woken up by the sound of bursting fireworks from behind the window. Next morning, the receptionist told me that those were Michael Jackson's fans celebrating after his concert at Budapest's Nepstadion – the same music-loving fans who later that day smashed the windows of a record store where the king of pop was shopping. The Great Friend of Children (especially boys) did not want to leave me alone on my East European journeys. Could it be that he had somehow come to fancy me and was following me around?

I got up at 6 a.m. My cold was no better. In fact, it had got worse. My nose which had been firmly, almost bathroom-sink-like, blocked the day before, was now – unlike the sink – running (God knows where to) and flooding me with snot.

Ten minutes later Attila rang up to say that he was not coming, because – surprise, surprise – he had had a car accident the night before. He was calling from a hospital, but assured me that he was OK – a broken leg and a couple of bruises, that was all. From the way he sounded, it was plain that his cold had not improved either.

'Get well soon! Ah-tishoo!' I said.

'Ah-tishoo!' echoed he, before hanging up.

26 OF NOBLE ROT AND IGNOBLE SNOT

There is the best wine in the world, called Tokay. There are no grapes like those in Hungary; the people say that the worst wine of Hungary is better than the best wine of France. This is not true, but everything grows well in Hungary.

Near Home or Europe Described,
Longmans, Green, & Co., London, 1910

It was not without relief that I took a taxi to the station. With Attila locked up in a hospital, Budapest roads were more or less safe.

The station hall was swarming with sleepy early-morning commuters. They were all silent and unsmiling, as if contemplating some inner guilt, and looked like sulky children who had been woken up in the middle of an enjoyable dream.

It took me a while to sort out that my train was to leave from platform 10. I was lucky, because platform 10 was next to platform 5, whereas platforms 6 to 9 were missing. They had probably been commandeered by another Budapest station.

I was standing near a coffee stall, sipping strong, boiling-hot black coffee, when I was approached by a stooping, angry-looking man. Staring me straight in the eye and gesticulating frantically in front of my face, he burst into a long and passionate monologue. Was he complaining about the missing platforms? Or was he saying something nasty, like, for example, 'These bloody Russians standing here drinking our nice Hungarian coffee, as if 1956 never happened! And the bloody trains which are never on time! And the bloody timetables from which you can't understand a bloody thing!'

I simply stood there, nodding in agreement. What else could I do? I wanted to say that I didn't speak Hungarian, but I couldn't. Why? Because I didn't speak Hungarian.

And again I was on the train, rocking back and forth in my seat, blowing my poor nose and swallowing aspirins. If by this point in the book you have started thinking that there are too many trains and train journeys in it, I don't blame you. The reality is that there are too many trains and train journeys in Eastern Europe, where trains, rather than private cars, are still by far the most popular means of transport. And in most East European countries, they are better, faster and cleaner than in Britain.

Trains crawl across the old and new East European borders – they always slow down before crossing a state frontier, probably to underline the significance of the occasion (on Romanian trains, they still switch off all the lights one hour before the border to enable frontier-guards to intimidate the passengers by flashing torches in their faces). After a series of epileptic twitches, they stop at the platform of some obscure city or town, and their coupled buffers make a clanking sound – like rings on the fingers of the East European new rich, when they shake hands.

I have always loved trains, and it was on trains that I met some of the most extraordinary characters of this book. One such encounter occurred on my return journey from Sarospatak, the centre of Tokaji region in north-eastern Hungary, to Budapest. But because by now you must be tired of trains and dying to taste some good Tokaji wines, I shall tell you about it in the next chapter.

'Quick!' said Zsuzsanna. 'Get into the car! We are running late!'

From the moment she met me at the station in Sarospatak, Zsuzsanna (pronounced 'zh-u-zh-a-nna') was firmly in control of things. Businesslike and bespectacled, she moved forward with the blunt determination of an ice-breaker ship and with the speed of a powerful hovercraft.

'Call me Zsuzsa,' she suggested, handing over her business card, which described her as a commercial manager of Tokaji Wines. 'Zsuzsanna is too long and takes too much time to pronounce.'

We sped through Sarospatak, an old college town, which was cosy and beautiful, not dissimilar to Cambridge, only much smaller. Perched behind the wheel of her Renault, Zsuzsa showered with sophisticated Hungarian curses every passing car and every pedestrian who took too long (in her view) to cross the road. 'They are all so slow!' she complained, tooting the horn. 'We must be in time for the tasting.'

'I am terribly sorry,' moaned I, 'but I can't taste wines, or anything else, because of my bad cold.'

I hated myself for being such a wimp, but I was no longer suffering from some trivial running nose. My whole body was literally overflowing with snot, and my condition could be best described as 'snotorrhoea'.

Zsuzsa threw a quick, pitiless look at me and pressed the brake. The car screeched to a halt in front of a small *gyogyszertar*, which, as you might remember from the previous chapter, means 'pharmacy' in Hungarian.

'There is only one thing that can cure you in no time,' she said authoritatively. 'Penicillin in ampoules. Selling it over the counter without a prescription is illegal, but I have a friend who works in this pharmacy.'

Before I could object, she ran inside the *gyogyszertar* and two minutes later reappeared with a parcel.

'How am I supposed to take it?' I asked her when we were back on the road. 'Before a meal, or, maybe, after?'

'Before and after, and instead,' she snapped. 'You have to break the top of an ampoule and drink it – like vodka, which you Russians like so much, ha ha ha.' She had a dry, if somewhat cruel, sense of humour, only slightly moistened by sweet Tokaji wines, in which she was an expert.

'You are being unfair,' I coughed out. 'It was thanks to Russians that your Tokaji wines were introduced to the rest of the world and gained international fame.'

I had done my research.

The Tokaji region's ability to produce sweet aromatic wines was first discovered by my escort's namesake Zsuzsanna Lorantfly, a local landowner, in 1650. Again, as in the case of Plzen beer, it happened through miscalculation. Fearing an attack from the Turks, the imperious Zsuzsanna (does authority go with this name?) ordered that the grape harvest be delayed that year. The Turkish attack never came, but another one did. During the warm and humid autumn, the unharvested grapes were attacked by a fungus called *Botrytis cinerea*, which later became known as Noble Rot ('*aszu*' in Hungarian). The half-rotten berries were shrivelled and dehydrated, but their sweetness increased dramatically. When they were finally harvested and added to the so-called 'base wines', the results were beyond all expectations: the new wine was full, sweet and fragrant. It soon became popular with the Habsburgs, who sent a consignment of Tokaji to the Russian imperial court as a gift.

Peter the Great, who was then Tsar of Russia, liked the wine so much that he gave an order for Tokaji grapes to be grown in the Caucasus, but they never caught on. It was in the reign of his youngest daughter, Empress Elizabeth Petrovna, that Tokaji won itself a truly international reputation and became known as 'the king of wines and the wine of kings' – *vinum regum rex vinorum* in Latin, a logo that can still be found on Tokaji labels. Like her father, the empress enjoyed the wine to such an extent that she ordered a Russian Military Procurement Committee under the command of Brigadier General Vishnevsky to be permanently stationed in Tokaji, although the correct name for the mission should have been Wine Procurement Committee, for its main and only purpose was to choose the best wines and to deliver them to the fun-loving Russian Court in St Petersburg. In one of her letters to Vishnevsky, dated 1745, Empress Elizabeth wrote:

Dear Brigadier General,
    We* have received your letter about your arrival in Hungary, in which you state that you cannot find wines suitable for Us because the last 8–9 years have produced a poor vintage. It is useless to search for good wine, even though some merchants advertise them, since these wines will not last. These merchants only serve to swindle the buyer. Consequently, do not waste time and effort looking for aged wines; buy those made of the best grapes of the current year. Buy as much as you can . . . If it is at all possible, send me by messenger three antals.† I am unable to obtain it anywhere, and as you know, I cannot live without it.

What better publicity for the Tokaji wines?

We were now driving through the Tokaji-Hegyalia region, which includes twenty-eight villages and the town of Tokaj. The foothills of the Carpathian Moun-

---

* She meant herself, of course. Royalty have always had a curious way of referring to themselves in the plural, as if suffering from a split personality.
† Small barrels of approximately 16.5 gallons each.

tains could be seen in the distance. The road was lined as far as the horizon with hillocks covered with straight and curved vine strips, which made the whole landscape look zebra-like. I could discern full, dew-covered berries on the vines close to the curb. Suddenly I felt an irrepressible itch to touch the cool, moist skin of a grape, to stroke this magic creation of Tokaji's volcanic soil.

'Can we stop for a second?' I asked Zsuzsa. 'I need to pee.'

I stumbled out of the car, and my boots immediately got stuck in the brownish, juicy mud, so that I was unable to go any further. But there was no need to, unless I really intended to pee (which I didn't). On the vine closest to me, some of the grapes were already touched with Noble Rot – they were greyish and shrunk like the skin on the hands of an old peasant woman. Other berries were still round and green. It was only September, and most of the grapes were not going to be 'nobly rotten' until mid-November. Here lay the main difficulty of harvesting in the region: choosing the right moment. One had to pick the berries when they were only half eaten by mould. Leave it for too long and Noble Rot would promptly become 'grey rot', making them absolutely useless. Due to the fragility of Noble Rot-affected grapes, harvesting could only be done by hand – berry by berry – which required gentleness and lots of patience and made someone like Zsuzsa (or myself) an unlikely harvester. It was only fair that they received a hundred times more money for berries affected by Noble Rot than for non-affected ones.

We stopped at the entrance to the famous Rakoczi Cellars, near Rakoczi Castle. Prince Ferenc Rakoczi (or Rakoczi Ferenc, if we are to stick to the topsy-turvy Hungarian order of things and of words) plotted and led a popular revolt against the Habsburgs in 1670. The revolt failed, but the prince became a Hungarian national hero anyway.

The sixteenth-century cellar was 800 metres long and contained 2000 oak barrels.

The moment we entered the damp, dimly lit underground corridor, my snotorrhoea had a boost. In despair, I broke open a penicillin ampoule and swallowed its awfully bitter contents, which made my whole body shudder with disgust.

The cellar walls and ceilings were covered with a thick layer of some fuzzy, sponge-like growth.

'This is our famous grey mould, or *Claudosporium cellare* in Latin,' said Zsuzsa. 'It serves as a natural air-conditioner, which helps to maintain a constant temperature of around ten degrees Centigrade.'

Having passed through an underground chapel with a mural depicting Bacchus, the god of wine, we found ourselves in a spacious candle-lit hall. A massive round table with half a dozen bottles of wine was in the middle. Next to it stood four throne-like wooden chairs, on to one of which Zsuzsa invited (or rather ordered) me to sink.

Everything was ready for the tasting – the first proper wine-tasting in my life. True, Evgeny Bulavin and I had once got very drunk on a cheap Tokaji (it was readily available in the Soviet Union) mixed with Biomedicine and Bulgarian brandy and chased with pickled gherkins, but to call that binge 'tasting' would be on a par with calling the sound of a flushing toilet a symphony. I was ashamed to tell Zsuzsa about it and decided to imitate everything she did and to keep my mouth shut, so as not to disgrace myself with an irrelevant question or comment.

'We start with Château Megyer Tokaji Furmint 1995,' said Zsuzsa. 'As you know, Furmint is our basic grape.'

I nodded and blew my nose.

'This dry white wine is fruity, well-structured and elegant,' she went on. 'It is fermented in barrels. It is suitable for aperitifs and goes well with fish and seafood.

Served at eight degrees Centigrade.'

Was she taking me for a bloody wine critic, or what?

During her monologue, Zsuzsa kept gently rotating her glass, then she lifted it, held it against the light of a burning candle and took a tiny sip of the wine, which she almost immediately spat out into a porcelain spittoon. I was glad that Evgeny was not there: he wouldn't have survived such an unforgivable waste of alcohol.

I repeated everything she did to the letter, but the only thing I could taste in my abused mouth was that damned penicillin.

Zsuzsa was already holding a glass with the next wine.

'This is dry Tokaji Szamorodni, which means "as it was grown". It is made with a mixture of grapes both affected and unaffected by Noble Rot. It has a distinctive taste of sherry, a typical hazelnut flavour and slightly dry predominance. Goes well with Hungarian soups.'

I sniffed the wine, but detected no distinctive flavour, let alone predominance. For some reason, I remembered that many years ago, during my visit to the Novie Maleshty wine cellars in Soviet Moldavia, my red-faced escort with a wine-glass corn on the bridge of his nose had told me about the celebrated Moldavian taster Konstantine, who, allegedly, tasted the wines only when in doubt, which didn't happen often, for he could describe their exact qualities by their colour alone. Once, his colleagues decided to play a joke on him and, in the middle of a tasting, gave him a test-tube with urine. Konstantine looked at it and said, 'I think it's urine.' Then he sipped from the tube and joyfully concluded, 'It is urine indeed!'

With my snotorrhoea still rampant, I was not sure whether I would have been able to tell urine from the best of Tokaji wines, even if I drank a full bottle of it.

The tasting proceeded smoothly (apart from the fact that I wasn't able to taste anything). Zsuzsa carried on talking about 'strong backbone', 'the crust of bread taste', 'green nut skin taste', 'aromas of tangerine and apricot', while I nodded, sneezed and imitated everything she did.

Having briefly shut my eyes after another powerful sneeze, I didn't notice that Zsuzsa had produced from somewhere a mould-covered bottle which she was now opening.

'This is Tokaji Château Pajzos 1991 – a collectors' item. We don't make it any longer, and there are only a few hundred bottles of it left in the world. Nineteen ninety-one was our best vintage year in decades. It is a dessert wine, good with goose liver and chocolate. A wine like this can live for ever. In our cellars we have three-hundred-year-old Château Pajzos which is still drinkable.'

'Stop!' I cried out, almost against my will. 'Don't open it! Don't waste this wonderful wine on me! I would rather drink another ampoule of penicillin.'

But it was too late: the cork was already out. With a doomed sigh, I had a big sip from my glass, and suddenly – for a fleeting moment – I could taste it all. The powerful bouquet broke through the shielding of my desensitised sensors and dead taste-buds like an armour-piercing shell through a bulletproof vest. I could feel in my mouth the aromas of tangerine and apricot, the taste of green nut skin, the delicate smell of the Alpine edelweiss and even the hint of the mysterious elderberries, which I had never eaten or seen. I could feel the dry after-taste, the fruity finish and the strong backbone of the wine that was going to outlive both Zsuzsa and myself and was likely to taste the same in the year 2300. It was like taking a sip of an elixir of life, or of eternity itself. And – miraculously – my own flu-weakened backbone felt stronger, too.

On our way back into the daylight, we passed through another, much bigger, tasting hall. A group of formally dressed men were sitting at the end of a long table tasting wines.

'Sh-sh!' Zsuzsa put her finger to her lips. 'There is a very important person there, the director of the town of Tokaji' (that was how she put it: 'director of the town').

She didn't have to hush me: I was silent savouring the exquisite taste of Château Pajzos. But her pusillanimous hissing and the setting itself (which, again, reminded me of the underground palace in Novie Maleshty reserved for the top Communist Party apparatchiks) made me think that it was not only the wines that remained unchanged in Hungary: old communist habits, just like old Tokaji wines, seemed to have a long life.

'Until 1990, we had mass production of Tokaji wines, and the bulk went to the Soviet Union. Nowadays, most of our wineries are owned by the French and other Western shareholders. The interest in our wines is so high that our government had to pass a law blocking further vineyard sales to non-Hungarian companies,' Zsuzsa said with a touch of sadness in her voice as we were driving back to Sarospatak.

The setting sun was painting the hills, the vineyards and the tiled roofs of the country houses in golden, Tokaji-wine-like shades. A picture of a wooden barrel decorated the gate of a whitewashed hut, which meant that a member of the dying cooper's trade lived there. A neat stack of plywood planks, destined to become wine barrels, was visible behind the fence. Everything in the Tokaji region meant wines, spoke wines and smelt of wines. It was clear why the French were so eager to buy into the secrets of Tokaji wine-making.

In the absence of 'slow' pedestrians on the road, Zsuzsa cursed her unsuspecting little car, probably for being slow, too. Her mood fluctuated easily between cheerful warmth and unprovoked anger – a typical Hungarian temperament, often compared to a bonfire in the wind.

It was the day of my son Mitya's sixteenth birthday – his first birthday that I was going to miss. He was in Melbourne, and I was thousands of miles away in the Hungarian town of Sarospatak. Theoretically, I should have got drunk, but in practice I couldn't even do that, because of the penicillin, which didn't go with alcohol.

Nevertheless, I was planning to have a celebration and invited Zsuzsa to join me for dinner. She accepted my invitation, only to change her mind two minutes later:

'No, I can't. I am in a hurry,' she said and, having hastily drawn a map of the town to help me to get to the station next morning, jumped into her car and sped off.

I shrugged, blew my nose and headed for the restaurant she had recommended, thinking that with my rampant snotorrhoea and with Kleenex tissues sticking out of my every pocket, like banknotes from the glittery suits of Russian new rich, I was not an attractive dining companion.

The restaurant, recommended by Zsuzsa for its 'good food and live gypsy music', had the longest name one could imagine: Bombi Discont Kavenaz Etterem Traffik, 1790. It looked more like a short newspaper article, possibly even an obituary.

Inside, it was clean and cosy. I was the only customer. The waiters were all students at Sarospatak's Calvinist College trying to earn some extra money to pay for their studies. They seemed to be enjoying their new capitalist reality and, not having much else to do, were adroitly spinning empty trays on their index fingers.

After some hesitation, I ordered Gypsy Roast Sarospatak-style and some hot chicken soup for my sore throat. My nose felt better, but – through some invisible connecting tubes inside my body – the cold had migrated to my larynx.

The Gypsy Roast tasted suspiciously sweet. Disgusted by my own imaginary cannibalism, I put it aside and asked for pancakes with cottage cheese, which sounded safer. I felt lonely and was desperate to talk to some-body. But the chances of finding an interlocutor in an empty Hungarian restaurant with a short obituary instead of a name were close to zero.

Having consumed two portions of crispy cheese pancakes in vanilla sauce, I was about to pay my bill and leave, when a fat, bearded man with a red scar in the middle of his forehead, slid into the restaurant from the street. Without taking off his coat, he proceeded to the piano in the corner, opened the lid and started tickling the ivories.

'This is what Zsuzsa meant by "live music",' I thought, although some old American blues the man was playing didn't sound like 'gypsy music' at all. Maybe it was she who had arranged for this strange musician to be sent here to entertain me while I deci-mated Sarospatak's weekly supply of cheese pancakes?

Having played a couple of tunes, the man moved over to a table next to mine. He beckoned a waiter and asked him in almost unaccented English: 'Can I play some more after I eat?'

'Are you British?' I asked him.

'No I am Dutch,' he replied without looking up from the menu. It was obvious he didn't feel like talking. Tough luck, because I did!

'Are you a musician?' I persisted.

'No. Piano-playing is my hobby. By profession, I am an inventor.'

'What have you invented, if I may ask?'

He put the menu aside. His hazel eyes were suddenly lit up with some wild inner spark. A similar light can be found in the eyes of a hungry dog which has spotted a T-bone. Or else in the eyes of a madman.

'I have invented interactive television,' he pronounced solemnly. 'Today I drove all the way from Warsaw, where I arrived yesterday from Frankfurt. And now I have to wait here for two weeks for them to take a decision and summon me to Dusseldorf, or, maybe, to

Istanbul. I am worried that while I wait here, someone will nick my invention. People steal ideas, you know.'

'I am awfully sorry,' said I. I still had some faint hope that the Dutchman was not as mad as he seemed to be. 'I am terribly sorry, but hasn't interactive television been invented already? Video telephones, for example. I saw one on sale in Gibraltar recently.

The sparkle in his eyes had burst into flame. 'Mine is different!' he shouted. 'It is interactive television with teletext!'

I thought that it would take him much more than two weeks of waiting until they decided to see him in Istanbul. Or in Dusseldorf.

'Do you travel a lot?' I asked, in an attempt to change the subject.

'Eastern Europe is my favourite hang-out,' he said. 'I've been travelling here since 1976. There is only one thing that pisses me off about it. I myself speak five languages, but here no one speaks Dutch, or even English!'

At that point I committed a mistake. As the grandson of a neuropathologist, I should have been familiar with the main rule of dealing with royalty and lunatics: never object to what they say.

'I disagree with you,' I said. 'Although I haven't been travelling in Eastern Europe since 1976, as you have, I have travelled enough researching a book. My experience shows that many people do speak foreign languages, especially English. Even here, in Hungary, my guides – both in Budapest and here, in the Tokaji region – had an excellent command of it.'

'I don't care about your bloody book and your bloody guides!' he yelled. 'Don't you tell me that they speak foreign languages, because they can't speak any! They can't, they can't, they *can't*!'

The young waiters were throwing worried looks at us. I was seriously afraid that the Dutchman could start biting any moment. But all of a sudden he calmed down.

'Now, if you don't mind, I'll have my soup and then play some more,' he said in a conciliatory manner.

I wished him good luck with his inventions and, still not believing that I had managed to escape the 'playing Dutchman' unharmed, went towards the exit. I could hear his mobile phone ringing behind my back and him shouting into it in Dutch. He was probably on the line to Dusseldorf. Or to Istanbul. Or, possibly, to Frankfurt. But, most likely, it was a call from a lunatic asylum in Amsterdam, from where he must have recently escaped.

That is how I 'celebrated' my son's sixteenth birthday: suffering from snotorrhoea in Sarospatak in the company of a mad Dutchman.

27 A COUPLE FROM HELL

It was a lovely September morning. I left my hotel early, anticipating an unhurried ten-minute walk to the station. Zsuzsa had assured me that it wouldn't take any longer to get there.

Sarospatak was basking in the fragile Indian summer sunlight. Gossamers hung in the sultry, mica-like air, faintly smelling of lime and of Tokaji wines. Polished chestnuts were falling from the trees with doomed thumping noises. Fiery autumn leaves crunched soothingly under my boots.

Flocks of joyful students with notebooks under their arms were hurrying towards the gates of their famous Calvinist College, which boasted, among other things, Europe's oldest library. Unlike them, I was not in a hurry – a fact that I soon came to regret.

I have always been of the opinion that the ability to get lost in an unknown place is the main quality of a travel writer. By that, I don't mean getting lost in a small Hungarian town ten minutes before your train is due to depart. And that is exactly what happened. Zsuzsa had obviously been in a hurry when jotting down her town plan the night before. Or else she suffered from a particular directional malfunction affecting one's sense of left and right (there is a special scientific word for it which I can't recall now). Whatever it was, after studiously following her directions to the railway station, I found myself at a local peasant market.

I looked at my watch: it was less than ten minutes before the departure of my train. The next one was not due until tomorrow. Panic seized me. Having forgotten that I was in Hungary, I spent the next five minutes trying to get directions from passers-by. I used all four languages that I could speak, including Russian, which a Hungarian tourism official in London had urged me not to resort to while in Hungary, in the interests of 'my safety'.

Having failed to make myself understood, I started making hooting and puffing sounds impersonating an outdated steam engine. My impersonation was probably not very convincing. A passing Hungarian granny offered me a dried red *paprika* (pepper), having probably mistaken me for a street busker. The mad Dutchman was right: they simply did not speak foreign languages, apart from Hungarian – foreign to me, if not to them. At least, in Sarospatak they didn't.

It was my ultimate confrontation with the Hungarian language, one of the world's most idiosyncratic tongues, with four different words for 'you'.

I was saved by the *Lonely Planet Eastern European Phrasebook*, which I dug out from the very bottom of my backpack: being a linguist, I had been dead sure I would never need it.

The *vasutallomas*, or the train station in Hungarian (I should have guessed!), was just round the corner.

I cannot give you a detailed description of the young married couple whom I met on the train to Budapest. Nor can I reveal their real names, for if they were recognised, they would be in trouble with the KGB back in the Soviet Union.

Before you start thinking that I had contracted a form of insanity from the playing Dutchman, let me reassure you that I was well aware of the fact that my native totalitarian monster-state had collapsed several years before and no longer existed. But . . . But there was (and still is) one small chunk of the 'evil empire' that had miraculously survived its demise, the so-called Pridne-strovskaya Republic. That was where my accidental travelling companions came from.

He was a qualified chef, she an accountant, but neither of them had a job back home: a small restaurant where he used to work and which he had also owned, was burnt down by mobsters after he refused to cough up protection money. The police didn't want to intervene, saying there would be more to come if he did not co-operate with the extortionists.

To make ends meet, they decided to go to Hungary to try and earn some cash, but ended up being mercilessly exploited by the owner of a Hungarian country inn, where they worked in the kitchen for a quarter of the wages paid to the lowliest Hungarian employee. Eventually, they were thrown out for having allowed a starving Romanian fellow-worker, who had been evicted by the proprietor, to spend a night in their vermin-infested hostel room. They were paid only half of what they had been promised. To afford tickets home, they had to slave for several months weeding tobacco fields.

They struck me as extremely likeable and decent folk, who had lost all hope of having a better life.

'I now realise why some people go crazy and go on shooting sprees,' said the chain-smoking husband. 'I sometimes feel like howling out of despair.'

The self-proclaimed Pridnestrovskaya (sometimes called Transdniester) Republic, where they had been living and to which they were reluctantly returning after their failed cash-raising expedition to Hungary, is a unique post-Soviet formation. Situated in the territory of Moldova, in the eastern part of the former Soviet republic of Moldavia, it remains the world's last truly communist Soviet enclave. Occupying a large and fertile area, it is populated mostly by ethnic Russians and Ukrainians who refused to be incorporated into the new, independent Moldova, which has Romanian as its official national tongue. A military conflict with Moldova followed.

The warring sides were eventually separated by the intervention of the 14th Russian Army under the command of the notorious General Aleksandr Lebed, a crew-cut martinet with the name of a bird (*lebed* means 'swan' in Russian) and the face of a gangster. The 14th Army was still there at the time of my encounter with the couple as the only guarantee of peace, although its husky-voiced commander had gone to Moscow to take part in high-level political games. When Lebed was leaving, local women threw themselves under the wheels of his car, trying to stop him, but the general's political ambitions took the upper hand.

The area, which used to be famous for its fine wine, incorporates two big industrial cities – Tiraspol and Benderi – as well as numerous villages and towns, all of which are still run by Soviets of People's Deputies and Communist Party organisations. Monuments to Lenin and Brezhnev still adorn the streets, and almost everything is under state control (or rather under state arbitrariness).

According to my travelling companions, life in the republic was dire almost beyond description. With an official exchange rate of more than 500,000 local coupons to one US dollar, cash was accepted in shops by weight – bundles of worthless paper coupons were routinely weighed on primitive scales. State shops offered nothing but huge containers of tomato juice. Bread queues were a feature of everyday life. All industrial enterprises were at a standstill and their workers had not been paid for several years. The average old-age pension was $6 a month, hardly enough to buy a kilogram of meat at a 'co-operative' food market.

At the same time, military hysteria was constantly being whipped up and youngsters faced compulsory recruitment to the local Cossack-style 'army' preparing for a final showdown with Moldova.

Corruption was the only way of existence, and the few remaining spheres of distribution and production were under the firm control of the mafia incorporating the police, the secret service (the KGB) and the local administration. The 'country' had its own 'president', a staunch communist called Igor Smirnov, and its own rubber-stamp 'parliament'.

Hope was dead in that God-forsaken Jurassic Park-like place, forgotten by the outside world. The West, not willing to aggravate its already strained relations with either Russia or Moldova (the latter increasingly leaning towards reunification with Romania), chose to ignore the plight of the more than 500,000 residents of the enclave, whose only means of survival was to flee to Hungary, Russia or any other place that would harbour them. But this, too, was next to impossible since, first, they had no money, and, second, they did not qualify as refugees.

'What are you going to do next?' I asked the couple as they were getting ready to get off at Miscolc, where they planned to catch a bus to the Ukrainian border.

They shrugged and, having picked up their battered rucksacks, started pushing their way towards the exit – two bright and energetic young people with shattered lives and no future.

The carton of Marlboro that I had offered them as a gift was left untouched on a small table in my compartment.

I spent the rest of the journey smoking and staring down at my boots, which were soiled with the magic silky clay of the Tokaji vineyards.

28 BALATON REFLECTIONS

*The Hungarians are handsome. Their bodies are supple
and elastic. Their hair and their bright eyes are generally
black . . . Just like England is divided into counties,
Hungary is divided into fifty parts, and each has its chief
town . . . The chief things made in Hungary are wine,
soap and tobacco-pipes. Hungary sends quantities of
corn, wine and pigs, to other countries.*

Near Home or Europe Described,
Longmans, Green, & Co., London, 1910

'The best wines are made in the land where grapes
can see themselves in Lake Balaton,' they say in
Hungary. This is not just a typically Hungarian
romantic metaphor, but also a scientific, or rather
enological, truth. The sun's rays, reflected by the lake,
easily penetrate the volcanic basalt soil of its shores and
keep the grapes warm during the night. The unique
micro-climate, created by one of Europe's largest freshwater reservoirs, accounts for the sophisticated
elegance of local wines. This is why I couldn't miss the
Balaton area when exploring the Wine Lands of Eastern
Europe.

I was sitting on the Balatonfured-bound train, ready
to depart from Budapest Deli (not to be confused with a
delicatessen) railway station, when a blonde middle-
aged woman got in. She stopped next to my seat and,
pointing at a luggage rack above my head where my

bursting backpack precariously rested, blurted out several angry sentences in Hungarian before moving on. Significantly, all the other luggage racks in the carriage were empty. A minute later the woman got off the train, and through the window I could see her pacing along the platform in the brisk purposeful manner of an alcoholic hurrying out of an off-licence. 'Mission accomplished' was written all over her satisfied face.

The train started with a jerk, and I sat there wondering what she might have said. After intensive pondering, I came up with four possible versions:

1. 'I collect luggage racks. Can I take this one? It will be the pride of my collection.'
2. 'This is what I do for a living: run along the trains and point at luggage racks.'
3. 'This luggage rack was stolen from another train last week. I am going to tip off the police.'
4. 'I want to warn you: this luggage rack is going to collapse upon your head in five minutes. I have installed a small explosive device in it.'

Having dragged my backpack off the rack, I moved to a different seat in the opposite end of the carriage. Better to be safe than sorry.

My room at Balatonfured's Marina Hotel had a lake view.

After years of extensive globe-trotting, I discovered that all inland countries with no access to the sea suffer from a common inferiority complex. This peculiar dry-land syndrome is illustrated by the following international joke. Question: 'Why do they have a Ministry of the Navy in Hungary, when they have no access to the sea?' Answer: 'For the same reason as they have a Ministry of Culture.'

I heard similar jokes about Slovakia, the Czech

Republic, Switzerland and even Luxembourg.* That is why I was not particularly surprised to learn that in Hungary they called Lake Balaton 'the Hungarian Sea'. Hungarians think that there used to be a real sea in its place in the days of yore. Whether it is true or not, at 77 kilometres long and 14 kilometres wide Lake Balaton could easily compete with a sea, if not in size, then definitely in beauty. Never before had I seen a lake whose waters changed their colour so dramatically several times a day – from dark brown to green, from steel-grey to pink, from pitch-black to aquamarine. Waking up every morning, I was never quite sure what sort of make-up this chameleon of a lake was going to put on.

The colour of Lake Balaton varied not only with the time of the day, but also depended on what, or who, was reflected in its still waters (*balaton* means 'swamp' in Hungarian). Like an enormous looking-glass, it mirrored the surrounding landscape (vineyards, white peasant huts, graceful churches) as well as the ever-changing life on its shores.

My guide's name was Tanya. She was Russian and was married to a Hungarian army officer, who had studied at a military academy in Kalinin, where they met.

'I am so nervous, so nervous,' she said (in Russian of course) when introducing herself in the hotel lobby. Her hands were trembling, and she kept adjusting her make-up and hair every now and then.

'Why don't you relax?' I asked her.

'How can I? I have such an important guest today.'

I looked around, expecting to spot her 'important guest' hiding behind one of the imitation marble columns, then realised that she meant myself.

No matter how hard I tried to persuade her that I was

* This last was especially pointed, for in Luxembourg the Ministry of Culture is also responsible for the country's agriculture.

not a VIP but a VOP (very ordinary person), she remained tense, and she even developed a nervous stutter, which was a pity because she was an excellent guide and knew a lot about the Balaton area, where she had lived for many years.

Tanya's constant nervousness never grew into shyness and did not stop her from being heavily opinionated. 'I suspect that Magyars are gypsies, although Hungarians themselves deny it' was one of her typical pronouncements.

One morning she greeted me with the following words: 'I am so nervous, I couldn't sleep all night, but I think that you have to pay me for my services.'

I replied that I would have been delighted to if: a) I had had enough money, and b) I had not been an official guest of her employers, the Hungarian Tourism Service, who were kind enough to provide me with free hotel accommodation and free guides.

'I am sure they are going to pay you,' I suggested.

'And what if they don't?'

She was probably used to being cheated. And I didn't hold it against her.

Russian to the core of her bones, Tanya harboured a huge dislike of the Russian new rich, who were now frequent guests on the lake's shores. She told me that she was once commandeered by two Russian fat cats, who 'had pockets full of dollars and kept drinking vodka all the time'. After a guided tour of the local sights, they started demanding 'other services' from her and offering her wads of banknotes.

'I am a married woman,' she said to them. 'You should be ashamed of yourselves.'

She didn't specify whether or not she had accepted their offer.

On the way to the Badacsony Wine-Growing Co-operative, we stopped in the village of Tyhany on the northern shore of Lake Balaton. Tanya insisted that we had a look at the eighteenth-century twin-towered Abbey Church, built in the style of 'peasant baroque', as she put it.

The altar of the church was decorated with gilded figurines of Christ and the saints, with their hearts exposed. Some of them were nursing their hearts in their hands, like glasses of red wine. Others were cradling them in the creases of their tunics. The hearts were made of ruby, which gave the impression that they were bleeding. Or oozing with red wine. Never before had I seen such an unusual 'cardiological' altar.

On the edge of the village, there stood a cluster of old houses, built in traditional country style, which had been turned into an open-air museum. The windows of some faced away from the lake to reduce the effect of cold winters. Others did not have windows at all: in the old days, peasants had to pay taxes on smoke and on daylight, and some chose darkness as a means of innocent tax-evasion.

I noticed that some windows had white circles painted round them.

'This is meant to say: "Our house is poor but clean, you can pop in for a drink, although we don't have a chimney",' explained Tanya.

The museum was empty, except for an old local lady in a white kerchief, probably a custodian. She spoke to me at length in Hungarian.

'What did she say?' I asked Tanya.

'Nothing much. She welcomed you to the village and called you "my little star" and "my jewel".'

'But I have never met her before,' I muttered bashfully.

'So what? Hungarian peasants are very polite and hospitable. They have a saying: "A guest is a king".'

How nice it was – at long last – to be able to understand some Hungarian!

German tourists, stoned and stone-faced, were singing in chorus outside the wine restaurant of the Badacsony

Co-operative. They were sitting at crude wooden tables
drinking *must* – an unfermented grape juice, flowing
from under an outdated manual wine press operated by
two local peasants. The juice was sour (the result of the
cold summer, according to Tanya) and non-alcoholic,
but the Germans looked very drunk. Or were they just
pretending?

Waiting for Gyula Lichtnecker, the president of the
co-operative, whom everyone called President Gyula
(pronounced: dju-la), we drank *must* with the Germans
and ate bread with lard, red pepper and onions, a
popular Hungarian chaser.

President Gyula was a tall robust man with the puffy,
weather-beaten face of a wine-maker (or of an
alcoholic). He showed us round the co-operative, which
made 3 million litres of wine a year.

It was the beginning of the harvesting season. Trucks
were unloading grapes in the winery's courtyard. Several
grim-faced workers, armed with spades, were tossing
the grapes into a rattling mechanical press, where they
were lightly crushed to release the 'first juice', and their
skins, stalks and pips were automatically removed. The
workers were soaked with grape juice from head to toe.
Heavy drops of volatile, sticky *must* flew at us from
under the press.

'We use old technology and traditional methods here,'
President Gyula said. 'Not everything old is necessarily
bad. Planting grapes is an old tradition in itself. It
requires faith in a good future, which we had under
socialism. We were part of the powerful Warsaw Pact,
and Hungary was entrusted with making wines and
exporting them to other socialist countries. It was a big
mistake that the Warsaw Pact was disbanded. As a
result, we have lost most of our foreign buyers.'

'But, surely, the free market has its advantages,' I
intervened.

'We are disappointed by the market. Who knows
what all these Western investors are up to? Formerly, we

used to have plans, socialist emulation, and now what? Free competition? The black market dictating its own conditions? Chaos, that's what it is! We had to stop planting new sorts of grapes, and not all private owners are good vine-growers. Some of them are just speculators. Next Monday a Frenchman is coming to us to launch a new bottling line. It is a risk, but we have no choice: the market dictates everything!'

'Do you allow your staff to drink wine while they work?' I asked, remembering the dismal faces of the workers.

'Never! If a worker is caught drunk at work for the first time, we send him home for four hours to contemplate. If it happens again, we sack him.'

No wonder the staff of the co-operative looked as if they were in a permanent state of sombre 'contemplation'.

The tasting took place in President Gyula's fairly unpresidential office: a desk, a book-case and a couple of chairs.

'This is our Italian Riesling,' declared the President putting a bottle on his desk. 'It is an elegant, sourish wine which is pleasant to drink during a conversation. We call it "democratic wine", or "everyday wine", because you can easily drink two litres of it without noticing any effect.'

'Speak for yourself,' I thought, unable to cope with a few sips of 'democratic wine', let alone two litres. After the second swallow, my eternal companion – my stomach ulcer, which had been lying dormant for the previous couple of weeks – gave a signal of slight discomfort, a gnawing premonition of serious pain. Clearly, my ulcer was not a democrat: it couldn't stand sour things.

'And now, something completely different,' the President pronounced, solemnly uncorking the next bottle. He didn't realise that he sounded *Monty Python*esque. 'Grey Monk, our flagship white wine.'

Even the way he spoke was unmistakably socialist.

The Grey Monk was seventeen years old. It was made in 1980, when my son Mitya was born; when Moscow was preparing for its showcase Olympics, boycotted by many countries after the Soviet invasion of Afghanistan; when Polish shipyard workers in Gdansk went on strike, orchestrated by Lech Walesa, in protest at rising food prices. The dying, senile Brezhnev, who could no longer pronounce 'socialism', was sitting in the Kremlin. Kadar's Hungary was happily stagnating alongside its Big Soviet Brother: living standards were declining at the same rate as the foreign debt was growing. These were the times President Gyula was so nostalgic for.

But the wine itself was lovely, subtle, refreshing and slightly astringent.

'Do you like it? Of course, you do. Remember: we made this beautiful, soft wine using our old primitive technology.'

'I think President Gyula should be renamed Chairman Gyula and addressed as Comrade Chairman. He would love that,' I said to Tanya after we left the co-operative.

We had some time to spare before proceeding to our next venue, the famous Esterhazy wine cellars. After a couple of hours in the Badascony Co-operative, my brain needed detoxication, not so much from the Grey Monk as from the grey man, President Gyula. According to my omniscient Slovak friend Fero, there was no better way to rejuvenate one's brain cells than by taking a plunge into a thermal bath. In a Hungarian tourist pamphlet, I read that the Balaton area was 'rich in sulphurous mineral waters which according to the locals very pleasantly mix with the wines of the region'. I was not sure whether I would be tempted by such a cocktail, but Tanya insisted that one thing I definitely had to try was a swim in Lake Heviz, Europe's biggest natural reservoir of hot water. She said that the healing thermal waters of the lake and its radioactive mud were the best cure for rheumatism and illnesses of the nervous system, and was disappointed when I assured her that I was not suffering from either. She was uncertain whether the therapeutic lake was capable of curing my persisting cold. But I decided to give it a go, or rather a dip.

The lake was covered with a thick cloud of steaming vapour. When the cloud was briefly dispersed by a gust of wind, I was able to discern a 'Tariff' sign at the cloakroom entrance:

3 hours – 280 F
5 hours – 140 F
8 hours – 80 F

It was probably the world's only price-list where the fare was in inverse proportion to the duration of the facilities' use. One could assume that those daredevils who were prepared to soak in hot water for ten or twenty hours were exempt from any fees and could boil themselves to death for free.

But what if someone decided to cheat and, having bought the cheapest eight-hour ticket, got out after three hours, thus robbing the lake authorities of 200 forints?

Although three hours were far too much for me, being an honest person I bought a ticket for the minimum stay – and hence had to pay the maximum fee.

The lake was full of elderly Germans in silly bathing caps made of pink rubber. They stood in the water in silence, staring in front of themselves into nowhere, as only Germans can do.

'Germans live here,' Tanya commented, as I emerged from the cloakroom wearing nothing but my Marks & Spencer underpants, which had to pass for swimming trunks on that particular occasion.

The water was hot and malodorous. I was surprised to see shoals of some minuscule sulphur-loving fry floating underneath. It would have felt like swimming in a bowl of fish soup, had the lake not smelt of donkey.

Suddenly, it started raining. And whereas my body from the neck down was submerged in the donkey-smelling soup of fish and Germans, my poor head was exposed to ice-cold raindrops, which was extremely unpleasant. Brushing against the steaming overcooked bodies of my fellow-bathers, I got out.

The brevity of my swim had to be kept secret from the lake's administration, who, in compliance with the 'Tariff', were likely to charge me millions of forints if they discovered that, instead of the compulsory minimum of three hours, I had stayed in the healing water for no more than a couple of minutes.

Beards of thick matted cobweb were hanging from the ceilings of the 230-year-old wine cellars that used to belong to the Esterhazy family.

'When did you last clean your cellars? In the eighteenth century?' I asked the cellar master sarcastically.

'We preserve the cobweb here deliberately. It helps to stabilise smells. Wine absorbs smells extremely well. One rotten potato can spoil the whole cellar. On the other hand, if you put wine into a cellar with bare concrete walls, the quality goes down.'

We walked past endless rows of massive old wine barrels and multi-tiered stacks of mould-covered bottles. I no longer felt like being facetious.

'The oldest wine here is Tokaji of 1811 vintage. Eighteen eleven was a very good year, with a long dry autumn.'

'So this wine could have been tasted by Napoleon?'

'It was. And not only by Napoleon, but also by Prince Ferdinand and by many Hungarian kings. The more sugar and alcohol the wine has, the longer you can keep it. If its alcohol content is over sixteen per cent, it might survive for several hundred years.'

'How do you decide how long you can keep this or that wine?'

'To determine the exact time of storing is hard. Wine is like a woman who gets prettier with age, but only up to a point. One of the main indicators is colour. That is why the bottles are kept in darkness.'

'And why did you put these bottles behind bars? Have they committed a crime?'

'This is our *vinothèque*, or wine library. Here we keep samples of the best wines for reference of colour and taste.'

'Can one borrow a book, sorry, a bottle from this library?'

'Yes, when we sell them at auctions. But they are expensive. A bottle of 1811 Tokaji, say, will go for two to three million forints, or twenty to thirty thousand US dollars.'

I was relieved that the cellar master hadn't offered me a tasting of it.

On the way back to Balatonfured, we stopped near an old house on top of the Badacsony Hill. Tanya said that it used to belong to Roza Szegedy, an eighteenth-century local beauty, who had inspired the poet Sandor Kisfaldy to write two collections of poems, dedicated to her. The first one was called *Bitter Love* and dated from the time when the couple were courting. The second, *Happy Love*, was written after they got married. From a modern point of view, it should have been the other way round – *Happy Love* followed by the post-marital *Bitter Love* – but in the poetic eighteenth century marriages were probably still made in heaven. At least, some of them were.

Roza Szegedy was a wine-maker. All her life she grew vines on the hill, where the first grapes were cultivated by the Roman legionaries, or rather by their hard-working slaves, two thousand years ago. The Romans were driven away by the Huns, the Huns by the Avars, the Avars by the Franks, the Franks by the Magyars, but all these fighters, conquerors and jingoistic nomads had one thing in common: they liked wine, so they had to grow grapes.

Looking at the row after row of terraced vineyards covering the hill was like looking at a chart of Hungarian history, on which each vine terrace represented a different generation. But the end product always remained the same: wine.

Roza Szegedy's former house was now a museum of wine-making. There, among barrels, hoes and old wine-presses, I saw a long mace-shaped wooden spoon called a *lopotok* (literally 'little thief'), which was used for taking small amounts of wine out of a barrel for casual tasting. It could have been used by the invading Turks, who had tried for 150 years to conquer Hungary. During a lull between battles, they would break the prohibition of the Koran and would – stealthily – savour Hungarian wines. Was it from them that the *lopotok* had got its unusual, sweet-sounding name?

'I am so nervous, so nervous,' Tanya said to me next morning. She looked genuinely distressed, and dark shadows under her eyes showed clearly through layers of make-up.

From her faltering accent, it transpired that her neighbour, a colonel in the Hungarian army, had committed suicide the previous night. He was married to a Ukrainian woman and had two children. The couple had a good (by Hungarian standards) flat, and all was well with his career. The only reason for his taking his life, in Tanya's view, was the fact that a family next door had bought new furniture, and he could not afford to do the same.

'How pathetic!' exclaimed I.

'Yes, but don't forget he was a Hungarian,' Tanya said. 'Hungarians are brought up on fairy-tales, on folklore full of saintly princes and noble brigands, on idealistic nationalism. In the first form of the Hungarian school where my little daughter studies, pupils have to repeat in chorus several times a day: "We are Hungarians! We speak Hungarian!" This is why Hungarians find it hard to cope when their ideals clash with everyday life.'

We were standing on the balcony of my hotel room. The sun was playing its endless hide-and-seck game with the Balaton – now hiding behind the clouds and now peeping out playfully – and the chameleon lake was reacting by changing its colour from dark green to pink, and then back. Wasn't it a reflection of the flighty and somewhat schizophrenic soul of Hungary, the country that, for many decades, had been an undisputed leader in a rather dubious unofficial world championship, the per capita rate of suicides?

The latest figures show an average of 38.5 suicides a year per 100,000 Hungarians, putting the country way ahead of runners-up Belgium (22.7) and France (20.1). By comparison, Britain lags far behind (thank God) with 7.9 suicides per 100,000 people.

A retired British diplomat once told me in London about an incident involving a newly appointed first secretary at the British embassy in Budapest in the early seventies. He arrived with his wife to take up his new posting and drove straight to the Budapest Hotel, where the embassy had booked temporary accommodation for them. He found a vacant parking spot in the street next to the hotel.

'Well, darling, let's try and enjoy Hungary,' he said to his wife as they were about to leave the car.

At that very moment, a body flew out of one of the hotel windows and landed on the roof of their car with a loud thump.

In a Budapest English-language newspaper, I read about a young couple from the town of Komlo in the south-west of Hungary, who both tried to commit suicide after their cleaning business went bankrupt. When their attempt failed, they resorted to infanticide, killing their two children aged 8 and 13.

There is no shortage of similar stories from Hungary, where the suicide rate keeps growing. Why?

'To be a Hungarian is a collective neurosis,' said Arthur Koestler, one of Hungary's most distinguished émigrés. Indeed, Hungarians, like no other national group, have somehow managed to combine pessimism and gallows humour with stoicism and survival strategies. They can be called a nation of compulsive over-achievers, infected with paranoia-tinged patriotism. Burdened by a long record of glorious defeats in war – by the Turks, Tatars and Habsburgs – and the failure of two major uprisings – in 1848, against the Habsburgs, and in 1956, against the Russians – Hungarians, like jilted lovers, tend to alternate easily between impulsive over-confidence and bleak fatalism and are always anxious to escape prosaic reality in search of their largely non-existent heroic past.

'Weeping, the Hungarian makes merry' is a popular Hungarian proverb. Pessimism is deeply rooted in the romantic Hungarian soul, which, according to Eszter Vecsey, a Hungarian art historian, has 'a rhapsodic nature'.

'The Hungarian will complain if his ice-cream is cold,' noted Yale Richmond, an American observer. 'When a Hungarian is asked how things are going today, he is likely to reply, "Worse than yesterday, but better than tomorrow."'

On top of it all, Hungarians have an obsession with death.

'See, brethren, with your own eyes what we are, merely dust and ashes are we,' moans *Halotti Beszed*, a twelfth-century poem, part of the curriculum in every Hungarian school. A huge chunk of Hungarian classical literature is concerned with dying, and the national anthem echoes a funereal march.

Each 23 October signifies the start of the annual 'season of the dead', which lasts for three weeks. During this period, Hungarians pay daily visits to cemeteries, where they grieve, meditate and read poems over the graves. Yes, poetry is another important part of the gruesome Hungarian psyche: besides having the world's highest suicide rate, Hungary boasts the world's highest per capita number of poets. I wonder if there is a connection?

To my mind, two other factors may lie behind the clear-cut Hungarian propensity to suicide. One is drinking. Hungary remains one of the seven heaviest-drinking nations on earth – a fact which, incidentally, prompted its inclusion in this book. As we all know, excessive and careless consumption of alcohol, be it beer, spirits or wine, leads to debilitating hangovers, depression and, as a result, suicidal moods. The second factor is the extremely complicated Hungarian language, a subject on which I have dwelt enough in the above pages (I think I'd sooner commit suicide by swallowing the mouse of my word processor than write a book in Hungarian).

'A society can forgive a murderer, but it never forgives a dreamer' is my favourite Oscar Wilde quote. But what if a whole society consists almost exclusively of dreamers, as in Hungary? Can it ever come to grips with itself? Or will suicide for ever represent its ultimate way of self-forgiveness?

From what happened to Tanya's neighbour, one may conclude that, for the majority of Hungarians, life remains a precarious tightrope-walking act. Even a relatively gentle push, such as the purchase of new furniture by a neighbour, is enough to upset the shaky balance and precipitate a deadly fall.

But isn't it often the same for many non-Hungarians, too?

'I like taking my guests to restaurants,' Tanya said dreamily on my last evening in the Balaton area. 'Why? Because as a guide I get a free meal, and the staff often give me money for having brought tourists to them.'

I took the hint and invited her to dinner at Csarda
Baricska, the area's most famous inn. It was rather
crudely stylised to resemble a den of *betyars* – good-
hearted highwaymen, robbers of the rich and givers to
the poor, popular figures in Hungarian folklore. The
most celebrated Robin Hood of old Hungary was Joska
Savanyu ('Joe the Sour'), whose memory still lives in
Hungarian hearts: his grave (not far from Csarda
Baricska) was flooded with flowers, and the inn which
he used to frequent hundreds of years ago still served
Joska's Favourite, a lentil soup with bacon and sour (*sic*)
cream.

The robbing traditions are also very much alive in
Hungary, if no longer on highways, then definitely in
some inns. In Csarda Baricska they were manifested by
a badly performing gypsy band, whose oily-eyed leader
was so insulted by my small (from his point of view) tip
that he threw the money back at me with the words: 'Go
and buy something for your woman!' dutifully translated by a blushing Tanya. It was obvious that her
chances of being paid by the staff of that particular
csarda were much smaller than my chances of being
fleeced by them.

The inn had a menu in English which started, 'Dear
guests, we welcome you and your respected society!'

Among the drinks was a cocktail called Sexy, Kicking
Legs, and the main course could be chosen from Devil's
Kick Lucifer-style, Nightmarish Dream of the Chef,
Final Tasty Morsels with Sausages, Brigand's Meat on
the Roast and Pork Loin à la Good Woman with
Mushrooms and Peas.

For the first time, I wished the menu had been written
in Hungarian.

We ended up having a Drunken Fish Soup and
washing it down with a Hungarian red wine aptly
named Bull's Blood. They seemed to go well together –
in contradiction to wine snobs' favourite truism that fish
dishes should be had only with white wine.

I saw Tanya off to the bus station in Balatonfured. We had about fifteen minutes to kill. Despite the late hour, a wine kiosk near the station was still open.

'Let's have one for the road,' I suggested.

We stood comfortably at a tall wooden table, with our elbows on it, and drank the local Szyrkebarat (pinot gris) from a big carafe. The wine cost 50 forints (20p) a glass. Cold, cheap and wonderfully refreshing, it was a real 'democratic' drink – the best wine I had had so far.

'Do you know what Pope Benedict said about Balaton wines sent to him as a gift by the Hungarian Queen Maria?' Tanya asked me.

'I did know, but have forgotten,' I lied. 'What did he say?'

'Blessed is the land that has grown you! Blessed is the woman who has sent you! Blessed am I who am drinking you!'

'He obviously didn't like the wines,' I concluded re-filling my glass.

Tanya laughed. She didn't look nervous any more.

I thought that there was no better way of drinking wine than standing with your elbows on the table – at night, at a bus station, and with a friend.

29 DINNER WITH SCEPTICS

Bulgaria is a land of high mountains and valleys, and great plains. It is very fruitful. In some parts, there are plenty of vineyards full of sweet grapes, which are made into preserves and treacle as well as into wine . . . Bulgarians do not work fast, for they are generally very slow in all they do, and they have no good tools.

Near Home or Europe Described,
Longmans, Green, & Co., London, 1910

The new private restaurant where I dined on my last night in Sofia with Christo and Nikolai, two young executives of Domaine Boyar, Bulgaria's first independent wine merchants, was called Across the Road Behind the Cupboard. One of the dishes on its English-language menu was Cock in Red Wine with Green Rice. None of us ventured to order it.

The otherwise delightful meal could be described in just three words: dinner with sceptics.

My hosts started by sceptically sniffing the cork of the bottle of Merlot Suhindol they had ordered. They made faces, wrinkled their noses and exchanged disgruntled remarks like 'Disrupted taste' and 'Acidic palate'. With horror, I realised that I had forgotten all the wisdom grasped in London from my invaluable book *Wine for Dummies*.

'Wineries often send bad bottles to restaurants,' explained Nikolai, returning the wine to the waiter and ordering another bottle of the same brand. 'Also, in restaurants, they don't store them properly.'

'In general, our best wines go to the West, and the worst stay in Bulgaria,' added Christo. 'Despite this, the British attitude to Bulgarian wines can be described as negative ignorance: I don't know and I don't want to know. Bulgaria's bad image affects consumption.' Having finished his tirade, Christo opened the second bottle, which proved excellent.

Throughout the evening, I had to play the unlikely role of an optimist trying to disperse the impenetrable doom and gloom emanating from my dinner companions.

My points were: 1. There was no more KGB in Bulgaria. 2. There was no real censorship and the elections were more or less democratic. 3. The reforms were slow but irreversible. 4. Bulgaria had a bright future. 5. My Sofia InterContinental Hotel was superb, even by Western standards. 6 (my last and weightiest argument). It takes a highly civilised country to produce such a beautiful wine (I meant the second bottle, not the first one).

Christo and Nikolai's counter-points were: 1. The West had forgotten Bulgaria. 2. Bulgaria was surrounded by enemies. 3. Bulgaria was very corrupt: the moment Domaine Boyar made public its production figures, the mafia knocked on their door. 4. They couldn't improve the quality of their wines until they had control of vineyards, which they didn't. 5. There was no real market in Bulgaria and no one knew who the land belonged to. 6. Things were still reversible, and Stalinism could come back. 9. Bulgarians could still be seen barbecuing meat (a sign of prosperity in Bulgarian folklore), but it was 'the meat of their fellow Bulgarians'.

As you see, their arguments outweighed mine. At least, in quantity they did. I knew that they had good reason to be negative. But negativity could only create more negativity and their sad prophecies could easily become self-fulfilling, whereas a bit of optimism and 'hope against hope', as I knew only too well from my thirty-five years in the Soviet Union, could work miracles.

My enthusiasm was, to a large extent, faked. Looking back on my first few days in Bulgaria, I thought I could be forgiven for having succumbed to some cautious pessimism myself.

'Be alert,' I had been instructed at the small London offices of Domaine Boyar a week before. The series of adverse happenings in Bulgaria prior to my departure was so extraordinary that I was seriously thinking of putting the trip off.

Three days before my scheduled arrival in Sofia, Andrei Lukanov, Bulgaria's former prime minister and one of the country's leading reformist politicians was assassinated in a mafia-style killing, which looked almost like a copy-cat version of the murder of Russia's leading TV journalist, Vladislav Listev, in Moscow two years earlier. The assassin, camouflaged as a tramp, was waiting outside Lukanov's house and shot him in the heart and in the head – precisely as in Listev's case.

Lukanov was an outspoken critic of the slow pace of reform in Bulgaria. Some time before his death, he claimed publicly that he had evidence pointing to a 'return to Stalinist methods' to be introduced by Bulgaria's ruling Socialist Party. His murder sparked off rumours of troops in the streets of Sofia, of an impending state of emergency and even of a possible military coup.

Almost simultaneously, nine of Bulgaria's biggest private banks collapsed, effectively destroying the country's financial network. Inflation reached truly cosmic proportions. According to a London broadsheet, ruthless leather-clad gangsters, nicknamed 'wrestlers', swarmed all over the place and 'have transformed Sofia's cityscape'. And my recently published *Lonely*

Planet guidebook warned that 'foreigners are robbed by locals who invite them for a drink', which didn't bode well for the purposes of my wine-familiarisation trip.

As if all that were not enough, an epidemic of meningitis, triggered by the plummeting living standards, was raging in many areas of the country – a fact that made me carry water-purification pills in my luggage.

I learnt more bad news from the Bulgarian newspapers offered on my Balkan Airlines flight from Heathrow to Sofia. The Bulgarian language is similar to Russian, and uses the same Cyrillic alphabet, so I could understand almost everything, although, on that occasion, I wished I couldn't.

The papers led with speculations about possible motives for Lukanov's murder: economic, political or mafia-connected. These were followed by the news of yet another death (this time, natural and non-violent), that of Bulgaria's legendary clairvoyant and fortune-teller Baba Vanga (Granny Vanga), reputedly consulted at various times by Hitler, Brezhnev, Gorbachev, as well as by generations of Bulgarian leaders, who all wanted to know what the future had in stock for them.

In 1943, the blind peasant oracle, who lost her sight at the age of 12 during a whirlwind, allegedly told Hitler 'to leave Russia alone or face defeat'. In 1992, she assured Yeltsin of his forthcoming landslide election victory. She was also able to brief many grieving parents as to the exact whereabouts of their runaway offspring. And so on. Blind Baba Vanga was one of the country's few remaining optimists (probably just because she was blind): she predicted the onset of bright and plentiful times for Bulgaria, without specifying when they were going to come. But the undisputed fact that she had been able to foretell correctly the time of her own death was encouraging.

There seemed to be no end to negative newspaper stories. One was entitled 'Plovdiv Residential Area

Attacked by Worms'. It was too much, and I put the papers aside.

A sumptuous in-flight meal, washed down by a glass of excellent Bulgarian red wine, cheered me up a bit. 'Surely, things cannot be that hopeless in a country that can produce such refined wine,' I mused in self-consolation.

From what I knew, despite all the political mess and economic instability, the wine-making industry of Bulgaria, one of the world's four top wine exporters, was doing well. Brits alone were drinking more than three million cases of Bulgarian wine a year. My research files were bursting with recent press cuttings, in which snooty and hard-to-please British wine critics described Bulgarian wines as 'fine', 'unbelievably good', 'gloriously juicy' and 'safest choice', while Bulgarian wine-makers were credited with 'delivering great wine under incredibly difficult conditions'.

The plane gently probed the ground with its wheels, as if to check whether it was firm enough for landing. In a few minutes, it taxied up to a dimly lit terminal with a 'SOF A' neon sign on its roof.

'I' was missing from the sign, but *I* was in Sofia – there was little doubt about it. And in 'SOF A', too.

'Don't lose it!' the immigration officer blurted out handing me a dreaded 'statistical card' – a leftover from totalitarianism. The card was supposed to be stamped in every hotel I was to stay at. The punishment for its loss was probably a prison sentence. Or a firing squad. It all made sense: communists calling themselves 'Socialists' were still in power in Bulgaria.

A stooping young man in a leather jacket took a step towards me the moment I stumbled into the arrivals lounge. Still under the influence of the gory newspaper stories, I decided he was a 'wrestler'. Having dropped my suitcase, I frantically tried to recall the latest tae kwon-do moves we had learnt at my martial arts class in London.

'Are you Vitali?' he asked me in perfect Russian, picking up my suitcase from the floor.

'Yes, and you must be from Domaine Boyar,' I said in English with relief.

He shook his head.

I was about to wrench my suitcase from the cheeky Russian gangster's grip, when I remembered that shaking one's head in Bulgaria means 'yes'.

The young man's name was Christo. A Domaine Boyar official, he had studied in Moscow and was married to a Russian woman. He spoke Russian with a good Moscow accent.

'Has the situation in Sofia stabilised a little?' I asked him in the car.

He nodded, which, in the peculiar Bulgarian body language, meant 'no'.

It was late afternoon, but the dark streets of Sofia were already deserted. Very few cars were on the road. Most traffic lights didn't work. The kerb was lined with hundreds of wheel-less and door-less Soviet-made Ladas abandoned by their owners, who could not afford to maintain them. Flags were flying at half-mast on lamp-posts with no lamps. It looked as if the whole city had retired into itself, waiting for more troubles to come.

'At this spot a bomb exploded the other day,' said Christo pointing at an intersection of two wide streets. 'No one knows why.'

At the money-exchange office of my InterContinental hotel, I was given a thick wad of greasy lev banknotes in exchange for £20 – an average monthly salary in Bulgaria, which I intended to use as a couple of days' pocket money. The exchange rate was in the region of 350 lev per pound.

'Yesterday, the lev suddenly rose slightly against the US dollar, for no reason. It's chaos,' commented Christo.

All telephones at the hotel were switched off by the city council as a punishment for a neighbouring factory, which had refused to dispose of its rubbish and dumped it in the street. The hotel had nothing to do with the slovenly factory, but was unfortunate enough to share the same telephone line.

The famous fountains of Sofia had been dead for over five years. 'No one cares any more,' explained a street bookseller, whose wobbly stall in the former 9th of September (the start of communist rule in 1944), now 3rd of March (the victory over the Turks) Square sagged under glossy Bulgarian translations of Western pulp which nobody was buying.

Old men, with tearful eyes and faces of brown parchment, sat on benches under acacia trees surrounded by begging gypsy kids, whom they waved away without looking – like flies. Khaki-painted military jeeps were parked here and there.

The faded totalitarian grandeur of Sofia's centre reminded me of Moscow in the eighties. The only restored building was that of the Bulgarian People's Bank. A long line of queuers eager to withdraw their shrinking savings was snaking towards its entrance. The nearby Italian embassy was besieged by crowds of visa-seekers. In a small park around the church of Alexander Nevsky, grannies were selling portraits of Lenin, old samovars and 'The KGB is Alive' badges. And on the opposite side of the former Russian – now King the Liberator – Street, there was a strip club. Posters of the forthcoming Miss Erotic and Miss Lingerie competitions were stuck to its walls.

Weeping female voices could be heard from the magnificent Byzantine St Sofia Cathedral, where a morning liturgy was under way. 'Dear foreigners. We thank you with gratitude for your donation,' said a handwritten English sign on its front door. The moan-like Orthodox prayer floated above the empty mausoleum of Georgy Dimitrov (the founder of the Bulgarian Communist Party had been reburied at Sofia's Central Cemetery); above the Stalinist wedding cake of the Communist Party headquarters; above the former

Park of Freedom, renamed the Garden of Tsar Boris; above the statue of a lion put up in 1981 to commemorate thirteen hundred years of the Bulgarian state. A stray dog sniffed the ground around the stone lion, then lifted one leg and desecrated the symbol of once-glorious Bulgarian statehood. The lion was unperturbed. Battered and unkempt, he himself had come to resemble an oversized homeless dog.

From the centre, I took a tram to the suburb of Vitosha, on the outskirts of the city, where Bulgaria's Communist Party elite used to reside, separated from the real world by the natural wall of the Vitosha hill. This exclusive area was now occupied by Sofia's new rich, many of whom *were* the former party elite, so they didn't even have to move out of their ivy-covered cottages with stunning mountain views.

There, in quiet Sekvoya Street, stood the villa of Todor Zhivkov, Bulgaria's communist dictator for thirty-five years, from 1954 to 1989. His rule was marked by unquestioning loyalty to the Soviet Union, to which he referred as Bulgaria's elder brother. This tanks-enforced 'brotherhood' was the subject of many sad jokes. Here's one. At an international exhibition the Soviet Union showed a red elephant carrying a slogan: 'The Soviet elephant is the best elephant in the world!' And Bulgaria displayed a smaller elephant under the placard: 'The Bulgarian elephant is the younger brother of the Soviet elephant!'

After the popular uprising of 1989, the ageing Zhivkov was charged with nepotism (among other things, he appointed his daughter, Lyudmila, Bulgaria's minister of culture), corruption and the dictatorial abuse of power; he was put on trial, but his failing health saved him from a prison sentence. A frail octogenarian, he now lived under house arrest in Vitosha with his middle-aged granddaughter.*

*Todor Zhivkor died in May, 1998

Zhivkov's villa, half hidden from view by thick foliage, was surrounded by a fence with security cameras on top. I wondered whether they were there to protect Zhivkov from the anger of the Bulgarian people whom he had tormented for thirty-five years, or to protect the people from the nasty Stalinist ghost lurking behind the walls of this nice-looking mansion in Vitosha.

Through my Sofia contacts, I obtained Zhivkov's telephone number, and I dialled it from my hotel as soon as its telephone lines were restored. The phone was answered by a woman, probably his granddaughter. I introduced myself and asked whether I could have a word with Mr Zhivkov (with the stress on 'Mister'). I wanted to ask him only one question: whether or not he had any regrets. 'Comrade Zhivkov is ill,' the woman said after a pause (with the stress on 'Comrade'). 'He is in bed and does not give interviews.'

I was not particularly upset, for I knew what the answer to my intended question would have been. Speaking at his trial several years before, Zhivkov had blamed the Kremlin and staunchly refused to repent.

My farewell-to-Sofia dinner at Across the Road Behind the Cupboard was coming to an end. After the fourth bottle of wine, the mood of my hosts had improved dramatically.

'There are no rules, but the game goes on,' said Nikolai. 'Nature is on our side, and the quality of our wines keeps going up.'

'This year's vintage is especially good, which means that politics does not affect wines,' concluded Christo.

'Grape types tend not to recognise political borders,' Angela Muir once noted in *Decanter* magazine. Whether wines were immune from politics or not, they were definitely capable of turning incorrigible pessimists into cautious optimists. If only until the following morning.

30 THE STONY ALYOSHA

Bulgarian women do not go to shops to buy their dresses, as women do in England; they spin and weave, and make them at home. You see how industrious they are. They are much happier than Turkish women, because they are always busy . . .

Near Home or Europe Described,
Longmans, Green, & Co., London, 1910

Domaine Boyar had appointed Christo my driver and escort in Bulgaria. Our car was a new Korean sedan called Espero which means 'I hope'. Well, so did I . . .

Bouncing on road bumps and flying over potholes, I Hope raced us through the drab suburbs of Sofia and out into the countryside. The highway was so empty that even I could have driven on it for a while without having an accident, although my ideal driving ground is an Australian desert during the night – when camels are asleep.

The Bulgarian countryside was barren. No one was working in the fields.

'Nobody knows who owns the land,' complained Christo. 'Commissions to liquidate state farms have been created, but they do nothing, apart from arguing about what's to be done.'

It was a no-man's-land, in the true sense of the term.

Before proceeding to Plovdiv, Bulgaria's second-largest city, we made a detour to visit a winery in the town of Assenovgrad, known as the home of Mavrud, the famous Bulgarian black grape.

Escorted by the winery's manager, we went down to the cellar and walked past rows of supine 9000-litre barrels, made of Bulgarian oak, in which Mavrud was maturing. Each barrel was supplied with a tag describing the characteristics of the wine – like a medical history sheet at the foot of a hospital bed.

'We have possibilities, but too many restrictions,' complained the manager. The state takes away seventy per cent of our profits, and we have almost nothing left to spend on grape-growing. I hope we'll be fully privatised one day.'

Hearing this, Christo gave a sceptical chuckle.

When we entered the tasting room, my heart fluttered, as if I had suddenly bumped into a schoolmate whom I hadn't seen for many years. In the middle of the table, covered with a white starched cloth, among the ready-to-taste red and white wines, stood a short, pot-bellied bottle of Slantchev Briag ('Sunny Beach'), a cheap Bulgarian brandy which used to be one of my and Evgeny Bulavin's favourite drinks. God knows how many bottles of it we had killed. I could almost feel its strong oily taste in my mouth – the taste of many a Soviet hangover.

My good friend Sasha Kabakov, now a celebrated Moscow author, once wrote about Slantchev Briag:

Let me pour you some more of this magic Bulgarian drink. God help them, our little Bulgarian brothers, God preserve their primitive technologies, according to which they make this grape moonshine – without any colourings and other technical crap. God bless them and let them keep sending us – by cargo-car loads – this magnificent 'Sunny Beach', which, even in the biggest rip-off of a wine shop, costs no more than ten thousand roubles . . .

'We produce this brandy exclusively for Russia,' the manager said apologetically, having intercepted my nostalgic look. He ordered an assistant to take the brandy away and assured us that it had been placed on the tasting table by mistake. What a shame!

We tasted Mavrud 1991, and Mavrud Special Reserve 1989, matured in small Californian-oak barrels; and the full-bodied Cabernet Sauvignon 1992. I was (almost) professionally swirling my glass before each sip of wine and dutifully spat all of it out into my personal spittoon. Well, almost all.

I wished they had offered us Sunny Beach instead.

Towering above Plovdiv was a huge statue of a Soviet soldier on top of a hill. With a sub-machine-gun slung over his disproportionately broad concrete shoulder, the soldier was looking down at the town, first liberated and then enslaved by him.

The statue, immortalised in a popular Soviet song, had a name: Alyosha.

> Alyosha, the Russian soldier in Bulgaria,
> stands above the mountain.
> He no longer brings flowers to girls –
> they bring flowers to him.

The flower-loving concrete Alyosha found himself in the centre of a long-lasting post-communist controversy. When the statue was erected in 1957, the pro-Soviet local authorities ordered the sculptors to make it into the city's tallest structure. It was a rushed and tactless decision. Plovdiv residents, for whom the memory of five centuries of Turkish rule, when no building was allowed to be taller than the mosque, was still alive, took it as an affront. From the moment the first democratic freedoms came to Bulgaria, there were numerous calls for the removal of the offending monument. In 1996, the fate of Alyosha went on public trial, but the Plovdiv regional court decreed that the statue had to be left alone. It was probably the first court case in history with a statue as a defendant.

In reality, it was not just the monument that went on

trial: it was the whole of Bulgaria's communist past that the Court had ordered should be left intact. And so, he was still there, the frozen Soviet soldier in enormous concrete boots.

With Christo, I climbed the hill to have a closer look. Alyosha was lost, forgotten and desecrated. Red paint was splashed all over the pedestal. Black graffiti covered the inscription: 'Glory to the Soviet Army, the liberator'. Grass and weeds grew in between the steps leading to the monument, a sure sign that girls were no longer bringing Alyosha flowers.

From close to, the statue had a Pisa Tower effect: it gave the impression of leaning at a precarious angle, as if ready to collapse and bury you under its massive weight. I could understand why the people of Plovdiv thought it was offensive.

Plovdiv was a stark contrast to the war-zone dreariness of Sofia. It was colourful, Mediterranean and bubbling with life. The unmistakably Turkish cobbled streets of the old town, with small shops, mosques and open-air cafés, ran up and down the hill. Tiny car parks were guarded by Adidas-clad 'wrestlers' who looked as though they had the word 'gangster' tattooed on their low, Neanderthal-like foreheads.

We had coffee in an empty Turkish coffee shop near the main mosque. The coffee jug stood on a small brass tray, next to a plate with Turkish biscuits and a glass of water with a spoon in it. The spoon contained a small amount of melted sugar, the so-called 'white jam' which you were supposed to put into your mouth and then wash down with the 'Bulgarian coffee'.*

For some reason, sitting on an old squeaky divan and staring at dirty rugs hanging from the wall, I felt as if I

---

* It was actually Turkish coffee, but in Bulgaria all references to Turkey were still frowned upon – just like in Greece, where the same drink would be called 'Greek coffee', or like the same popular Russian dish which is known as Chicken Kiev in Moscow and as Chicken Moscow in Kiev.

was in a Turkish harem, although I had never been to a real harem (Turkish or not), and neither had Christo.

Like a fairy-tale oriental town from the *Arabian Nights*, Plovdiv was full of ancient magic. That was why I was not particularly surprised when, on the slope of a hill, we stumbled upon the beautifully preserved Roman theatre built in the second century BC, complete with columns, marble terraces and toga-wrapped statues; it made the Colosseum look like a small, insignificant ruin. The Romans constructed the theatre in an attempt to elevate Trimontium (Plovdiv) from a vassal town to a provincial capital, and they certainly succeeded.

For an hour, we climbed up and down the theatre's marble steps, trampled by the legionaries' soft sandals. We sat on time-beaten stone seats, polished by the flabby behinds of the patricians. A sudden return to modern times was provided by the entrance sign: 'Local – 20 lev; foreigner – 100 lev', although no one had bothered to charge us any fee at all.

More Adidas-covered 'wrestlers' stood in the lobby of our Novotel hotel in the evening. They behaved like bosses and were busily answering telephones at Reception.

The hotel's basement bar, where we went for a nightcap, was full of young mini-skirted prostitutes under the supervision of an old hook-nosed witch, probably their 'madam'. They were targeting two brandy-tossing German businessmen at a corner table. The more the Germans drank, the more interested they seemed in the girls, who were hypnotising them with moronic grimaces intended as lascivious looks. At one point, one of the girls stood up from her seat, pulled up her mini-skirt (there was nothing much to pull up) and showed the Germans her knicker-less behind. I was not sure whether it was a gesture of contempt, or her special way of after-dinner flirting.

One thing was certain: she was not the sort of girl who would bring flowers to stony Alyosha.

31 SQUIFFY NOTES IN MY TASTING LIST

'Do you want to hear a joke?' asked Christo. We were driving through south-eastern Bulgaria, overtaking puffing Trabants and unhurried, self-important donkeys. 'In Britain, they once had a travel quiz with the first prize being one week in Bulgaria and the second – two weeks in Bulgaria.'

Christo's humour was more than self-deprecating. It was masochistic. But, despite (or, maybe, because of) his constant alternations between pessimistic scepticism and sceptical pessimism, I was enjoying his company more and more. It was like catching up with an old Moscow buddy.

A big wine day lay ahead of us: we were expected to visit three wineries. I was bracing myself for more of the wine-bluffer's six essential 'S's: Swirling, Sniffing, Staring, Sipping, Swilling (without Slurping!) and Spitting.

Stara Zagora winery was a happy little place. Clean, well-kept and efficient, it was a good argument in favour of capitalism, simply because it was Bulgaria's only fully privatised wine factory.

'Privatisation was a real blessing for us,' its jolly

administrative manager told us in English. 'We now work for a real market and can invest in grape-growing and production. Two per cent of our shares are owned by the workers, whose motivation and responsibility have increased greatly. As a result, we are able to export ninety per cent of our wines to the West.'

'What are your best wines?' I asked him.

'It is hard to say. They are like children to us. We love them all. Even years ago, when we were forced to export the bulk of our production to the Soviet Union, the quality of our wines was good.'

At the mention of the Soviet Union, the manager shuddered, but he quickly regained his composure. 'Gorbachev taught us a good lesson in 1986, when he adopted his crazy anti-drinking regulations: never to rely on one market alone. Do you see my grey hair? It went grey then, in 1986, when the Soviet Union, our main buyer, stopped ordering wine from us. For eight months after that stupid decree Bulgaria did not export a single bottle! God, we suffered. Of course, Zhivkov aped everything done by Big Soviet Brother and introduced a similar law in Bulgaria. Until 1989, we were not allowed to plant new grapes. But we have survived. How? By being optimists. It takes an optimist to make a good wine. All the pessimists have left Bulgaria already.'

'Have they really?' I thought, throwing a furtive look at Christo, whose body language showed total and complete scepticism about everything the manager was saying. I suddenly realised why he was an executive, not a wine-maker.

The manager's anti-Russian feelings manifested themselves again during the tasting, which started with Aligote and Rkatsiteli, white table wines to which Evgeny Bulavin, who liked using them as chasers for more serious drinks, affectionately referred to as 'sukhen'koye' ('little dry').

'These wines mostly go to Russia, since their quality is

not as high as that of our famous reds from the Oriachovitza region,' said he.

'They must have good reasons to treat Russia like a big spittoon and send their worst and cheapest wines there,' I thought, spitting out (not without pleasure) the sour Rkatsiteli into my personal small spittoon. After years of drinking in the Soviet Union, I knew exactly what those reasons were.

Our visit to Iambol, the next winery on our route, was dominated by one person, who wasn't even there. His name was Simeon Coburgotski. He was 58 and worked as a business consultant in Madrid. I nearly forgot to mention that, outside office hours, he was also known as His Majesty King Simeon II of Bulgaria. Simeon left Bulgaria in 1946, when he was 9, clutching his mother's hand. By that time, he had already been on the wobbly Bulgarian throne for three years: his father King (or Tsar) Boris II died of a heart attack after returning from a visit to his good friend and ally Adolf Hitler. Rumour had it that his Nazi buddy had poisoned him for trying to win greater autonomy for Bulgaria within the Third Reich.

According to another Bulgarian rumour, the pickled, broken heart of King Boris had been lovingly preserved by the former royal gardener throughout the communist times.

Fifty years later, Simeon came back to his motherland on a short private visit. Thousands of Bulgarians came to welcome him and his Spanish wife, Margarita, at the airport. The communist-dominated government, however, did not send anyone to meet him and refused to provide the exiled monarch with bodyguards. Unguarded but happy, Simeon undertook a tour of Bulgaria. A connoisseur of good wines, he visited Domaine Boyar and granted it the exclusive right to use his royal coat of arms on their best labels, which, from then on, read, 'By Appointment to His Majesty King Simeon II'.

The wine-loving king made a special detour to visit the Iambol winery. We had to spend a long time looking through a weighty album of photos taken on that memorable day. In the photos, Simeon was shaking hands, touching grapes and tasting wines, of course.

The wines at Iambol were good. The winery's director assured us that they made the best merlot and cabernet sauvignon in Bulgaria, while their whites were successfully exported to Japan, where they were mixed with local wines (sakei), and – naturally – to Russia.

'Our Cabernet 1993 is the best-selling wine in Norway,' the director said proudly. Having visited Norway more than once, I knew that severe restrictions on the alcohol trade, together with high prices, had made booze-hungry Norwegians not particularly choosy about what wines (or spirits) they could grab after queuing in the country's few state-monopoly shops: the cheaper, the better. In the director's shoes, I wouldn't have mentioned that as an achievement of his distinguished Simeon-endorsed winery.

Peasants were bringing grapes by donkey to the winery in the village of Slaviantsi, our last visit of the day. The donkeys were queuing near the winery gates in an obedient and orderly fashion, like customers at a London post office.

As opposed to Stara Zagora and Iambol, Slaviantsi specialised in white wines, whose main difference from the reds, from the wine-maker's point of view, was not so much in colour but in the lower temperature of fermentation. From the vodka-drinker's point of view, however, there was no difference at all.

Here I must confess that after two previous tastings, during which I was unable (and sometimes unwilling) to spit out every wine I had to try, I was feeling somewhat tipsy and could not care less whether the wines in Slaviantsi were red, white or turquoise.

In the tasting room, each of us was given a tasting list,

a sheet of paper with the names and main characteristics of the wines we were to try. I was slightly disturbed by the Notes column, which was blank and was supposed to be filled in by the taster, i.e., myself. I was worried that at the end of the tasting our notes would be collected for appraisal, like test papers in a primary school.

We tasted Misket, a local white wine made of black grapes, and Merlot, a local red wine made of white grapes.

The company's vice-president told us that their Misket won a royal gold medal in 1898, which was not surprising: Bulgaria was then ruled by Prince Ferdinand of Saxe-Coburg-Gotha, who had the reputation of being not too discriminating a drinker. 'Wines win medals – like soldiers, horses and dogs,' I wrote in the Notes column of my tasting list.

Another revealing thing about Misket was that it was exported to Scandinavia, Poland, Russia and the UK – clearly, Europe's most wine-ignorant nations.

We tasted a sparkling wine of 1951 vintage (three years older than I and still bubbly!) and polished it off with a shot of *rakia*, a burningly strong grape brandy by which they swear in Bulgaria. The last squiffy note in my tasting list was 'Rakia is a Russian woman's first name'. I was glad that no one bothered to collect it from me, or I would have ended up with a very bad mark.

The overloaded I Hope was slowly chugging up the steep mountain road towards the Black Sea coast town of Nesebar, where we were to stay overnight. The number of people inside I Hope remained unchanged – me and Christo – but the quantity of crates of souvenir wine bottles in the boot had grown in direct proportion to the number of wineries we visited.

The poor I Hope was sagging and striking sparks from the asphalt with its metallic belly. It had also acquired a considerable backward tilt due to the gallons of white, red and sparkling wines in dozens of cheerfully clinking bottles inside its uncomplaining boot.

We didn't know what to do with this liquid load. Certainly, we were unable to drink it ourselves, and I was not planning to take it back to London. Christo did not need it either: as a senior official of Domaine Boyar, he never experienced shortages of wine. Nor could we commit the sacrilege of throwing the bottles out on to the road. In short, we had to carry this alcoholic white (and red) elephant with us.

I have always been of the opinion that a long journey can only succeed if one travels light. Alas, in reality it often proves difficult because of the burdensome gifts you pick up on your way. Especially if you are a travelling journalist. In the West, publicity-hungry officials force tons of pamphlets and brochures on you. Normally, you can dump them in a rubbish bin the moment you leave their offices, but at times this may be embarrassing.

Once, in Andorra, I ended up with a bulky tome of Andorran medieval laws in Catalan, presented to me by the country sub-syndic general (deputy prime minister). Dumping it in tiny Andorra, where everybody knew each other, could upset the country's government and, possibly, even lead to the worsening of Andorran–British, Andorran–Australian, Andorran–Ukrainian or Andorran–Russian (depending on whom they preferred to take me for) bilateral relations. So I had to drag the unnecessary volume all the way to Monaco. The helicopter which was supposed to fly me there from Nice had problems taking off. It was with great relief that I finally abandoned the brick-heavy volume in my hotel room in Monte Carlo.

As an investigative journalist in the Soviet Union, I constantly had to rebuff clumsy attempts by corrupt apparatchiks to force a bribe, camouflaged as a souvenir, on me. One had to be especially careful in Georgia and other republics of the Caucasus, notorious for their violent hospitality.

In Georgia, there existed (and still does) an old custom, according to which any object praised or complimented by a guest was supposed to be immediately presented to him. The guest's failure or reluctance to accept such a gift could seriously upset the host and, occasionally, even lead to stabbing the ungrateful guest in the chest with an old family dagger.

Once, in Tbilisi, the Georgian capital, I unwisely complimented my host's wife – a fat, moustached woman – on her cooking, after which her husband started hinting at his willingness to give her to me as a gift, and it took me considerable effort to persuade him that such a present would have been too precious and too bountiful (which was true) for me to accept.

On another occasion, in Vologda, where I was sent to investigate embezzlement at a local furniture-making factory, they kept offering me chairs, tables, cupboards and even a double bed as 'souvenirs'. After I had adamantly refused all of those, they – in a devilishly clever gesture – presented me with a souvenir wooden board with a portrait of Lenin engraved on it!

The board – more than a square metre large and weighing over ten kilos – was a classic example of a gift that one could not refuse, for dumping something with Lenin's portrait on it could easily lead the dumper to jail. So I had to carry the stupid, useless board all the way back to Moscow. Naturally, at the very first opportunity, I gave it away as a birthday present to a really nasty person. You should have seen his face when he unwrapped it. I was sure that he would promptly present it to someone else, and so on – and dreaded the possibility that one day, having gone through thousands of hands, the blasted board could return to me like a boomerang, which would have almost certainly happened, had I not left the Soviet Union in January 1990.

With travel to and from the former USSR getting easier by the day, I dread that it will eventually find me in the West one day.

32 REDISCOVERING OLD BUDDIES AND OLD TASTE-BUDS

The forest-covered hills along the road were touched with a brownish autumn rash, as if they were suffering from some ecological form of measles. Compact Bulgarian cows were grazing in the fields.

'It is good that we still have cows,' muttered Christo sarcastically. 'Soon we won't have any . . .'

'In all normal countries people have credit cards,' he droned on. 'Only we in Bulgaria don't have them. We have nothing!'

'Look how beautiful your Bulgarian autumn is,' I said trying to stop his whinging.

'So what? Spring is better.'

I gave up.

We were 40 kilometres from Varna when I Hope, whose boot, after a quick visit to the Pomorie distillery, was burdened with a crate of Pomorie brandy, came to an abrupt stop in the middle of a highway. We had to get out and push it over to the kerb. This time the breakdown looked terminal. Since the RAC had not yet come to Bulgaria, we had to abandon our faithful I Hope and hitch-hike to Varna, where we could seek help.

Bulgaria's main port and third-largest city, Varna felt more like a capital than Sofia did. Crowds were milling along its pretty plane-tree-lined boulevards. Teenagers were dashing past open-air cafés and 'snek-bars' on their rattling skateboards. Street stalls were selling books and popcorn, which in Bulgaria was aptly called '*pukalka*' ('fartie'). On the promenade, a chained tame bear was swilling beer from the bottle – to the delight of the crowd and of the corpulent and bearded trainer, who looked very much like his bear, only more drunk. In its fuss, buzz and never-say-die spirit, Varna reminded me of Odessa, the Ukrainian city of wits, poets and seafarers, which was just across the Black Sea.

Christo put himself in charge of the operation to save the disabled I Hope. With the help of his Varna-based friend Pyotr, I Hope was towed into the latter's garage, where it was left overnight. A 'car wizard' mate of Pyotr's promised to have a look at it the following morning. For me, it was as moving to see that friendships still mattered as much in Bulgaria as they did in the Soviet Union, where you could always rely on friends when everything else failed (which was not uncommon), and they could rely on you. Friendship was one of the few bastions which the system could neither penetrate nor shatter. Sadly, many seemingly impregnable liaisons collapsed with the advent of capitalism. Individualism, selfishness and isolation came in their stead.

Christo, Pyotr and I had dinner at the Happy English Pub, where the only 'English' dish on the menu was 'Smashed Potatoes'. Happy stray dogs kept running in and out of the pub as we ate *tarator*, a Bulgarian yoghurt soup with cucumbers.

'See that house across the road?' Pyotr said, pointing to a four-storey baroque building covered with scaffolding. 'It has just been bought for six hundred thousand dollars. The buyers paid cash, for there is no mortgage system in Bulgaria, and banks charge three hundred per cent a year for any credit.'

A naval engineer by education, Pyotr was now a businessman with his own design and printing company. He also owned a local radio station – 'just music, no politics'. 'The worse off Bulgaria is, the better off my business is,' he said somewhat enigmatically.

It was at this point that Christo mounted his favourite hobby-horse.

'Pyotr is an optimist,' he said, slurping his *tarator*. 'Our freedom is stillborn. The atmosphere is too bad, too polluted.'

To my surprise, Pyotr responded in kind, and the two friends spent the rest of the evening discussing the devilish plot of Russia and Israel, whose teams had deliberately drawn their World Cup qualifying football game in order to undermine Bulgaria's chances.

It was hard not to agree with Bulgaria's former prime minister, Filip Dimitrov, a psychotherapist by profession, who once collectively diagnosed his compatriots as suffering from a 'passive feeling of total helplessness'.

Next morning, we towed I Hope to the 'car wizard', who lived in a sunlit seaside suburb. Multicoloured rags were drying on the balcony of his ancient sandstone cottage.

The wizard's conclusion was grave: the alternator had to be replaced. I had no idea what the alternator's function was, but it looked as if without it I Hope would only alternate between immobility and motionlessness.

After an hour of phone calls and strenuous net-working, Pyotr managed to track down a mechanic who would replace the mysterious alternator by the following morning.

On the last leg of our journey towards the Romanian border, we stopped at Suhindol, Bulgaria's best-known winery. Unlike all the other wineries we had visited, Suhindol was a co-operative, owned by its workers and independent of the state. Besides making wines, it made its own cheese and bred its own pigs and chickens. Each worker was entitled to fifteen free loaves of bread a month, and the prices in the co-operative's canteen were heavily subsidised. Suhindol had its own kindergarten, a nursing home and a football team. It even had its own private roads. In short, it was a paradise on earth that could easily have been mistaken for a blueprint of Bulgaria's bright future, had it not been for one simple fact: it was the country's *only* co-operative of its kind. To call a spade a spade, it was a showcase.

The table in the tasting room was sagging under food produced by the co-operative. But it was not for us: Bulgaria's vice-president was expected any moment, with a suite of factotums. Like their communist predecessors, the new Bulgarian elite knew which places were worth visiting.

It looked as if wine-making was the last item on the busy agenda of our hosts, who were more preoccupied with problems of pig-breeding and politician-feeding.

The winery's speciality was Gamza, a red wine made only in Bulgaria, of which we tasted three different vintages.

I had seen too many showcases and too much window-dressing in my life to be impressed by them any longer (in the Soviet Union, they used the word '*pokazukha*', which I would translate as 'boasting of non-existent achievements'). But I couldn't help being favourably affected by the excellent wines, for which I had developed if not exactly a craving, certainly an interest and a taste. True, I was still not well versed in the wine critics' sophisticated terminology – all this 'smooth-minty-taste-with-a-hint-of-the-pastilley-fruit-of-yesteryear' gibberish. But, for the first time in my life, I was definitely enjoying wine. It was like classical music: to appreciate a symphony, you don't have to know the score.

In a previous life, I was probably a cat in a medieval European town: I love side-streets, narrow lanes and smelly gateways leading to dark and smelly courtyards, full of historical nooks and crannies. Veliko Turnovo, the ancient capital of the Bulgarian kingdom, where we stopped overnight, had plenty of those. The tiled roofs of tilted old houses criss-crossed above our heads as we walked through the old town, which smelt of freshly washed linen and cats' poo.

Near the former Ottoman police station, we saw a group of people sitting on the empty terraces of what looked like a small stadium and staring down silently into pitch darkness. Christo explained that it was the spot of the famous 'light and sound show', which functioned only in summer.

Well, it was early autumn, but they were already sitting on the 'light and sound' spot, which had neither light nor sound, looking into nowhere and waiting for the show to commence next summer. How very Bulgarian!

There was only one thing that I hated about the old town: its fragile, ancient façades were covered with Marlboro signs and stickers. The bold black letters on the red background screamed at us from every wall, every door and every window. Their per capita rate in Veliko Turnovo was probably the highest in the world, even if homeless cats were included in the overall figure of the town's population. Bulgaria, even without Marlboro, has always been among the world's heaviest-smoking nations. Putting up Marlboro ads in the windows of Veliko Turnovo was on a par with pro-moting the benefits of AIDS in the red-light district of Bangkok.

We marked my last evening in Bulgaria by dining at the Arbanassi Palace, formerly a hotel for the Bulgarian Communist Party top brass. We were driven there by a teenage taxi driver in a battered Moskvich (I Hope was enjoying a well-deserved rest) with an 'I Love Marlboro' sticker on the windscreen.

To me, the interior of the Arbanassi was recognisable from similar Soviet establishments: wood panels, columns, chandeliers and parquet floors, from which the polish didn't have time to fade. Communist functionaries in the former Soviet-bloc countries seemed to have similar taste, or rather a similar lack of it.

We sat in a spacious restaurant, which had only one copy of the menu – as transferable as the red communist banner of honour. Several dozen oak tables stood outside earshot of each other – as in a Pall Mall club. An old, sad-faced piano player was tickling the ivories gently. He must have played here for years ignoring the shouts and insults of the carousing party bosses.

'Have any of the former communist leaders of Bulgaria, apart from Zhivkov, been tried for their crimes?' I asked Christo.

'No, they haven't. They can't be tried by the laws of a civilised country, because they didn't live by those laws. In Romania, they did the right thing – they shot the Ceausescus on the spot, and that was it.'

The old piano player was soon replaced by three Russian female dancers in darned tights. One of them, with feathers in her hat, was no less than fifty years old. I christened her Babushka ('Granny').

At the end of the meal, we ordered the expensive Black Sea cognac. I had a sip from my glass, and, as Igor Pomerantsev would say, I couldn't believe my tongue: my mouth felt that it was not Black Sea, but a much simpler and cheaper stuff, possibly diluted with real Black Sea water. My semi-dead taste-buds must have been revived by all those tastings. I called the waiter over.

'This is not Black Sea!' I said with unexpected authority.

'Terribly sorry,' the waiter mumbled. 'There has been a mistake. I'll bring you the real thing in a moment.'

'Well done,' said Christo. I myself was impressed by

the sudden awakening of my old, vodka-ruined taste-
buds.

Babushka did a belly dance, and the two others a half-
hearted can-can. Then all three of them sang 'Summer-
time' in a faltering chorus.

The show was over.

33 THE QUAINTEST CITY IN THE BALKANS

Though the Bulgarians are very industrious, their religion led them to laziness, for it required them to keep holy more than a hundred days in the year. It also told them to fast more than two hundred days; that is, to eat neither meat nor cheese, eggs nor butter, but only bread and vegetables. The Bulgarians are very brave, and often conquered their enemies.

Near Home or Europe Described,
Longmans, Green, & Co., London, 1910

One place in Bulgaria that I couldn't possibly miss was Gabrovo, a town that had won international fame for its cruelly self-deprecating humour, directed at the extreme miserliness of its own residents. Supposedly, it was the economical Gabrovians who had invented mini-skirts and narrow trousers, gliders and Bulgaria's smallest-denomination coin (the stotinka), a matchbox with only one side for striking, and clocks that stopped during the night. According to Gabrovo jokes, the locals carried their shoes when climbing the Shipka mountain, to avoid wear and tear. They always travelled in third-class carriages because fourth-class ones did not exist. They added flour to face-powder to make it last longer, and insisted on seeing their guests to the door simply because they enjoyed doing so. They made horses wear green-tinted glasses to encourage them to eat sawdust instead of oats and let a cat down the chimney rather than hire a sweep. They split a match in two before lighting a cigarette and warmed the knives before a party to make it difficult for the guests to help themselves to butter.

A cat with a docked tail was the town's official emblem: the Gabrovians, always eager to cut their heating expenses, calculated that it would take a wee bit less time to let a tail-less cat inside a house in winter than a cat with a full-length tail.

I was anxious to see whether the troublesome times had affected the famous Gabrovo wit, and, although the town was not on our wine-tasting route, Christo magnanimously agreed to make a detour.

'This is my favourite Gabrovo joke,' he said from behind the wheel. 'A student from Gabrovo writes a letter home from Sofia complaining that he is so poor that every morning he has to run after a bus to save five stotinki. His father replies, "Why don't you run after a taxi instead and save a lev?"'

I chuckled, happy to hear Christo joking. But my joy didn't last long.

'These days stotinki exist only in jokes,' he added with a deep sigh.

'There is a similar Georgian joke,' I said to cheer him up. 'A Georgian student writes home to his mother from Moscow: "Dear Papa" – "*papa*" is "mother" in Georgian, by the way – "I feel very ashamed. Every morning all my fellow students go to the university by bus, and only I travel by car. They all laugh at me." His mother replies, "My poor bicho" – "*bicho*" is "boy" in Georgian, contrary to what you might have thought – "why can't you be like everybody else and buy yourself a bus?"'

It was nice to realise that humour could travel.

In accordance with Gabrovo's space-saving traditions, a statue of the town's founder, Racho the

Blacksmith, stood on a tiny island in the middle of the River Yantra. Economical horse-drawn carriages and carts outnumbered cars in the town's narrow streets. It was necessity rather than choice that kept some of the old humorous traditions alive.

We parked near the Palace of Humour and Satire, an imposing modernistic structure dominating the town-scape. The palace was the venue of the international Biennial Festival of Humour, which used to attract leading satirists from all over the former communist bloc. They competed for the prestigious award, the Prize of Sly Pyotr. Selected jokes from the festival would appear in *A Propos* magazine, of which I had once seen a copy.

It looked as if those times were firmly in the past. The square in front of the palace was deserted, apart from the statues of Don Quixote astride a horse and his faithful squire, Sancho Panza, following him on a donkey. The palace itself was closed.

An elderly duty woman in a woollen kerchief finally responded to our frantic knocking. She agreed to let us in on condition that each of us bought two tickets.

'Why two?' I asked.

'Because very few people come here these days, and the palace is closed,' she retorted.

I made the mistake of flashing my press card in her face, hoping that this would persuade her to go down to the normal one-ticket-per-person fee.

'Ha, you are with the press,' she mumbled con-tentedly. 'It means I can charge you extra for taking photos.'

We were in Gabrovo, after all . . .

The darkened interior of the palace smelt of toilets and decay. The duty woman followed us assiduously as we walked from one empty hall to another, counting every photo I took. Some of the cartoons and sculptures on display were truly witty. I was taken by a drawing of an egg with a water-tap attached to it, which struck me as an adequate symbol of modern Gabrovo humour. The tap was screwed on tightly, meaning that there was nothing much to laugh at.

We lunched in I Hope on 'apricot rolls', bought at a local petrol station. Having consumed the rolls, we failed to find any trace of apricots. We were in Gabrovo.

The town's only bookshop, the House of Books, now traded in saucepans and vacuum-cleaners. There were as many books left in the House of Books as there was humour in the House of Humour.

The road out of Gabrovo, which was described by an insightful turn-of-the-century British traveller, Harry de Windt, as 'undoubtedly the quaintest city we saw throughout our wanderings in the Balkans', was lined with ugly Soviet-era apartment blocks, a living illustration of the world's shortest and cruellest joke: communism.

The town of Ruse was split into two by the River Danube, which marked Bulgaria's border with Romania. My Romanian driver was waiting for me in the lobby of the Riga Hotel.

It was time to say goodbye to Christo. We embraced.

'We shall meet again one day,' I said.

'I doubt it very much,' he muttered.

I patted I Hope on its warm, crackling bonnet and jumped into the waiting car with Bucharest number plates.

As we drove across the Friendship Bridge, I felt a tinge of sadness at leaving Bulgaria – the land of blind profits, incorrigible sceptics, parsimonious wits and resourceful wine-makers. If Gabrovo was 'the quaintest city . . . in the Balkans', Bulgaria was definitely the Balkans' quaintest country.

'As the geese saved Rome, wines will save Bulgaria,' Margarit Todorov, Domaine Boyar's managing director, had told me in London before my trip.

I hoped very much that he was right.

34 SHIATSU OF THE SOUL

Romania is one of the most fertile countries of Europe.
It is full of corn-fields and wide pasture lands. It yields
beautiful fruits, especially grapes and lemons . . . The
peasants have pieces of land of their own. They eat
nothing but a kind of flour, called polenta . . .'

Near Home or Europe Described,
Longmans, Green, & Co., London, 1910

Having negotiated the Friendship Bridge, we drove
straight into a huge dirty puddle, almost the width of the
Danube. It was that puddle that effectively separated
Bulgaria from Romania.

My first impressions of Romania could be sum-
marised as culture shock in reverse. It was like driving
through the Soviet countryside of the '50s. The road,
which felt as if it consisted solely of bumps and potholes, was crammed with horse-drawn carts loaded with
hay. Peasant women with rakes in their hands were
sitting on top of these slowly moving haystacks.

For the first time since leaving the Soviet Union, I saw
women with yokes over their shoulders, bent under the
weight of the buckets of water they were carrying.
Roadside villages were literally drowning in dirt, and all
the huts along the road were in different stages of
collapse and decay. The not-too-prosperous Bulgaria I
had just left looked like a modern superpower in
comparison to this time-forgotten land. Had the ever-

whinging Christo been with me, I would have reminded him of a wise oriental proverb: 'I complained that I had no shoes, until I met someone who had no feet.'

I recalled one of the opening sentences of Bram Stoker's *Dracula*: 'The impression I had was that we were leaving the West and entering the East.' Associations with *Dracula* were bound to be frequent in Romania.

I was dying to use the toilet. The driver did not share my enthusiasm, but I insisted.

We stopped near a half-ruined shed with the sign 'Bar' above the entrance.

The Bar was empty, apart from an overpowering stench, mountains of rubbish covering the floor carpet-like, and mounds of cigarette ends on the tables.

The toilet . . . Describing it would take the angst and wrath of the great proletarian writer Maxim Gorky, author of *The Lower Depths,* who had an extremely deprived childhood. It was the worst toilet I had ever seen (and I have seen some pretty disgusting ones, I can assure you). The collapsing door, with its broken, semi-detached door-handle, hung on one rusty hinge. One could almost see with the naked eye all the world's deadliest bacteria horror-dancing and having a picnic on its filthy, scratched surface. I pushed the door aside with my shirt sleeve, trying not to touch it, but, having slipped on the slime-covered floor, ended up grabbing it with both hands. My palms immediately started itching, as if tickled by millions of naughty microbes and viruses which had happily abandoned their quarters on the door and re-settled on my skin.

Since I am no Maxim Gorky, I will spare you a description of what was behind the door.

When I emerged back into the Bar, my way was blocked by a buxom woman. 'Taxa!' she pronounced threateningly. Capitalism had come to Romania, and now one had to pay 500 leu (10p) for the privilege of using the world's filthiest toilet.

This episode added a new meaning to one of Evgeny Bulavin's memorable expressions: 'A toilet is a great purgatory for thoughts.'

We drove through the tree-less outskirts of Bucharest – past rickety, unkempt housing blocks wrapped in washing and surrounded by piles of debris; past dark, subdued crowds of shabbily dressed people waiting for non-existent buses and trams; past packs of ragged and bony dogs fighting over pieces of garbage on street corners; past flocks of ragged and bony street kids, who besieged our car at each set of traffic lights, asking for money or food.

It was getting dark. The crimson rays of the setting sun, filtered through thick, heavy clouds, made the apocalyptic urban scene even more tragic and surreal. It was like moving inside a gaping wound, inflicted on Bucharest (whose name – ironically – means 'the City of Pleasure' in Romanian) by twenty-four years of Ceausescu's tyranny, a wound that showed no sign of healing.

Closer to the centre, an occasional brightly lit window of a Western shop, at which pedestrians were gaping, or a blinking neon sign could be spotted.

The centre itself was livelier: its wide streets and boulevards, reminiscent of the pre-war times when Bucharest was known as the Paris of the East, were now lined with grey, massive buildings of the Ceausescu era – dark, abandoned and sinisterly out of place.

The interior of the newly renovated and Western-owned Majestic Hotel, where I was disgorged, was dressed in marble. It was a chunk of a different world, which had nothing to do with the tramps, beggars and stray dogs lurking outside its spotlessly clean corridors, restaurants and lobbies, patrolled round the clock by broad-shouldered security guards, all looking 'too strong for their suits', to use the polite euphemism of London shop assistants.

The porter immediately offered me a massage – the last thing I needed under the circumstances. The shock of my first encounter with Romania had already resulted in a complete shiatsu of my soul, and the Majestic Hotel's massage (whatever that might imply) was superfluous.

The mini-bar in my room stocked 25-milligram vodka bottles for $7 each – an average weekly salary in Romania.

I had been invited to dinner at the newly restored Casa Vernescu Casino by Basil Zarnoveanu, director of Vinexport trading company, my Romanian hosts.

White limos with French and Italian number plates were parked near the Casa Vernescu's plush entrance. As I was told later, Western fraudsters liked to come to Bucharest's twenty-two new casinos, where – for a bribe – they could obtain a certificate that they had won millions of dollars. What better way of laundering dirty money?

We sat in a luxurious baroque dining hall with mirrors on the ceiling. Whenever I looked up, I could see the restaurant patrons, myself included, suspended from the ceiling like peculiar human stalactites.

We ate with silver and off silver. The waiters synchronically removed silver lids from our silver plates. The soft, velvety Romanian red wine was poured into silver goblets from a bottle encased in a silver holder. After the shock of Bucharest's streets, I could hardly taste my food, which could have been made of silver, too. The tacky silver luxury of the Casa Vernescu increased my awareness of the indescribable third-world misery outside.

Basil Zarnoveanu was a young Westernised business-man with warm and clever hazel eyes – as only Romanians and Italians have. His manner was gentle, but firm and self-assured.

'Making wine is an art,' he said in his almost impeccable English. 'Under communism, Romanian wine-makers were dominated by the state plan, so there was no question of being artistic. Their mentality remains largely unchanged, and we have to rely on young people, untarnished by Ceausescu's regime, whom we send to study abroad. Our main task is to re-create the artistic side of wine-making.'

Our conversation was spoilt by the presence of Basil's other guests, an elderly Swedish wine writer and his wife, both of whom never stopped complaining.

'Romania is not France,' the wine writer pronounced with faked perspicacity. 'Why don't they wash their cars? Why don't they have toilet paper? Can you believe it: I was unable to get a roll of toilet paper at my hotel!'

'Yes, yes,' his skinny wife assented. 'I feel so homesick. Here they don't speak Swedish. They don't even speak English. They don't communicate.'

From Basil's strained face muscles I could see how furious he was. It was only his role as host that stopped him from giving them a worthy rebuff. Unlike him, I had no reason to contain my mounting anger.

'You must be forgetting that Romania has only recently freed itself from the yoke of one of the cruellest dictators in human history,' I told the Swedes, trying to look calm.

'Unwashed cars have nothing to do with Ceausescu,' the wine writer insisted. 'Why don't they wash them?'

Like a blinkered horse, he was incapable of looking back or sideways and could only stare blankly in front of himself.

'Ceausescu would have explained to you why,' I muttered, and I stood up to leave. I had had too many shocks and contrasts for one day to keep maintaining this pointless conversation.

Next morning, I waited for Cornel, my Vinexport escort and interpreter, in Revolution Square, the heart of the 1989 uprising. In front of me was the oblong white-stone edifice of the Romanian Communist Party former headquarters, still heavily pockmarked with bullet holes. It was from the balcony of that building that Ceausescu, the self-proclaimed 'Genius of the Carpathians', made his last fateful speech, during which he was booed and jeered by 150,000 demonstrators in the square. Next to it – in a tragic irony of post-communist Romania – stood an unremarkable building, a former library, now dominated by a large English sign: Bingo Club. The walls of the Bingo Club were pasted with portraits of candidates in the forthcoming presidential elections. The most prominent face was that of the incumbent president, Ion Iliescu, a reform communist who had been Ceausescu's heir-apparent until he fell out with him in 1970.

A group of small, sad-faced children from an orphanage, chaperoned by their teacher, stood near the – either still half finished or already half ruined – monument to the 'Martyrs of the 1989 Revolution'. Dressed in identical mass-produced pink pyjamas, the kids were silently holding hands.

Cornel was a pale, middle-aged man with curly hair and deep, dark shadows under his eyes – an indicator of a serious liver (read 'drinking') problem.

'All the people in the so-called revolution were drunk' was his first remark.

'Were you here that day?' I asked him.

'Nah. My mother told me: go and fight! But I didn't want to. I had two sons, and I thought they would be better off with a coward father than with a hero father who was dead!'

I didn't like Cornel at the beginning – another proof of how misleading first impressions can be. In the course of our travels round Romania, we forged a friendship, and I ended up admiring him for his irrepressible sense of humour and for his honesty, which I had initially mistaken for the opportunism of a disgruntled ex-government apparatchik.

Under Ceausescu, Cornel used to occupy a privileged and highly coveted position as head of the meat department of Prodimport, Romania's sole importer of food. His thriving eighteen-year career, which even allowed him to travel abroad, came to an end after a colleague denounced him to the Securitate (Ceausescu's secret police) for having entered a casino while on a trade mission in Beirut. He said he did not gamble, and just 'wanted to have a look', but that was enough.

'Thank your lucky stars for not being arrested,' a Securitate investigator advised him back in Bucharest.

Cornel was sacked from his post and blacklisted: he was unable to find a proper job until the revolution.

'Why do you refer to the revolution as "so-called"?' I asked him in Revolution Square.

'Because there are lots of mysteries around it,' he replied. 'No one knows who was the first to start shooting, who set the Securitate archives on fire, why the Ceausescus were so quickly executed, without a trial, and so on.'

Like so many conspiracy-minded Romanians, Cornel was inclined to think that the revolution was plotted by Ceausescu's old communist rival, Iliescu, to grab power, which he eventually did, whereas I was of the opinion that of all the East European 'revolutions' the Romanian was the only genuine one, in which the hated dictator was overthrown by a people driven to the limits of poverty and despair.

To drive me round Bucharest, Cornel commandeered the services of his buxom neighbour Elena and her antediluvian Dacia, in which she took enormous pride. Owning a car under Ceausescu was a rare privilege: private owners were only allowed to use their cars on two Sundays a month and not in winter ('You can only drive in winter if you put your car on a sledge,' they used to joke). The monthly ration of petrol could not exceed 20 litres. Forced to carry yellow ('private') number plates, private cars were banned from driving outside the immediate area of their owners' residence (for instance, Bucharest drivers could not leave the boundaries of the capital, and drivers from the country were not allowed to enter Bucharest). If caught, the trespassers could face imprisonment without a trial.

Elena's Dacia could best be described as an oversize tin on wheels. It was rusty and battered, not just outside but inside as well. Elena would have been an excellent driver had it not been for her religious zeal. She would cross herself fervently every time we passed a church or a spot where a church once used to stand, of which there were hundreds in the post-Ceausescu Bucharest.* While crossing herself, she would momentarily let go of the wheel and shift her gaze from the road to a faded paper icon above the dashboard. Thus she managed to combine two things, praying and driving – with the emphasis on praying.

'Ceausescu ruined my liver,' said Cornel, pouring himself another glass of Petroasa Merlot 1988, a year when Ceausescu was still around. 'We drank methylated spirit and other rubbish which made people lose their eyesight. Good wines were not available – they all went abroad, and we didn't need them, for all we wanted was to escape the nightmares of our lives and to keep ourselves warm. What else could we do in our dark, freezing flats, with no heating and no electricity after eight p.m.? I had to send my two sons to my mother, who lived in the country. At least she had a stove.'

'How about now? Do people still drink to escape?' I asked him.

'No. Now we drink to forget.'

We were sitting in the state-run Casa Alba restaurant in the Bucharest suburb of Baneasa. An Australian

* The dictator had set himself the formidable task of demolishing all Bucharest's churches, which he would have certainly completed, had he himself not been 'demolished' in December 1989.

'flying wine-maker', who worked for Vinexport, was supposed to join us for dinner, but he had stood us up and flown somewhere else for the night.

On the stage in front of us, dancers in folk costumes were jumping around to an accompaniment by Romanian musical instruments: *hai* (wooden flutes), *limpoi* (bag-pipes) and *buciu* (long horns). The dancers outnumbered the restaurant customers.

Unlike the fiery music, the service at the restaurant was slack and slow. I had to tell the waiter off for putting a bottle of red wine into an ice bucket. Cornel looked at me with respect. 'You are an expert,' he said.

I wished I were. Cornel himself had just joined Vinexport, and his knowledge of wines was not much better than mine.

'Ceausescu didn't have good taste in wines,' noted Cornel, ordering another bottle. 'He didn't like champagne, but had to drink it because Elena did.'

There was no escape from Ceausescu in Bucharest, and our conversation kept coming back to him every ten minutes. At times, it felt as if he was our third dinner companion – a proxy for the elusive 'flying wine-maker'.

'No more Ceausescu talk for tonight,' I suggested, and we agreed to pay each other a 1000-leu (20p) fine for every subsequent mention of the dictator's name.

'During our trip, you should be very careful,' Cornel said didactically. 'Four hundred and twenty cases of meningitis have already been recorded in Romania. It is transferred through water, dirty hands, dirty plates, dirty cutlery, toilets and mosquitoes.'

I thought that I had already been exposed to the whole lot of the risk factors, apart from mosquitoes and cutlery. Having carefully scrutinised my bread knife, I determined that there was only one factor – the mosquitoes – left to try.

Cornel told me that, due to the meningitis epidemic, some local councils had started fining people for blowing their noses in public and that so far over fifty people had been convicted, including a woman who had accidentally sneezed on a policeman, and a man who had been fined double for blowing his nose on a leaf in a park.

At that point, I concluded that meningitis was no more appetising a subject for dinner conversation than Ceausescu. I had to do it silently to avoid paying the fine.

35 CEAUSESCU'S PLONK

At Vrancea winery, not far from the town of Focsani, I was offered a tasting of Galbena Odobesti, a locally produced sweet white.

'This is our best-selling brand, the so-called "*grand cru*", although you might not like its taste,' said the winery's director, somewhat apologetically. 'Before the revolution, we made only small quantities of it for the VIPs. It was Ceausescu's favourite wine, and we used to send regular consignments of it to all his residences. We had to do it secretly, because Ceausescu never drank in public and tried to portray himself as ascetic and teetotal. Galbena is very popular in Romania now, because it is cheap and also because in people's minds it is associated with Ceausescu's lifestyle. We sell one hundred thousand bottles of it a day. Shop owners come here pleading for it, and it brings us a lot of profit.'

I was not in a hurry to take a sip from my glass. I already knew that the dictator's tastes in architecture and interior design were tacky, unsophisticated and reeking of megalomania. I was wondering what his favourite wine would taste like, and hoping that

Galbena's amazing popularity in the impoverished post-communist Romania had more to do with its low price than with Ceausescu himself. After a guided tour of 'Ceausescu's Bucharest' several days before, I was finding it hard to imagine that anyone in Romania could feel nostalgic about him.

We had started with the House of the Republic (also known as Ceausescu's Palace), the world's second-largest building after the Pentagon, although much uglier.

The Italians have an interesting way of conveying the size of an object with the help of suffixes alone. For example, 'casa' is a normal house, 'casetta' or 'casino' is a smallish house, 'casaccio' is a huge house, and 'casuccio' is a huge, ugly house. The Palace of the Republic, which jumped at us in all its mind-boggling monstrosity at the end of Bucharest's Unirii Boulevard, was an archetypal casuccio. The 101-metre-high building was the shape of a giant wedding-cake disfigured by drunken guests (Ceausescu had copied its design from a much smaller palace of the North Korean dictator, Kim Il Sung, in Pyongyang). For six years, twenty thousand workers and four hundred architects toiled twenty-four hours a day on its construction. Only Ceausescu's execution in December 1989 stopped him completing the project.

Next to the Palace of the Republic, stood the somewhat smaller Palace of Science, housing the National Institute for Science and Technology, of which Ceausescu's semi-literate wife, Elena, a virago with a passion for French champagne, American fur coats and expensive jewellery, had been president.

Even after their death, the vicious Ceausescu couple dominated Bucharest's city-scape, if now only in stone.

I was surprised at the entry charge to the Palace of the Republic: 3000 leu ($1) for the locals and 15,000 leu for foreigners, who were also allowed to use photo- and video-cameras inside the building for the additional fee

of 100,000 lei. Charging people for looking at the
excesses of Romania's recent tragedy did not seem right
and was made even more bizarre by the fact that the
post-Ceausescu Romanian government had made the
palace a venue for conferences, receptions and other
state occasions. To me, this partially explained why
democratic reforms had not taken off in Romania: how
could the government take reformist decisions in houses
swarming with the ghosts of the country's not-so-distant
totalitarian past?

'Welcome to the Palace!' said an unsmiling female
guide, addressing our small English-speaking group,
which, apart from Cornel and myself, consisted of two
bewildered Indians with camcorders.

Leading the way along the 150-metre-long, 18-metre-
high neo-Baroque gallery, with marble floors and
mahogany walls, she bombarded us with astounding
statistics. The total volume of the palace's interior was
2,500,000 cubic metres, more than that of the largest
Egyptian pyramid. The 330,000 square metres of floor-
ing were covered with 220,000 square metres of hand-
made Transylvanian carpets. Three thousand massive
crystal chandeliers, on which Elena Ceausescu had been
especially keen, hung from the ceilings. The foundations
of the palace, which was connected by underground
tunnels with numerous Ceausescu residences around
Bucharest, were 500 metres deep, and housed an
earthquake-resistant bomb-shelter. A special underground mini-train was always ready to take Ceausescu
and his wife to their private airport in case of emergency.

With a touch of pride in her voice, the guide informed
us that the Ceausescus were the palace's main architects
and interior designers: every single detail had to be
approved by them.

'How many rooms are there in the palace?' asked one
of the dumbfounded Indians.

'No one counted,' she answered.

The interiors of the sumptuous palaces of the Russian

tsars, of which I had seen many, looked like barren peasants' huts in comparison with this cornucopia of tasteless extravagance. With disgust, I looked at tacky golden roses hanging from the chandeliers, at curtains embroidered with gold and silver, at columns made of pink marble, at flowery patterns on the carpets, repeating in minute detail the ornamentation of the ceilings above them. The crude 'little girl's' hand of Ceausescu's overbearing wife was felt everywhere. If architecture was indeed music in stone, the palace was a dull and pretentious cacophony played by a madman. It was the world's biggest monument to wasteful, aggressive and authoritarian kitsch, created by imbecile parvenus. The illusion of the Ceausescus' ominous presence was almost complete under its lavish ceilings. Being there was like conversing with the horrible couple at a pompous and meaningless reception.

Feeling tiny and humiliated, I looked out of the window. Debris and devastation were everywhere. In front of the palace, the building of the former Radio Centre lay in ruins, its dark glass-less windows gaping at the world like empty eye-sockets. Next to it, stood the iron and concrete carcass of an unfinished fast-food factory, another crazy project of the Ceausescus, who had ordered that dozens of such factories, popularly known as 'starvation clinics', be built in Bucharest (one could still see their abandoned stone skeletons with protruding fittings here and there). The idea was that people would pop in there after work to buy pre-cooked and pre-packaged warm meals, which they would consume in their dark, cold flats, thus saving precious energy. Under Ceausescu, Romania, which had supplied the whole of the Luftwaffe with petrol during the Second World War, was able to offer its citizens water, heating and electricity for just two hours a day. All the country's resources went to accommodate the perverse needs and tastes of the Ceausescus – rulers whom the Romanian people did not deserve.

'Have a good stay in *my* country!' the guide said with a scowl and with emphasis on 'my'. It made me start with recognition: her farewell remark could have been borrowed from Dracula, who, in Bram Stoker's book, ended one of his letters to Jonathan Harker with 'I trust that you will enjoy your stay in *my* beautiful land!'

'You know why I don't want to take my two sons to the palace? I don't know what to tell them.' Cornel said to me, back in the car. 'They will ask me, "How come all this money was wasted? How come you, Daddy, were a member of the Communist Party? How come you kept silent all those years?" I don't know what to say.'

We were heading for Ceausescu's last abode: two cubic metres of solid earth – and no chandeliers. His wife, Elena, was buried in the same cemetery. Only a couple of weeks before my tour of 'Ceausescu's Bucharest', the vicious couple were joined there by their wayward son Nicu, an alcoholic and a skirt-chaser, who had died of cirrhosis of the liver in a Viennese hospital.

I felt as if I had known the Ceausescu family for years. It all started in Moscow in the late '80s, when, quite by chance, I bought several English books, printed in the US, from a drunken Soviet ex-diplomat. One of them was called *Red Horizons*. It was written by Ion Pacepa, Ceausescu's closest adviser and former head of the Romanian intelligence service, who had defected to the West. For many years, General Pacepa was a trusted confidant of the Ceausescu family and was able to observe their everyday life from behind the scenes. The stupidity, grotesque drunkenness, nepotism, scheming, brutality, greed and corruption described in the book were hair-raising and bordering on wild fantasy, even for someone like myself, hardened by many years of life in the USSR, which did not look half as terrifying as Ceausescu's Romania as portrayed by Pacepa.

The self-proclaimed Romanian president, referred to by his underlings as 'the Comrade' (what an irony), was shown routinely ordering assassinations, masterminding global terrorism, dancing with anger when things went wrong and drinking unchilled wine in generous quantities. He wore his suits only once, fearful that devious Western intelligence services would impregnate them with a cancer-inducing agent. He made his beloved black labrador, Corbu, a colonel in the Romanian army and gave him his own car and driver. And so on . . .

Elena, officially dubbed 'The Romanian people's most esteemed daughter', was portrayed as an alcoholic, a nymphomaniac, a devious ignoramus and a compulsive hoarder, who was firmly in control of her weak-spirited husband and, through him, of Romania. It was not she who was Ceausescu's second-in-command, but the other way round.

The most disgusting real-life character in Pacepa's book was Nicu, who spent his time carousing at nightly saturnalia, smashing whisky bottles against walls, abusing everyone around him and screwing everything that moved.

My drinking trainer Evgeny Bulavin used to go to the neglected and run-down Kharkov zoo in the moments of despair which usually coincided with hangovers: the sight of the poor caged animals never failed to reassure him slightly. As he used to say, it was good to see living creatures whose life was even more miserable than his own. Prior to getting hold of *Red Horizons*, I used to rely for the same purpose on the North Korean magazine *Korea Today*, readily available at Soviet newsstalls, after which a *Pravda* editorial read almost like an erotic novel.

Everything was relative indeed, and nothing could evoke the life-saving feeling of the relativity of suffering like Ion Pacepa's extraordinary book. It was one of the few treasured volumes of my Moscow library which I took with me when I had to defect to the West. It survived my numerous moves between Britain and Australia. Bedraggled and dog-eared, it lies on my desk as I am writing these lines.

A kiosk at the cemetery's gate was selling flowers and crude wooden coffins. I wondered what type of customers the florist-cum-undertaker could attract. Someone who wanted to buy a bunch of flowers to put on the grave of a loved one and suddenly decided to get a coffin, too – for himself? Or someone who came to bury a relative and forgot to bring a coffin?

Behind the gate, two rough types sat on a bench, taking turns to swig a brownish liquid that looked very much like the Biomedicine of my youth, from the all-too-familiar 'fire-extinguisher' bottle, the size and the shape of a surface-to-air missile. They turned out to be grave-diggers enjoying their break between burials. One of them volunteered to take us to the Ceausescus' graves, located in three different parts of the cemetery.

A simple stone cross with a red star on top stood on the grave of one of the twentieth century's vilest dictators. The cross was half covered with flowers and faded wreaths. 'Ceausescu Nicolae 1918–1989' was written on it. Half a dozen grave-faced and black-clad women huddled around. They crossed themselves frantically and stuck burning candles – a sign of respect – into the mellow soil.

'He was a very good man,' whispered one of them, and her eyes under her black kerchief filled with tears.

How much suffering do people have to go through to reach the point at which they stop worshipping their dead tyrants?

A handwritten note on a sheet of paper from a school notebook lay under the cross. I asked Cornel to translate it for me. 'Personal experience is an expensive school. Those who are not very clever study at this school. Clever people learn from the experience of others,' it said.

This meaningful note on the grave of Nicolae Ceausescu, whose monument in the shape of the monstrous Palace of the Republic still dominated Bucharest and whose vicious ghost had not been exorcised from the country's mutilated soul, gave hope that the people of Romania would one day be able to draw the right lessons from their own tragic past.

Elena's grave was in the cemetery's opposite corner. Inseparable during their lifetime, the Ceausescu couple were finally separated in death. This arrangement corresponded to the popular perception of Elena as a manipulating witch, who held the main blame for Ceausescu's crimes. At least in death Nicolae was spared the constant presence of his dominating wife. There were neither mourners nor flowers at her grave, which was decorated only with a bare stone cross. It was strange to see crosses on the graves of the couple, who didn't believe in anything but power and made sure that hundreds of Romanian churches were blown up. Was it a truly Christian attempt at forgiveness of the atrocious sinners who had died unrepentant and as such were impossible to forgive?

On Elena's grave, there was a note, too. 'Oh, Mother, sweet Mother, when leaves fall down from the trees, you are calling for me. Your beloved son, who has made lots of mistakes in his life.'

The fresh grave of Nicu, the Ceausescus' maverick son, was overlaid with wreaths, most of which hadn't had time to fade, and was surrounded by a crowd of mourners.

'Nicu is widely perceived as his parents' victim and a good guy,' explained Cornel. 'Tens of thousands turned up at his recent funeral.

Standing at Nicu's grave, also decorated with a cross, though only a wooden one, I remembered a scene from *Red Horizons* describing a state banquet, at which drunken Nicu, 'a good guy', was enjoying himself in his habitual manner. I knew it almost by heart:

A waiter came in with a silver platter full of oysters. 'Put it here, in the middle,' ordered Nicu, pointing toward the table. 'Is there any seasoning on them?'

'They are just fresh and raw, Comrade Nicu,' replied the waiter.

'They need seasoning, you idiot . . .'

He precariously climbed up on to the table and started urinating on them, careful to 'season' every oyster. 'Come on, comrades. Let's have an oyster,' he urged the guests . . . 'Nobody's eating? Who doesn't like my seasoning? Nobody? Then I'll wash them off.' And Nicu started squirting with a siphon bottle over the oysters and over the rest of us sitting around the table . . .

We left Nicu pushing a waitress toward the edge of the table while tearing off her blouse. 'I want to f— you here. Right here on this table, you slut.'

Having had to share a Moscow communal flat with the drinking and womanising son of a top Soviet functionary for several years, I knew how correct this seemingly improbable description was.

Unlike the mourners, I didn't feel like paying my respects to Nicu Ceausescu, simply because I didn't have any.

Having paid the grave-digger off with enough leu to allow him to buy another surface-to-air alcohol-fuelled rocket, capable of briefly propelling him and his colleague-in-spade away from the earth they had to dig, we drove to the Memorial Cemetery of the victims of the 1989 revolution, during which eleven hundred people were killed in Bucharest alone. Romania's recent history went hand-in-hand with death.

The fresh burial ground in north Bucharest was surrounded by hideous beehive-like apartment blocks. It was deserted, except for packs of hungry stray dogs scouring among the graves, pissing and copulating on them.

The 'victims of the revolution' were mostly teenagers, brutally killed by the Securitate during pro-democracy demonstrations in November–December 1989. Their faces looked reproachfully out from mass-produced obelisks (not crosses), as if saying, 'What have you done to us? We do not belong here. Our photos should be in school albums, not on tombstones.'

They could now communicate with this world through epitaphs only.

'I didn't leave this life because I wanted to. What I am now, you will become. My dear parents and brothers, please forgive me for leaving you when I was only 13. Octavian Burcioaila – "Tavi"' (a young bespectacled boy, with a know-it-all look on his face, who was probably bullied at school as a nerd).

'His train of life had only two stops – Revolution and Death. Stan Bogdan, 1970–1989' (a rugby ball lay on his grave).

'She was killed by the tyrants of the Ceau clan when peacefully demonstrating for free Romania. Gabriela Popescu, 1968–1989' (what a stunningly beautiful girl she was).

'We thank you and wait for you to be born again – sister, mother, father. Elin Marinescu, 1976–1989'.

'I loved my country. Vali-Valeriu Miu, 27 years old. Student. Died December 1989'.

I wished the nagging Swedish wine writer with whom I had had dinner on my first night in Bucharest were there with me. But he was elsewhere – probably eating lunch, paid for by his Romanian hosts, and complaining of the lack of toilet paper at his hotel and of the abundance of unwashed cars in the unswept, dirty streets. He didn't realise that it was not dirt that the cars and the streets of Bucharest were covered with. They were soaked in human blood.

Nursing a glass of Ceausescu's favourite drink in the tasting room of Vrancea winery, I recalled another passage from *Red Horizons*, in which Ion Pacepa described a typical drinking evening with Ceausescu in one of the dictator's personal wine cellars:

Before we were able to reach a table, a waiter in black tie materialised out of nowhere holding a tray with a newly opened bottle of wine and one large glass. Known as 'Odobesti Galbena' ['Odobesti' means 'Yellow'], it is Ceausescu's favourite, a flavourful wine of the same colour and consistency as sunflower oil, which is made in very limited quantities in Odobesti, a Moldavian village renowned for its wines. Ceausescu downed two glasses on his feet, then sat down in his favourite easy chair beside a heavy, round oak table. The waiter refilled Ceausescu's glass and set the bottle down beside him in an ice bucket containing no ice – Ceausescu does not want his drinks cold, in order to protect his vocal cords.

When I finally tasted the drink, I realised that Ceausescu's favourite wine was indeed similar to sweetened sunflower oil, not just in 'colour and consistency' but in taste as well. If the kitsch interior of his Palace of the Republic could be somehow liquidised and expressed in wine-making terms, it would result in Galbena Odobesti.

My Prague-based friend Igor Pomerantsev was right: wines – just like humans – could be immoral.

'Can you find me a spittoon, please?' I asked the winery's director.

36 BUMPY WINE ROADS OF ROMANIA

The main difference between Bulgarian and Romanian wineries (for me, at least) was that the latter had no spittoons in their tasting rooms. The reason for that was simple: until several years before my visit, the bulk of Romanian wines went to the Soviet Union, where no one cared what they tasted like. So the Romanian tasters would just get drunk, without bothering to spit the samples out. This is my personal explanation, of course.

Rovit winery in Dealul Mare was 70 per cent state-owned and looked it. It was the last day of grape harvesting. Since peasants could not be bothered to work in the fields for the miserly pay the impoverished state was able to cough up, local schoolkids were mobilised to do the job. We saw lots of them in the fields playfully picking up the grapes and throwing them into aluminium buckets, or – more frequently – into their mouths.

'It was a bad year: too much rain, and many grapes are affected by grey rot,' the winery's engineer told us.

It was there, at Rovit, that I was reintroduced to Feteasca, a wine made only in Romania, which was a popular hangover cure in the USSR. In his *Pocket Wine Book*, Hugh Johnson, the world's best-known wine guru, describes it as a 'light wine made coarse by clumsiness'.

We were lucky to bump into Emilian Mihalca, deputy technical director of the Romanian Vines & Wines Research Institute and one of Romania's leading enologists, who was visiting Rovit. He joined us for the tasting.

'Under Ceausescu, quantity, not quality, mattered,' said the respected enologist. 'Ninety-five per cent of our wines were exported to the Soviet Union. It was a shame for Romania, the country with the world's eighth-largest area of vineyards.

'By the way,' he added looking at me. 'You are sitting in the very chair where Ceausescu sat in 1981.'

I choked on my Feteasca and nearly fell off the chair. Once, I had a chance to spend a night on a couch that used to belong to Hitler and I couldn't help feeling that it still carried the imprint of his thin, bony buttocks. Suddenly, I felt uncomfortable, as if I had inadvertently sat on a drawing-pin.

To conceal my annoyance, I put forward my regular question: 'Do people in Romania now drink more than under Ceausescu?'

'Yes, they do. And mostly low-quality stuff. The main reason is growing insecurity about everyday life. It is impossible to support a family of three, but after you drink a glass of *tsuica* [Romanian plum brandy] your reality starts looking better.'

The answer was no less regular than the question.

I made some incredible achievements during the tasting. First – unexpectedly and without anyone's help – I scribbled two words, 'long' and 'oaky', in the Notes section of my tasting list against Feteasca Alba 1995. Mihalca himself confirmed that my appraisal was correct. Second, I was able to determine that another wine (I think it was a merlot) was barrel-matured. Third, I rightly concluded that the pinot gris we were tasting was semi-dry. Those might look like insignificant accomplishments to a wine critic with a well-practised, knowledgeable palate, but I was ready to cry, 'Eureka!' like Archimedes in his famous bath.

We drank (sorry, tasted) a local cabernet sauvignon, which, we were told, used to be drunk three times a day by the crews of Soviet nuclear-powered submarines to diminish the effects of radiation. A similar myth was fed by the authorities to the residents of the contaminated Chernobyl area, who were generously supplied with cheap, strong red plonk shortly after the reactor's explosion. Entering the 30-kilometre contaminated zone around the reactor in 1994, I saw a group of reactor workers, all legless after their shift, throughout which they had been drinking in the false officially encouraged belief that alcohol (red wine mixed with vodka) could fend off radiation, whereas the only thing it really did was help one forget about one's ruined health (or life) for a while.

We tasted (no, let's be honest: drank) Busuioaka De Bohotin, a rosé wine, which Romanian wine-makers call BB, or Brigitte Bardot, although, to me, it tasted much younger.

At the winery's impressive *vinothèque* (wine library), we were told how, in 1942, they hid their best wines from the liberating/invading Soviet soldiers, 'who drank everything around them', by pouring them (the wines) from the bottles into empty oil barrels.

'Did you wash the barrels well?' I asked the winery's manager sternly.

'We certainly did. In 1981, we sent two bottles of that very wine as a birthday present to Ceausescu,' he concluded with pride.

'What a shame you had washed the bloody oil barrels!' I exclaimed in Russian – a sure sign of having drunk (sorry, tasted) too many wines.

My room at the Vrancea Hotel in the town of Focsani, where we stopped overnight, was damp and freezing:

the heating did not work. In the deceptive light of a dusty, naked bulb under the ceiling I could discern empty bottles and cigarette packets on the unswept floor and a skull-and-crossbones picture on the wall. 'These premised are poisoned from 13 October' read a sign under the portrait of the Jolly Roger.

'They fumigated the hotel to drive the cockroaches away,' said Cornel, entering the room. His room had exactly the same sign.

'If so, they must have lost the battle,' I observed, pointing at an agile soldier of the victorious army crawling from under the bed and waving its ugly antennae triumphantly.

We had dinner at Pepsi Intim, a private restaurant with a 'Marlboro-push' sticker on the front door. There were no Marlboro (or any other) stickers on the toilet door, simply because it was missing from the hinges, and the dark hole in the floor (which was the toilet) could be clearly seen from the main restaurant hall, basking in a brothel-like light of blinking neon. The loudspeakers were blasting out the 1974 hits of Boney M, a half-forgotten Jamaican band of my Soviet youth.

'The restaurant's musical repertoire needs updating,' I said to Cornel, who suddenly got angry.

'We are not in America!' he snapped back. 'Ceausescu didn't allow the playing of any Western music in public places, and now – for the first time in our recent history – people can dance to a Western band, even if it is an old one!'

I felt ashamed. Like the empty-headed Swedish wine writer, I had forgotten for a moment that I was in Romania. Even senile Soviet rulers didn't go so far as to ban all Western music from restaurants.

'How about at home? Could you listen to Western music there?' I asked Cornel.

'In my flat, there was no Ceausescu, and even he could not stop foreign radio broadcasts. I used to listen to the heavily jammed Western music every evening.'

It was another proof of Newton's third law of motion: force breeds an equal counterforce. In other words, the stricter the ban, the harder people try to break it.

It was a dreadful night. The sheets on my bed were grey, wet and full of holes. In the flashes of light from the street, I could see the Jolly Roger scowling at me from the wall like a sinister mug-shot of the room's previous tenant.

At about 4 a.m., I was woken by a characteristic high-resolution buzz.

'Mosquitoes – the carriers of meningitis,' I thought in panic, and jumped out of bed.

It was no longer cold in the room: the heating was working, and the sudden warmth must have attracted squadrons of stinging mini-Draculas, who should have all been hibernating (or whatever they do in autumn). Never before had I seen so many mosquitoes in one hotel room. Were they Romania's national animals, like kangaroos in Australia? And didn't the word 'mosquito' sound a bit like a typical Romanian last name? Ion Mosquitou . . .

The situation was hopeless but not serious, as my vodka don Evgeny Bulavin used to say. I trudged into the bathroom, which the mosquitoes had made their main headquarters: they were swarming all over it. The water was switched off (it probably alternated with the heating). I washed my face, swollen with mosquito bites, with the remains of some fizzy mineral water from a plastic container and spent the rest of the night fighting a holy war against the mosquitoes, which grossly outnumbered me in both personnel and equipment. Besides, they were all airborne.

By dawn, the enemy had lost 158 officers and men, whereas I was still alive (if only just) and slapping.

We drove through the Vrancea wine region, a flat plateau to the east of the Carpathians. The closer we came towards the mountains, the more narrow and winding the roads became. Often we had to overtake horse-drawn carts loaded with hay, with Moldavian peasants sitting in them in their tall *caciula* sheepskin hats.

The Panciu winery is one of Romania's largest producers of sparkling wines, made using the traditional French method of double fermentation, known as *méthode champenoise*. It was then the only winery in Eastern Europe using not only the French method but French-made machinery, too.

The winery boasted spectacular two-kilometre-long champagne cellars, the Caves of Stefan the Great. Stefan was a jingoistic fifteenth-century Romanian king, nick-named 'the Athlete of Christ', who in the forty-seven years of his reign led forty-seven wars against the Turks, most of which he lost. A portrait of him wearing an elaborate crown now decorated the labels of Panciu sparkling wines and was initially mistaken by me for a 'by appointment' seal of royal approval, similar to King Simeon of Bulgaria's.

Romania, too, had a king in exile, but he was not in a position to give his seal of approval to anything. The 75-year-old King Michael of Romania, now living in Switzerland, was forced to abdicate in 1947 and was stripped of his Romanian citizenship in 1948. He tried to visit Romania in spring 1992, when a crowd of one million people came to greet him at Bucharest's Otopeni airport. Iliescu's authorities, however, refused him permission to step on to Romania's soil, and the exiled monarch had to look at his native land through the porthole of his plane before taking off. How sad.*

* King Michael's citizenship was restored in February 1997, after Iliescu's defeat in the elections, and for the first time in 50 years he was able to come back to Romania properly and even to spend Christmas there that year. King Michael must have been impressed by the women he met in Romania, for on his return to Switzerland he announced a new dynastic law allowing – for the first time in Romanian history – female succession, which would make his eldest daughter, Princess Margarita, a university friend of Gordon Brown, the next heir to the still exiled Romanian throne.

In the Caves of Stefan the Great, Panciu sparkling wines were undergoing their second – 'definitive' – fermentation in thousands of horizontally stacked bottles. At the end of it, each bottle had to be 'riddled', i.e., changed from the horizontal to 90 degrees position. Then it had to be twisted and shaken (twice daily) to move sediment into the neck, from where it was later removed by 'disgorgement', i.e. passing it through a freezing solution.

I learnt that 'riddling' was normally done by hand and took weeks to complete. To me, being a 'riddler' sounded like one of the most tedious occupations on our planet, worse than picking potatoes or filing one's tax return. I got bored out of my mind 'riddling' just one bottle in the caves. It was a riddle to me how one could 'riddle' for days on end, as some of the winery workers did.

I had never been a fan of champagne, which Evgeny Bulavin, my Soviet drinking Pestalozzi, used disdainfully to call 'shampoo'. In my student days, it made sense only in two cases: when mixed with vodka to form a near-lethal cocktail which we called Starlit Night, and when you wanted to make a girl drunk (for some reason, they seemed more susceptible to champagne's mildly intoxicating effects than the vodka-hardened Soviet young males were). Of all Russian writers, only Chekhov preferred champagne to other drinks. He liked it so much that his last wish before dying was to have a sip of champagne, and his last words (after he had had a sip) were 'Ich sterbe' ('I am dying' in German).

In a piece about Yeltsin's grandson Boris's days at Winchester school, the *London Courier*, a Russian newspaper published in London, quoted one of his schoolmates: 'I once asked Boris what his grandad's favourite drink was. He thought for a while and said, "Champagne." And then added, "With vodka."'

We looked at the winery's French bottling line. The bottles, with their necks frozen, were moving along the

conveyor to the machine which removed their temporary caps. The sediment was forced out of them by
internal pressure. The next machines on the line topped
the bottles up and corked them, while the last one stuck
labels on to their glassy bellies.

I was so fascinated by the process that I did not notice
I'd reached the very end of the bottling line, where
labelling was in progress.

I could not believe my eyes: the machine in front of me
was pasting the familiar 'Sovetskoye Shampanskoye'
('Soviet Champagne') labels on to the bottles full of
Romanian-made sparkling wine! I picked up one of the
labels from a stack. It said – in Russian – that the semi-
sweet 'Soviet Champagne' was produced and bottled in
the Republic of Moldova (which was not part of
Romania). A Russian sorting code was printed in the
corner.

It was only then that I noticed that the bottles were
sealed with typically Soviet (or Russian) plastic corks.
Something fishy was going on . . .

'Come on! What are you doing here? Everything is
ready for the tasting.' It was our host, engineer Marcu
Dinica. His voice brought me back to reality.

'Why do you put Russian labels on bottles of
Romanian sparkling wine?' I demanded.

'How do you know?'

'Because I am Russian.'

The engineer was visibly embarrassed. 'It's . . . it's . . .
a . . . special order for our Russian partners.'

'But the labels say that the wine was made in the
Republic of Moldova, which is not true!' I insisted. My
old instincts of an investigative hack came to life. It felt
as if I was back in the Soviet Union unmasking yet
another fraud.

'I . . . I . . . can't explain.'

'What do you think about it all?' I asked Cornel when
we were back on the road.

'It is very simple. Exporting Romanian sparkling wine

to Russia through Vinexport is risky and unprofitable: the Russians seldom pay on time. Besides, export duties are high. One day, a Russian mafia man comes to Panciu with labels, corks and a nice stack of dollars and offers to pay them, say, a dollar per bottle in cash two days prior to each shipment, provided they use his corks and labels. Out of this dollar, one cent might go to the pockets of the winery's management. When we talk millions of bottles, it adds up to a substantial sum. Especially by Romanian standards.'

'But what is the gain for the Russian mafia? And why do the labels say "Made in Moldova"?'

'There is no export–import tax between Romania and Moldova, and customs controls are slack. The consignment is first taken to Moldova and only then – with "Made in Moldova" labels – to Russia, which does not impose import duty on Moldovian goods. Thus the fraudsters manage to avoid paying any tax whatsoever. Also, Moldovian wines have a very good reputation in Russia and sell like hot cakes.'

It was a classic mafia scheme. Someone must have been making millions out of it.

'How come you know what's going on and keep silent?' I demanded. 'Why don't you raise the alarm? Go to the police, alert the press? These gangsters are robbing your country!'

Cornel turned his face to me. It was red with anger. 'Stop telling me this rubbish about "my country"! "My country" does nothing for me, so why should I do anything for her? Let the mafia do their dirty business – it is not my concern. My concern is how to pay for my sons' textbooks, which were free under Ceausescu, and now they cost a fortune!'

I did not press the matter any further. It was not only the 'Soviet Champagne' that had outlived the Soviet Union. The old servile thinking, which had made the state and the individual into secret lifelong enemies, was still rampant in Romania. I knew it would take a long time for it to change – much longer than it took for a good wine to mature in the Caves of Stefan the Great.

During an evening walk around the Moldovian town of Iasi, the venue of our next overnight stop, we were attacked by a pack of dirty stray dogs. Cornel drove them away after a good deal of shouting and kicking. An experienced dog-fighter, he had to rebuff similar canine attacks every morning on the way to work in Bucharest.

'They are so hungry they can easily maul you to death,' he commented as we moved on.

In the main square, next to the regulation equestrian statue of Stefan the Great, we stumbled upon a modest memorial plate to the local victims of the 1989 revolution: a piece of plywood with sixteen names written on it in black ink.

'Not one of the bastards who killed them has been identified, let alone arrested,' muttered Cornel.

Ironically, across the road was a former Securitate building – much smaller than in Bucharest, but equally grey and disgusting.

'What's in this building now?' I asked Cornel.

'No one knows,' he shrugged.

No wonder the murderers had not been arrested. While 'no one knew' what was happening at their former headquarters, while all the macabre offices of the communist secret police were not turned into memorials to their victims, the butchers were bound to remain unpunished, and the restless souls of the murdered freedom fighters were destined to roam around in the dark – like stray hungry dogs in the streets of Iasi.

At Cotnari, Romania's biggest winery, we were shown a small wooden barrel of Pastorel Teodoreanu intended as a birthday present to Ceausescu in 1989. As they were preparing to send it over, the dictator was arrested and shot. The gift remained unclaimed.

'Giving presents to Ceausescu was not our own

initiative,' explained the winery's chief enologist. 'It was done on orders from our local party committee and from Ceausescu's own staff in Bucharest.'

The barrel, with 'Long Life!' carved on its elaborate cover, stood there as a wooden memento of the carefully engineered popular love for 'the Comrade', whose 'long life' was cut short several days before his seventy-first birthday.

Cotnari's tasting room looked like a United Nations conference hall. A small flower bed in the middle was enclosed by a polished circular table, lined with throne-like wooden armchairs. A floodlit sculpture of a slender peasant woman with a basket of grapes on her shoulder stood in one corner. I looked around and froze: another sculpture – an exact copy of the first one – was pouring Tamuoasa Romaneasca into my tall tasting glass. Having noticed my consternation, she smiled: 'I am Valeria. I was a model for this sculpture. But it was ages ago. Now I am more of a Rembrandt-type woman.'

Indeed, she had put on a bit of weight, which only enhanced her beauty and made her correspond to Bram Stoker's description of Romanian women, who, in the words of his hero Jonathan Harker, 'have pretty faces but are a bit clumsy around the waist'. I wouldn't put too much trust in that portrayal, for Bram Stoker had never been to Romania.

'Is it true that in Britain a GP is obliged not just to treat people but also to feed them when he visits them at home?' Valeria asked me suddenly.

A thorough knowledge of the British way of life was obviously not among the main attractions of an archetypal Romanian beauty.

We had a good time at Cotnari, where a barrel of Ceausescu's wine stood undrunk in the *vinothèque*. And although I didn't taste many wines there, I met a sculpture that had come to life.

*

If I had had any doubts as to whether we were in Transylvania, they were bound to evaporate at the sight of a massive road-side billboard 'Coca-Cola – Transylvania – Coca-Cola'. There was little doubt that, given the chance, Coca-Cola's makers would happily rename that romantic Romanian province 'Transcocacolia'.

We drove through the Transylvanian hills, lush and superb in their golden autumn splendour. There was only one place which was in stark disharmony with this impressive parade of shades and colours: the town of Copsa Mica, with a huge chemical plant tirelessly belching clouds of black smoke into the crisp Transylvanian air.

I had never seen anything like it: the smoke and soot hung in the sky. Pitch-black houses. Black birds. Charred black churches. Black haystacks. Black birch trees. Black, doomed faces of little kids.

We stopped at a rail crossing to wait for a train to pass. From the road, we could see a large gypsy camp half a mile away. The camp consisted of several dozen rickety sheds made of cardboard boxes and broken roof-tiles. Some of the sheds had no roofs, others no walls.

In no time, our car was surrounded by small gypsy beggar-kids dressed in rags. At some distance, stood an adult moustached gypsy, patting the head of his son, no older than 5, who was smoking a cigarette.

One of the gypsy boys ran up to our car and screamed, pointing at my head, 'Dai! You are like me: we have the same curly hair!'

When the swing-beam went up and we drove on, I threw a 500 lei note out of the car window, hoping that the clever boy would get it first. No such luck: older kids pounced on it and pushed him aside.

The boy was right: I was a gypsy, even if not an ethnic one.

It was in Brasov, Romania's second largest city, that the flame of the anti-Ceausescu revolution was ignited in

November 1987, when ten thousand workers at the Red Flag tractor factory turned on party officials after learning that their pay had been cut. They marched down Bucharest Boulevard into the city centre, shouting, 'Down with the dictators!' and 'We want bread!' By the time the marchers reached the main square, twenty thousand people had joined them. When they reached the city's party headquarters, they found a meal had been prepared for the *nomenklatura* (party elite). On seeing all those delicacies for the first time in years of rationing, the workers plundered the food and threw oranges, furniture and files out of the windows. Then they set fire to portraits of Ceausescu and his wife.

In response, Ceausescu sent in the troops, who ringed the area and barred all visitors. Food and electricity supplies to Brasov were stopped. The leaders of the riot were arrested and thrown into prison.

In a subsequent speech, Ceausescu dismissed the Brasov demonstrators as 'a bunch of drunkards'. I am sure he had more than his normal intake of Galbena Odobesti on that particular day . . .

Brasov struck me as an extremely pleasant town. Flanked on both sides by forest-covered hills, it seemed more civilised and more European than Bucharest. Even its Ceausescu-style apartment blocks did not look quite as disgusting.

As we were driving through the lively city centre, I read aloud to Cornel an extract from a front-page piece of the *Sunday Times* travel section of 7 April 1996 which I had copied into my notebook in London: 'Brasov has bears the way Britain has urban foxes. Every evening, lured by the irresistible reek of garbage, they emerge from the woods . . . kerb-crawling in search of an easy meal. A fairy-tale setting it isn't, but where else in Europe can you see wild bears in the streets?'

'Where are the bears?' I demanded.

'They have all run away to London and now write for the *Sunday Times*,' he said. 'I'd like to send a congratulatory letter to the editor to thank him for the realistic coverage of modern Romania. No wonder we haven't been admitted to the EU, if that's how you perceive us in the West. Also, it would be interesting to know how many glasses of *tsuica* it takes to start seeing bears in the streets of Brasov.'

In a suburb of Brasov, we noticed a cluster of nice chalet-like cottages surrounded by a fence.

'This is our famous orphanage, Poiana Soarelui,' said Cornel.

Poiana Soarelui was the only privately funded orphanage in Romania. Founded in 1994 by Brasov-born millionaire and former tennis star Ion Tiriac, now living in Monte Carlo, it had ninety-nine children, looked after by forty-three staff.

The orphanage consisted of eleven cottages, each housing a 'family' of nine orphans, their permanent 'mother' (social worker) and a part-time 'aunt' (house-keeper). The cottages had Western furniture, bright, spacious playrooms and modern kitchens.

'We have a strict selection process,' Poiana Soarelui's manager, a kindly bespectacled man, told me. 'Children should be between three and twelve, with no mental or physical handicaps, and no parents alive. We have to vet them carefully, for many parents deliberately send their children here, telling them to pretend they are orphans.'

Those ninety-nine kids were by far the luckiest among Romania's estimated 350,000 orphans – the saddest legacy of Ceausescu's dictatorship, when abortion and contraception were banned, and children were routinely dumped by their parents, who were unable to feed them. There were not enough orphanages to accommodate all of them, and thousands of homeless, often AIDS-infected, kids ended up in the streets, begging, stealing and sniffing glue. It would take more than one Monte Carlo-based millionaire to provide them all with a simple roof above their heads.

A group of happy small kids were crossing the yard, with colourful rucksacks on their backs. Escorted by a 'mother', they were returning from school.

And I remembered the gypsy children at the railway crossing near the black town of Copsa Mica, who deserved normal childhood no less than the carefully selected ninety-nine alumni of Poiana Soarelui.

A sign saying 'Motel Dracula' flashed outside the windows of our car. We had entered Dracula country, the area around the medieval Castle Bran, which should have been long ago renamed Castle Bram, for it was Bram Stoker's wild imagination that made it into the residence of the world's most famous vampire, Count Dracula.

Due to the extraordinary popularity of Bram Stoker's book, Count Dracula became an international superstar. Over 250 feature films, 800 documentaries, over 1000 scholarly studies as well as hundreds of novels, ballets, musicals and operas were inspired by Dracula, or rather by the original Bram Stoker book. There are also thousands of Dracula societies world-wide, which include the New York Count Dracula Fan Club and the Bram Stoker International School in Dublin. The so-called 'Drakpaks' actually explain how to become a vampire ('the first qualification for a vampire is that you have to be dead') and these are mailed around the globe by a certain Jeannie Youngson, president of the International Dracula Fan Club. There is even an international chain of 'Transylvania' restaurants serving 'Hot Bat' burgers, 'Blue Blood' cocktails and 'Dead Body' buns (one of them – in London's West Hampstead – cordially invites customers to celebrate their own funerals there: no wonder it is permanently empty).

Bram Stoker's Irish descendants still happily live off the proceeds from the book, for which the author was paid no advance in 1897 and only received 1s. 6d. after the first 100 copies were sold.

Bram Stoker based his creation on Vlad Tepes, a fifteenth century Romanian prince and a founder of Bucharest, nicknamed 'Dracul' (which means 'devil' in Romanian), who had a predilection for impaling his enemies on wooden stakes. In Romania, Vlad the Impaler was always regarded as a national hero, a connoisseur of good wines and a keen bat-keeper, whose cruelty and the number of impalees had been crudely exaggerated by vilifiers. In Bucharest, I bought a Romanian tourist brochure on Bran Castle, which was trying to shift Dracula's blood-drinking habits onto the sixteenth century Hungarian Countess Elisabeth Bathor, who lived in Transylvania and, allegedly, enjoyed biting into the flesh of her female servants.

It is interesting that in the years of Ceausescu's rule, all references to Dracula were strictly taboo, probably because the analogies between the two were too strong. In the eyes of ordinary Romanians, Count Dracula became a double victim – of Bram Stoker's vilification and of Ceausescu's paranoia.

Shortly after the revolution, a campaign to restore Dracula's good name was launched by Vlad Tepes enthusiasts. It was soon joined by Romanian tourist authorities, who decided to capitalise on Dracula's dark fame and began promoting Transylvania as 'Dracula Land' to attract foreign visitors. The Transylvanian Society of Dracula was formed 'as a reaction to the multitude of sub-human, cheap productions, draped in blood and blind terror, in the generic name Dracula'.

The society proclaimed itself 'a non-political, non-governmental, non-profit organisation' with the twofold aim: 'the analysis of the penetration of the Western myth of Dracula into Romania and the world at large', and the establishment of Prince Vlad Dracula's true role. The alleged 'non-profit' character of the society caused me some doubt, since half of the Articles of its 'Statute' dealt with membership fees and control over Dracula paraphernalia.

Under the auspices of the society, dracula tours of three different grades were drafted. They promised fearful initiation rites, live witch-hunts, visits to haunted cemeteries, 'goblins, trolls and pixies roaming the domain'. The tips for the courageous included:

• Hope nothing
• Trust your guide more. Not that we see another choice
• Take an umbrella

In the end, each visitor was guaranteed a Dracula Certificate saying: 'This is to certify that the courageous (so-and-so) has followed a Grade (such-and-such) Twilight Zone Dracula Tour and survived.'

This over-the-top PR campaign ended in a spectacular failure. It succeeded in frightening the potential tourists away *before* they had a chance to visit 'Dracula Land'.

The closest I ever came to a real-life vampire was in Australia. In 1991, all Australian newspapers wrote about Tracy Wiggington, a dysfunctional young woman from Brisbane who avoided mirrors (she was ugly, too) and once on a beach – probably out of boredom – stabbed a drunken businessman and drank some of his blood. Engrossed in blood-sucking, she didn't notice how her credit card, which was later picked up by the police, fell out of her pocket. She was arrested on the following day.

My advice to all would-be vampires in this: before venturing on a blood-sucking expedition, make sure you have left your credit card at home. I hope Jeannie Youngson will include it in her 'Drakpak'.

In 1995, Castle Bran was the venue for the first World Dracula Congress, which lasted for five days and brought together Dracula experts from all over the globe, but mostly from the USA. Among the papers presented to the Congress were 'The Image of Dracula in

Juvenile Literature', 'The Cult of Dracula and the New
Age Religions', 'Links Between Vampirism and Satanic
Scares', 'Dracula as a Classic Wandering Jew Figure'
and (last but not least) 'Bram Stoker's Work as a Book
of Menstrual Taboos'. The titles alone make it clear that
the congress was a treasure-trove for an ambitious
clinical psychiatrist.

Castle Bran was eerie. For half an hour we trudged
along its squeaky floorboards and climbed its dark,
winding staircases. I was most impressed by Dracula's
own spacious four-poster bed, made of black wood.
And although I knew that Bram Stoker had chosen
Castle Bran at random and described it from photos he
had found in the British Library, the illusion of the
count's presence was almost complete, and I wouldn't
have been surprised had he suddenly emerged from
under the bed and greeted us 'in excellent English, but
with strange intonation': 'Welcome to my house! Enter
freely and of your own will!'

At the museum shop downstairs, they sold statuettes
of Dracula, with his lips heavily covered either in blood
or in raspberry jam, Dracula Vodka (which was red, of
course), Dracula goblets, and Draculina soft drinks.

I opted for a modest postcard with a portrait of Vlad
Tepes (alias Count Dracula) a plain-looking moustached
man in a silly hood. His typically Romanian brown eyes
had the puzzled and somewhat peevish expression of a
grossly misunderstood person.

The nearby Peles Castle had seen many more real-life
vampires and blood-suckers than Castle Bran. Built by
King Carol I in 1883, it was used as a private retreat for
leading communists under Ceausescu. It had 365 rooms,
one for each day of the year. And further up the
mountain stood the Villa Foisor, one of the many
summer residencies of 'the Comrade' himself, who had
made sure he was properly segregated even from his
closest factotums and was always on top of them.

Our climb to the villa was blocked by a very young

corporal of the Romanian army, with a Kalashnikov behind his back.

'You can't enter,' he told us sternly. 'The villa is closed to public.'

A bottle of wine (we had some in the boot) softened his protective resolve.

'Sorry, but I still can't let you pass,' he said accepting the gift (which was clearly intended as a bribe). 'But I have been inside, and I am prepared to tell you what I saw.'

It was raining. We stood under a tree in the middle of a thick Transylvanian forest, listening to the youthful corporal.

'The things you can see there . . .' he started with a dreamy expression on his childish face. 'It is a different world . . . Swimming pools in each room . . . Artificial water-falls . . . Mirrors . . . A greenhouse with lemon and orange trees . . . It is like a dream . . . I simply cannot express it.'

'What is there now?' I asked him.

'No one knows. The house belongs to the government. Prime Minister Vacaroiu stayed there recently with his family for ten days.'

As we walked away, I looked back. The corporal stood at attention, with a radiant smile of recollection on his round peasant face. In his imagination, he was still movinging through the mirrored interior of the villa.

His Kalashnikov sub-machine-gun no longer looked threatening, for the corporal had a bottle of good wine in his hand.

37 THE LAST FEW DROPS OF WINE

Like the English, the Germans can make useful things well. They make clocks and watches, knives and swords, cups and plates . . .

Near Home or Europe Described,
Longmans, Green, & Co., London, 1910

'**G**o through my backside and then turn left,' said the buxom blonde receptionist at my Dresden hotel when I asked her for directions to the railway station.

That was how my search for East German wines started: through the backside of a hotel receptionist (she meant the hotel's back door, of course).

In actual fact, it had started earlier – in London – when I rang up the London office of the German Tourism Board.

'*Was*? East German wines? Do they exist?' asked a bewildered female voice with a sexy German accent.

Germans are notorious for their precision and punctiliousness bordering on boredom. A sign I spotted on the door of the Espresso Café in Dresden can serve as an illustration:

> **Opening times:**
> Samstag: 10.01–02.02
> Sonntag: 10.01–22.21
> Montag–Dienstag: 10.01–00.31

The conscientious German Tourism Board contacted another punctual organisation, the German Wine Information Service, which, after a month of thorough pain-staking research, supplied me with a list of several East German wineries – all situated in Saxony. That is why I found myself in Dresden.

The difficulties of my German contacts were easy to explain. 'East Germany was twelve enormous Liverpools handed over [to West Germany] and marked "From Russia with Love",' my eccentric acquaintance (and a hearty drinker) Professor Norman Stone once said of German reunification.

Wine culture in the communist-run and Stasi-controlled GDR was limited to Rotkäppchen ('Little Red Riding Hood'), a mass-produced red sparkling plonk, to which schnapps was routinely added to enhance the bouquet. Most of the 'Ossies', eager to obliterate their communist reality, however, would rather go for schnapps on its own, or for *Braunie*, schnapps diluted with water and chased with beer. In the GDR, just as in the USSR, wine had either been totally dismissed or treated with scorn, and this attitude has survived reunification: the only wine restaurant in post-communist Dresden was called The House of Fools (whereas beer pubs had such enticing, nice-sounding names as Ass and Cholera).

Yet, almost unknown to the locals, dry and fruity Saxony wines did exist in the GDR. Produced in small quantities, they were mostly exported to the unsuspecting West or consumed by the East Berlin party elite, whose corrupted reality was pleasant enough not to require any obliterating. Saxony wines were one of the GDR's best showcases, on a par with multiple Olympic medals won by specially trained running, swimming and jumping steroids camouflaged as athletes.

Having successfully negotiated the receptionist's ample backside, which stretched for a good couple of miles, I took a sterile double-decker train to the town of

Radebouil to meet my contact, Herr Hardenberg, who had described himself on the phone as 'fat and wearing glasses'.

The description was in the best tradition of socialist realism, which implied a precise photographic image with the worst bits thoroughly re-touched. Not only was Herr Hardenberg bespectacled and fat ('I drink beer and eat a lot') but he also had a fondness for telling black German jokes such as: 'A man is making love to a woman on the beach. Another man approaches him and says: "What are you doing? Don't you see that she is a drowned woman?" "No," the first man replies. "I thought that she had been murdered."'

Otherwise, Herr Hardenberg was a lovely man. He spoke fluent English, only occasionally making little slips like 'cooked water' instead of 'boiled water'. On his wrist, he proudly wore a solar watch, totally useless in permanently overcast Saxony, and kept asking me the time every five minutes. A Westerner (or 'Westie', as they say in East Germany), he grew up in Munich and had come to the East six years before to teach the 'Ossies' 'how to advertise their wines'.

'The difference between West German and East German wines is like the difference between Westies and Ossies,' he told me as we were driving through the hilly terraced vineyards of Saxony. 'In the GDR, Saxony wines played the role of a third currency, alongside West German and East German Deutsch-marks. Now, they have to compete with West German brands, which requires a lot of marketing. They don't know how to do it and don't want to be bothered. They are not used to taking decisions and accepting responsibility for them. Eighty per cent of the Ossies are wine-dead anyway.'

That was the word he used: 'wine-dead'. I liked it.

Despite all the difficulties, adventurous wine-makers from the West were trickling to Saxony to open small private wineries, which also functioned as *Weinstuben* (small wine restaurants) and hotels. We visited one such winery, run by Walter Schun and his wife, Sabine.

'I want to remain small and to do everything myself,' Walter said, leading me through his spotlessly clean model-like mini-winery lined with small egg-shaped (very German) wooden barrels and plastic (exclusively German) fermentation vats. A small battery of empty *Sachsen-Flaschen*, elongated Saxony wine bottles, stood in the corner waiting to be filled.

'My friends from East Germany think I am crazy to have come here,' he added with a sad smile.

Unlike Walter, Joachim Lehmann had spent all his life in Saxony. He used to run a winery under communists.

'The East German government wanted to make sure that East Berlin had plenty of Saxony wines for party meetings and Interhotels, where they could be sold for hard currency,' he told me. We were talking inside his *Weinstube*, next to the winery, which he now owned.

'If formerly the winery was frequented by GDR communist VIPs and the Stasi agents who spied on them, now the EU officials from Brussels come here,' he concluded.

At least the Stasi agents were no longer around, although – in their destructive power – EU bureaucrats were only marginally less dangerous.

Herr Lehmann's winery stood on the bank of the Elbe river, which flowed quietly past – a reminder of the simple philosophical truth that bureaucrats and systems change but rivers and wines keep flowing, no matter what.

Herr Lehmann's biggest pride was that his wine was regularly requested by the official representative of Saxony in Bonn for presentation purposes.

It was there, in Saxony, that I was taught my most important personal lesson in wine culture: wines could act as ambassadors, as liquid envoys of democracy and civilisation, unlike *Braunie* and *bormotukha*, which represented only tyranny and despair.

Grapes may not recognise political borders, but they do recognise political systems, which change the touch of the human hands that grow them.

As to the taste of Saxony wines . . . Well, to be absolutely frank, I didn't like them, especially the reds. Taste, like choice, is a category of freedom and cannot be dictated by critics or imposed by rules or rulers – another important discovery I had made during my bibulous East European travels.

One thing was certain: unlike 80 per cent of East Germans, I was no longer 'wine-dead'. On the contrary, I was very much 'wine-alive'. It was a wonderful feeling!

'I feel as if I am living my second life here in Saxony,' said Herr Hardenberg while we waited for my train in the Radebouil station buffet – scrubbed and lifeless as a hospital ward. 'Everything I knew in my previous Western life I now have to forget.'

'With me, it is the other way round: I try not to forget my previous Eastern life, for it makes my new, Western one so much richer,' I wanted to say, but didn't: my train was already pulling into the station.

THE FINAL TOAST
WITH MINERAL WATER

On 29 January 1998, the Loafer diary column in the *Guardian* began with the following entry:

> Vitali Vitaliev, the Loafer hears, has been working hard on a new book entitled *Borders Up!*. A play on the toast 'Bottoms up!', VV's book . . . views Eastern Europe 'through the prism of the bottom of a glass'. The travelogue divides the continent not by conventional frontiers but by local drinking habits – hence 'Beer Lands', 'Wine Lands' and 'Spirits Lands'. But the research has taken its toll, for Vitali . . . is now on the wagon. Perhaps there will have to be a new section entitled 'Mineral Water Lands'. Cheers!

What can I say? The Loafer had done his research well. Having completed my East European drinking journey, I decided to give up alcohol. In actual fact, I had made up my mind to do so much earlier – during my excursion to Munich's famous Bierfest in an attempt to understand the roots and meaning of beer culture. Still under the influence of that wild bus trip from London in the company of aggressively drunk young Aussies, I was walking back to my hotel one evening, when I noticed a brightly lit '*Reform-Haus Vitalia*' neon sign in Wiener Platz. Having come closer, I saw that it was a health-food shop.

I stared at it, mesmerised. For me, it was not just a shop sign but a cabalistic sign from above. For years, I had been joking about my rootlessness and lack of clear-cut national identity by saying that my home country was 'Vitalia' and my nationality 'Vitalian', but I never imagined that one day I would see the name of my invented one-person mini-state in blazing neon letters above a German health-food shop.

'Maybe, it is time for Vitalia, along with other post-communist East European countries, to move into a *Reform-Haus* and to stage a mini-revolution of its own,' I mused.

The nature of the shop left little doubt as to what sort of 'revolution' it had to be. I had to give up excessive drinking, which, according to Dr Thomas Stuttaford, the *Times* medical expert, could cause 'gastritis, ulcers, damage to the liver, impotence, cancer, stroke, pancreatitis and brain damage among many other things'.

I already had a stomach ulcer, a souvenir of my Soviet past, and was not looking forward to tasting the rest of Dr Stuttaford's gruesome menu, especially the frighteningly euphemistic (and euphemistically frightening) 'many other things' – a dish spiced not with chillies but with the chill of a freshly dug grave.

For a maximalist like myself, giving up excessive drinking meant giving up drinking altogether, for I always found it hard, if not impossible, to drink (and to do many other things) in moderation.

It is nice to realise that, having become a teetotaller, I can still continue drinking. I can drink coffee or tea and even frequent bars, provided they are 'oxygen bars' of the type that is gaining popularity in the USA and Canada. I saw a photo of one of them in a magazine:

happy patrons sit around the bar, with rubber tubes
stuck into their nostrils, as if they are all connected to
one and the same life-support machine (and they are).
The oxygen addicts (oxyholics?) call their new pastime
'gassing up' and assure one that they get a great buzz out
of it. I am determined to try it one day – as soon as I find
an oxygen bar that allows smoking while 'gassing up' (I
haven't given up cigarettes yet).

Being a teetotaller, I can still attend tastings, if not of
wines, then of mineral waters, like the one organised by
the *Sunday Times* in August 1997, when a group of wine
and food critics were invited to taste and to grade Evian,
Perrier, Buxton, Highland Spring and other bottled
mineral waters, to which – clandestinely and unbe-
knownst to the tasters – several samples of plain tap
water had been added. In the end, the experts
unanimously graded tap water higher than any of the
famous bottled ones. The tap water, which, by the way,
had come from the public toilets of Birmingham, was
described by different wine and food gurus as
'refreshing', 'tasting of pink grapefruit', having a 'fresh
lemony aroma' and even 'having a giggly feel to it',
which proves that a snob is always a snob, no matter
what he or she drinks – wine or water.

As you see, I haven't lost much (except, perhaps, some
extra weight) by being on the wagon.

As an abstainer, I can also pronounce toasts. A non-
imbibing toast-master is a welcome guest at any
drinking party.

Thinking of the final toast for this book, I had to
discard as too scholarly the favourite drinking salute of
Evgeny Bulavin, my University of Youth learned lecturer
in Applied Boozology: 'To this glass not becoming the
last one, to more frequent drinking – long live, alcohol!
Hooray!'

There is a lovely toasting custom in the small
Caucasian republic of Abkhazia: each person at a table
is supposed to toast each of the other guests and to clink

VITALI VITALIEV

glasses with him or her in a separate toast, which cannot fail but turn complete strangers into good friends by the end of the party.

Please allow me to raise my glass of the best British mineral water from the public toilets of Birmingham to the improving social health and the growing economic fitness of the seven new dipsocracies of Europe:

- The Czech Republic – Na Zdravi!
- Slovakia – Na Zdravie!
- Poland – Na zdrowie!
- Hungary – (breathe in) Egeszsegedre! (breathe out)
- Bulgaria – Nazdrave!
- Romania – Noroc!
- and the former GDR – Prost!

I am sure it won't be long before all of them grow into true democracies, for dipsocracy is but the last and final stage of communism.

Disproportionate doses of booze are still much better than thoroughly proportioned and equally distributed measures of tyranny and fear.

Let's have a drink of water, for, as Mark Twain used to say, water taken in moderation cannot hurt anybody. Cheers! Skoll! Down the hatch!

And Borders Up!

POSTSCRIPT

As a writer, satirist, broadcaster and traveller Vitaliev is conscious of having had experience enough 'for several lives' but still retains an ongoing fascination with the lives he hasn't experienced.

Born in Ukraine in 1954, Vitaliev writes as confidently in English as he does in Russian. His books are an exploration of language and landscape written with a generous spirit and a profound sympathy for the displaced.

As a former Moscow investigative journalist, once-committed boozer and Soviet dissident, Vitali Vitaliev is perhaps uniquely qualified to survey the drinks and drinking habits of Eastern Europe. In *Borders Up!* Vitaliev cuts across the usual geo-political alignments, employing a novel tool of assessment, namely alcohol. A countries' adherance to making and taking particular tipples can evoke aspects of daily realities which are difficult to divulge through dry reportage. The somewhat distorted view through the bottom of a glass is often a peculiarly accurate way to observe a schizophrenic reality.

Borders Up! is a striking mix of travel book, memoir, political history of Europe and meditation on drink and drinkers. It is a union of not only the grape and the grain but also of the personal and the political. Inevitably the journey reminded Vitaliev of drinking sessions and drinking friends from his past in Moscow, where a bottle of Almagel (a medicine for ulcers) was routinely placed in the middle of the table next to a bottle of vodka.

During his early days in Moscow Vitaliev discovered his first literary passion, namely poetry. The son of a nuclear physicist and a chemist, he was born and brought up in Kharkov, in Ukraine. His mother loved literature and his parents insisted, when Vitaliev was only seven or eight, that he learn English from a private tutor. Although at first he reacted against it, preferring instead to roam the streets, by his teens he was an ardent Anglophile and fluent enough to read English classical poetry as well as Russian literature.

At the age of fifteen he had begun to write his own romantic poetry. 'My problem was that I decided to do it seriously,' he reflects. By the age of eighteen he had enough for a collection. He sent the poems to Moscow for publication but the publishers deemed his work to be politically incorrect. 'In Soviet literature you had to write patriotic poems. Anything else was regarded as decadent.'

It was at around this time that literary translation presented itself as a creative alternative: 'I didn't know at the time that translation was the way many writers in the Soviet Union chose to work. Not being able to publish their own writing they expressed themselves through someone else's work. So we had Shakespeare translated by Boris Pasternak.'

At Kharkov University Vitaliev translated Henry Longfellow into Russian, principally because it was the only book of English poetry that he could find. It was a bulky leatherbound and beautifully illustrated pre-

Revolutionary edition (which Vitaliev acquired for just three roubles). Vitaliev found the poet's lyrics inspiring and his enthusiastic translation prompted praise, both at the university and amongst the Moscow literati. Vitaliev still considers it to be amongst his finest works to date.

In the mid-Seventies Vitaliev took a job as an interpreter for the Soviet Ministry of Culture but remained unrepentant in his views on the government and state. This antipathy was compounded with the invasion of Afghanistan in 1979, so he resigned his position.

Vitaliev decided to write again. Whilst he had always regarded journalism as a 'shameful profession, in that newspapers all toed the party line', he found that he had an aptitude for satire which enabled him to subvert the status quo from within. He began to write satirical articles and won the Golden Calf, the highest satirical award of the Soviet Union.

With the coming of glasnost during the mid-Eighties, Vitaliev was able to extend the range of of his writing. At some danger to himself he was the first to write about neo-fascism and the growing threat of the Russian Mafia. In 1988 he made his first visit to Britain, at the invitation of Martin Walker, then the *Guardian*'s Moscow correspondent. He stayed for a month, not knowing that the trip would change his life forever, and wrote his first articles in English.

During the same year Vitaliev also became the Moscow correspondent for Clive James' *Saturday Night Clive*. Initially informed that it was a serious political talk show, Vitaliev appeared wearing his best suit and a 'sombre Soviet expression' and for the first transmission took James very seriously. This misplaced solemnity quickly subsided.

Back home, glasnost notwithstanding, Vitaliev began to be seriously harassed by the KGB for his penetratingly satirical writing, so he decided, finally, to defect. In January 1990 he left the country, on the very day he was made Soviet Journalist of The Year.

After a short spell in England Vitaliev, doubtful that he would obtain permanent residency, moved to Australia. Having settled in Melbourne he soon realized that he was missing Europe. Australia was made bearable only by his frequent trips to Tasmania, an ersatz-England, but after a difficult time in Australia, in which his marriage broke up, Vitaliev returned once more to London.

Vitaliev's dromomania, his 'passion for purposeless travel', and his rootlessness has never left him. Wherever he is, he cannot shake the feeling that he is 'not a stranger but not at home'.

Since coming to the West Vitaliev has made TV travel documentaries, written for various national newspapers and reported regularly for Radio 4's Breakaway. He has also written five books: *Special Correspondent*, *Dateline Freedom*, *Vitali's Australia*, *Little is the Light*, and *Dreams on Hitler's Couch*. 'I like travel books because the travel genre has no rules', he explains, 'but when you travel too much you lose a lot of things on the way. The temptation with non-fiction is to give answers. I resisted that in *Borders Up!*. I decided to write the book to explore the fact that with their new freedom people in Eastern Europe are drinking more not less. But I don't attempt to say why people drink so much. We all know why.'

Vitaliev lived for thirty-five years of his life in a system which brutally regulated life at every turn. As Andro Linklater noted 'the individualism that drove him to find a way round, and eventually an escape from, Soviet restrictions, also prevented him accepting any limitations on his freedom'.

Anna Kiernan